3–16

Postcards from Stanland

Author David Mould meets an eighteenth-century Kazakh warrior chief (*batyr*) in the Tian Shan Mountains.

Postcards from
Stanland

Journeys in Central Asia

David H. Mould

Ohio University Press   Athens

Ohio University Press, Athens, Ohio 45701
ohioswallow.com
© 2016 by Ohio University Press
All rights reserved

Printed in the United States of America
Ohio University Press books are printed on acid-free paper ⊗ ™

26 25 24 23 22 21 20 19 18 17 16   5 4 3 2 1

Cover image: You're in the Polygon nuclear zone, but you wouldn't know it.

Unless otherwise noted, photographs are by the author.

Library of Congress Cataloging-in-Publication Data
Mould, David H. (David Harley), 1949–
Postcards from Stanland : journeys in Central Asia / David H. Mould.
    pages cm
Summary: "Central Asia has long stood at the crossroads of history. It was the staging ground for the armies of the Mongol Empire, for the nineteenth-century struggle between the Russian and British empires, and for the NATO campaign in Afghanistan. Today, multinationals and nations compete for the oil and gas reserves of the Caspian Sea and for control of the pipelines. Yet "Stanland" is still, to many, a terra incognita, a geographical blank. Beginning in the mid-1990s, academic and journalist David Mould's career took him to the region on Fulbright Fellowships and contracts as a media trainer and consultant for UNESCO and USAID, among others. In Postcards from Stanland, he takes readers along with him on his encounters with the people, landscapes, and customs of the diverse countries—Kazakhstan, Kyrgyzstan, Tajikistan, and Uzbekistan—he came to love. He talks with teachers, students, politicians, environmental activists, bloggers, cab drivers, merchants, Peace Corps volunteers, and more. Until now, few books for a nonspecialist readership have been written on the region, and while Mould brings his own considerable expertise to bear on his account—for example, he is one of the few scholars to have conducted research on post-Soviet media in the region—the book is above all a tapestry of place and a valuable contribution to our understanding of the post-Soviet world"— Provided by publisher.
    Includes bibliographical references and index.
    ISBN 978-0-8214-2176-5 (hardback : acid-free paper) — ISBN 978-0-8214-2177-2 (paperback : acid-free paper) — ISBN 978-0-8214-4537-2 (PDF)
    1. Asia, Central—Description and travel. 2. Mould, David H. (David Harley), 1949— Travel—Asia, Central. 3. Kazakhstan—Description and travel. 4. Kyrgyzstan—Description and travel. 5. Tajikistan—Description and travel. 6. Uzbekistan—Description and travel. 7. Post-communism—Social aspects—Asia, Central. 8. Asia, Central—Social life and customs. 9. Asia, Central—Social conditions. I. Title.
    DS327.8.M68 2016
    958'.042—dc23
                    2015036332

Cover photo:
Photo by Robert Kopack

Dedicated to my wife,

Stephanie Hysmith, my lifetime traveling companion,

and to the late Hubert Wilhelm, who taught me to see

the world around me in new ways

Contents

Illustrations

Figures

Maps

Preface

I wrote my first travel journal at the age of nine. It had a circulation of precisely three—my father, mother, and sister. I'm not sure they actually read it, although they encouraged me to keep writing. It was run-of-the-mill stuff, a prosaic accounting of towns and sights visited, meals eaten, weather, and beach conditions—the predictable literary output of a nine-year-old. However, I would not have written anything, or asked my father to have my notes typed (with carbon copies), if I had not had the opportunity to travel.

In Britain in the 1950s and 1960s, most middle-class families took a summer vacation at the seaside, hoping the sun would peep through the clouds. Usually it did not. I have memories of cold, rain-swept South Coast resorts, with families huddled in their cars, the parents drinking tea from a thermos and reading the tabloids, glancing occasionally at the grey skies and the cold waves crashing on the stony beach. The children fidgeted and fought in the back of the car. There were no handheld gadgets to distract them; after they got bored with their toys, there wasn't much else to do but start destroying the upholstery or tormenting the family dog, if it was unlucky enough to be on the trip. Occasionally, a parent would say: "Children, we're at the seaside. Aren't we all having a lovely time?" No one was, but no one wanted to admit it. On rare sunny days, the kids could play on the beach, perhaps even finding a patch of sand, but most days it was too cold to swim; the main seaside attractions were the funfairs on the piers.

Most years my parents headed for France or Spain, where the weather was predictably better. We strapped the family tent—a heavy, complicated canvas affair with many poles, pegs, and guy ropes, which looked as if it had been salvaged from a M*A*S*H unit—onto the roof rack of the Vauxhall Velox, and set off for Dover to take the ferry across the English Channel to Calais or Boulogne. We drove south, buying baguettes, butter, cheese, and tomatoes for picnic lunches and camping every night, my parents enjoying a bottle of *vin ordinaire* over dinner.

I sat in the backseat, noting the kilometer posts, the terrain, and the historic landmarks, and taking notes. "Rouen," I earnestly remarked, "has a large cathedral." I helped navigate, a serious responsibility in the days before France built its equivalent of a motorway or interstate highway system. I was fascinated by the road maps and the names of towns, villages, and rivers, and I loved to plot our route. Often I enjoyed the trip—reading maps, getting lost, and asking for directions in shockingly bad schoolboy French—more than the destination.

I made my first solo trip at the age of seventeen, spending three months at student work camps in France, hitchhiking across the country and religiously writing postcards home. Unlike the typical "Weather lovely, wine cheap, *pate de foie gras* gave me indigestion, wish you were here" greeting, my postcards were crammed with details of my observations, now more insightful than "Rouen has a large cathedral." I bought cards with the largest possible writing space, and usually managed to cram more than one hundred words into the left-hand side. Over the next decade, traveling with my then-wife, Claire, through France, Spain, Portugal, Italy, Switzerland, Germany, Greece, Turkey, and Morocco, I wrote many more postcards. Looking back, I wish I had sent some to myself because they were the only records of our trips to Fez and Marrakech (where I picked up both a full-length Berber *djellabah* and head lice) or of lingering too long on a Greek island, missing the bus at Thessaloniki and having to hitchhike the 1,250 miles back to Ostend on the Channel.

In the early 1970s, I worked as a newspaper reporter for the *Evening Post,* a large-circulation daily in Leeds, the main industrial and commercial center in West Yorkshire. My work travel was largely confined to mining and textile towns, with two trips to Northern Ireland, not exactly a tourist destination in the 1970s. I wanted to write about what I'd seen in Southern Europe, but my editor wasn't interested. People didn't want to read about the Basque Country or the Bosphorus, he said. Perhaps I could write about bed-and-breakfasts in Scarborough or renting a cottage at Skegness? Neither was on my holiday list, so my dream of being a travel writer was stymied. In 1978, I moved to the United States for graduate school, and in 1980 took a faculty position at Ohio University. It would be another fifteen years, after my first trip to Central Asia in 1995, before I started travel writing again.

When I did, I had more to say about cathedrals or mining towns or railroads or architecture or just about everything I saw about me. Credit goes to my teacher, mentor, and friend Hubert Wilhelm who taught cultural and historical geography at Ohio University for thirty-five years. His courses and our later collaboration on three video documentaries on the settlement of Ohio taught me to ask questions about the landscape. Who settled the land, where did they come from, and why? Why were houses and barns built in distinctive styles? Why was the land divided in certain ways? How were towns aligned to transportation routes? Although Hubert's research was on vernacular architecture and settlement patterns in the US Midwest, the techniques can be applied to any region. Without his inspiration, I would not be asking questions about Central Asia's gerrymandered borders, Soviet public architecture, or the impact of Stalin's mass deportations on the ethnic mix.

By the mid-1990s, I was looking for a new challenge. Drew McDaniel, a faculty colleague, asked if I would be willing to travel to Kyrgyzstan to set up a media training center in Osh, the main city in the south. Drew had been to Kyrgyzstan a few months earlier and said he found it fascinating to observe the changes in the country as it emerged from over seventy years of Soviet rule. I said I'd love to take the opportunity. I didn't admit to Drew that I had no idea where Kyrgyzstan was.

Since the mid-1990s, I've traveled to Central Asia, mostly to Kyrgyzstan and Kazakhstan, more than a dozen times to teach at universities, lead workshops for journalists and educators, consult with TV and radio stations, and conduct research. My visits have lasted from a couple of weeks to three months, with longer stints for Fulbright Fellowships—sixteen months in Kyrgyzstan in 1996–97 and six months in Kazakhstan in 2011. I've made three trips to Uzbekistan, and two to Tajikistan; unfortunately, I haven't had the opportunity to visit Turkmenistan.

As I traveled, I made notes on everything from landscape, culture, history, politics, environment, media, and universities to the challenges of communicating and staying warm. Recording first impressions was important because what struck me as interesting on first encounter would, after a week or two, seem commonplace. Every week or so, I assembled the notes—recorded in a cheap *tetrad* (school exercise book) from the bazaar or, less systematically, on napkins, credit card receipts, ticket stubs, and pages ripped from airline magazines—and wrote a rambling e-mail letter to a growing circle of family, friends, and colleagues. These letters were the inspiration for this book; they documented what I experienced while the memories were still fresh. I've also written op-eds, essays, and features on Central Asia for the *Christian Science Monitor, Times Higher Education, Transitions Online,* the *Montreal Review,* and other print and on-line media, some of which are reproduced here, in whole or in part. The book also draws on research on journalism and media for academic papers. Thus it presents Central Asia from several perspectives, from the wide-angle views of geopolitics—the contest for political and economic power—to the close-ups of travel, work, eating, and shopping.

A note on spelling. Language is a sensitive issue in Central Asia, and there's no way that I will satisfy everyone with my choices because we are dealing with three language groups: Russian is a Slavic language; Kazakh, Kyrgyz, Turkmen, and Uzbek are Turkic languages; and Tajik is a Farsi (Persian) language. When a word or person's name has a clear origin, I use a transliterated spelling that approximates how it would sound in the original language. For example, my friend Asqat Yerkimbay prefers to use "q" in his name because it is closest to the guttural "қ" sound in Kazakh; the Russian spelling of his name is "Askhat" with the "kh" a transliteration of the consonant "x" which does not exist in English or Kazakh. However, to apply that principle to the name of the country, Қазақстан, and people, Қазақ, gives you Qazaqstan and Qazaq, names that might confuse some readers. In this instance, I sacrifice consistency and correctness for convention, while noting that the "kh" was a colonial convenience, used by the Russians to distinguish the Казах of the steppe from the similar-sounding Cossack people. I use Russian names for places such as Karaganda (Kazakh—Qaragandhy) and Kostanai (Qostanay), simply because the Russian spelling remains widely used. There's less linguistic confusion in Kyrgyzstan, where most places have Kyrgyz names.

This book, combining personal experience, interviews, and research, is not intended as a travel guide. It's not an academic study or the kind of analysis produced by policy wonks, although it offers background and insights. Think of it as a series of scenes or maybe oversized postcards (with space for one thousand rather than one hundred words) that I might have sent to friends and family if the postal system in Central Asia had been reliable enough. They feature observations of places and people, digging into an often complex and troubled past and, on occasions, offering an educated guess on the future. Postcards to ponder.

Charleston, West Virginia, November 2014

one

Travels in "Kyrzakhstan"

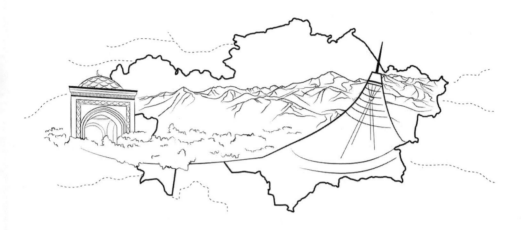

From the Osh Bazaar to Maryland Malls

On Christmas Eve 1995, my wife, Stephanie, picked me up at Washington's Dulles airport. I had been traveling for almost two days and was exhausted. I had arrived at Almaty airport in southeastern Kazakhstan at 11 p.m. after a six-hour drive on icy roads across the border from Kyrgyzstan. Although my flight to Frankfurt did not leave until 4:30 a.m., the US embassy advised me to allow enough time to navigate the Soviet-era airport bureaucracy and, if necessary, pay a small bribe. It was good advice. The journey through the airport was almost as stressful as the road trip, and I barely made my flight.

Stephanie and I planned to spend the holidays with her sister and family at their home on the Maryland shore before driving home to Ohio. After almost a month in Central Asia, I looked forward to returning to the United States. Instead I experienced, for the first time in my life, reverse culture shock. We drove past brightly lit suburban malls, crowded with shoppers

1

buying last-minute presents and stocking up on holiday food and alcohol. Billboards and neon signs were already advertising the postholiday sales.

One of the blessings—but also one of the curses—of international air travel is that in the space of a few hours (or, in my case, about forty hours) you are transported from one world to another. The place you leave and the place where you arrive differ not only in the predictable ways—the skin color and features of the people, the landscape, architecture, language, food, and money. More fundamentally, the everyday concerns of people are usually completely different.

In the malls, people were making standard American consumer choices. "What should I buy for your mother? She's *so* difficult!" "Which video game do the children want?" "How large a turkey? "Will anyone notice if we serve boxed Chardonnay?"

It was a stark contrast to the world I had just left. In suburban Maryland, the shops were open, and open late. In Osh in southern Kyrgyzstan, where I'd spent most of the past month, almost all the shops were closed, and had been closed for several years; what was left of the retail economy had moved to the bazaar and street corners.

In suburban Maryland, lights blazed from malls, streetlamps, and Christmas house and lawn displays. In Osh, the lights were off for at least several hours each day. No one was sure why there were power outages in a country with enough hydroelectric capacity to be a net exporter, but the usual culprits were named—corrupt government ministers, incompetent local officials, the mafia, the International Monetary Fund, or some cabal of all of the above.

In suburban Maryland, the restaurants were crowded; in Osh, the few restaurants that were still open had only the occasional customer and most of the items on the menu were not available.

In suburban Maryland, people were spending their Christmas bonuses and maxing out their credit cards. In Osh, teachers, civil service workers, and others who had not been paid for months were wondering when (or if) they would ever get a paycheck again.

In suburban Maryland, people were buying gifts for the holidays. In Osh, some people were selling all they had to buy food; in subzero temperatures, they squatted on the broken concrete sidewalks, their possessions—kitchen utensils, auto parts, school textbooks, old clothes, Soviet memorabilia—spread out on blankets. I don't know who was buying because most passersby were just as poor as the sellers.

In suburban Maryland and throughout the United States on Christmas Eve 1995, people were looking forward to the new year with hope. In Osh and throughout Central Asia, people were simply hoping that 1996 would not be as bad as 1995.

Not in the Holiday Spirit

When we arrived at Stephanie's sister's home, the party was in full swing. I was not in the party mood but could not explain why I felt depressed. "It's the holidays," guests said. "You're supposed to be happy." I tried talking about what I had seen in Osh, but they soon changed the topic. I excused myself, saying I was tired, and went to bed early. On Christmas Day, I put on a brave face as the children opened their presents and the family kitchen crew swung into action. It was a sumptuous spread. Social conditions in southern Kyrgyzstan were not a talking point over dinner.

I have no one to blame but myself for not working harder to make relatives and friends, all of them good and sincere people, think or care about what I had seen and learned. About shattered families where husbands, robbed of their jobs and the dignity of work by the collapse of the Soviet economy, turned to the vodka bottle. About *babushkas* and children, begging at the bazaar. About declining social and medical services, schools without heating or textbooks. About ethnic unrest, and the breakdown of the rule of law. But also about the resilience, spirit, and hospitality of people who, after many years of Soviet certainty, had suddenly seen their world turned upside down.

After years of media coverage of famine and conflict, the problems of the developing world can seem relentlessly wearying. Poverty, suffering, and conflict are comfortably encapsulated in five-paragraph or ninety-second narrative chunks, with the requisite quotes or sound bites. You could not understand southern Kyrgyzstan in 1995 from the occasional media coverage or even from my photos and stories. You simply had to be there.

I was there, and then I left. That was perhaps what disturbed me most. I had the freedom to travel, to move between the worlds of southern Kyrgyzstan and suburban Maryland. Most people in Central Asia were simply stuck, trying to survive. That Christmas Eve made me see my own world, career, and life in a new way.

As a US citizen and taxpayer, it's my duty not only to criticize government officials but to recognize when they do something useful. I happily acknowledge the contribution of US Secretary of State John Kerry to this introduction.

Kerry is probably unaware of my debt, because it was unintentional. On the eve of his first foreign trip as Secretary of State in February 2013, Kerry, in a speech at the University of Virginia, praised the staff of the State Department and US Agency for International Development (USAID) for their work in the "most dangerous places on Earth."

> They fight corruption in Nigeria. They support the rule of law in Burma. They support democratic institutions in Kyrzakhstan and Georgia.[1]

Come again, Mr. Secretary? *Kyrzakhstan?* Aren't you confusing volatile Kyrgyzstan, where popular protests overthrew two authoritarian leaders in less than five years, with its stable neighbor Kazakhstan, where President Nursultan Nazarbayev has ruled almost unchallenged since independence in 1991?

The State Department transcript of the speech helpfully clarified matters, replacing "Kyrzakhstan" with "Kyrgyzstan." But not before reporters picked up on the gaffe. Kerry was teased for "creating a new country." The flub was "all the more awkward," said the British newspaper *The Telegraph,* "because Kyrgyzstan is a key ally in the US-led war in Afghanistan and a major recipient of US aid."[2]

Russians poked fun in online forums. Among the comments: "I think we need to restore the USSR, so that the American Secretary does not confuse the names." "Well, if the USA decided so . . . Let there be Kyrzakhstan." "So what? Kyrzakhstan is a regular country. It's to the east of Ukrarussia and south-east of Litonia. Not far from Uzkmenia. You should learn geography." A cartoon depicted Kerry, cell phone to his ear, looking intently at a globe. "Where is that Kyrzakhstan? I've been trying to call there for three days."

The gaffe was fodder for TV talk shows and the late-night comics. Stephen Colbert picked up on a comment Kerry made the next day in a lecture on freedom of speech to students in Berlin: "In America, you have the right to be stupid if you want to be."

"Yes, in this country we are endowed with the inalienable right to be stupid," said Colbert. "It's right there in the Constitution between the peanut doodle and the ranch dressing stain. Folks, John Kerry doesn't just talk the dumb talk, he walks the dumb walk. Here's what he said last week [excerpt from speech at University of Virginia]."

> Yes, Kyrzakhstan. And there's just one thing about Kyrzakhstan. It does not exist. Of course, he's got some ribbing in the press for making up a new country. And folks, it is well deserved. I mean, how could anyone ever confuse Kazakhstan [shows map] with its neighbor when everyone knows that in Kyrgyz-stan [shows picture of yurts, the traditional tent-like dwellings] they play a fretless stringed instrument called the *komuz* which is nothing like Kazakhstan's *dombyra,* also a fretless stringed in-strument with a slightly thinner neck. And what are you going to do, Kerry? Go to downtown Bishkek and use a bunch of tenge to buy a new *kolpak* [shows picture of kolpak, traditional Kyrgyz men's felt hat, and Kazakh tenge bills]. Not without first exchanging into soms [shows Kyrgyz currency], you're not. Quit embarrassing yourself, John Kerry.[3]

Of course, Kerry was not the first US official to be, as the *Telegraph* put it, "tongue-tied by post-Soviet geography." "Stan-who?" President George W. Bush is reputed to have asked when Secretary of State Con-doleezza Rice briefed him about Uzbekistan. In August 2008, he mixed up Russia and Georgia, which at that time were at war, when he warned against possible efforts to depose "Russia's duly elected government."

I'm prepared to forgive Kerry's gaffe, but I can also use it to make a point. The confusion is symptomatic of a more general geographical malaise, caused by the collapse of the Soviet Union and the proliferation of countries whose names end in -stan. Kerry is not the first and will not be the last public official to become lost in Stanland.

Lost in Stanland

So where is "Stanland?"

The imprecise reference is to a vast swath of Asia, stretching from Turkey to the western border of China, populated by a bewilder-ing assortment of ethnic groups that give their names to an equally bewildering collection of provinces, autonomous republics, and countries. Remembering them all—not to mention finding them on a map—is a challenge, even for people who are supposed to know these things, such as diplomats and international relations experts.

I don't claim to be an expert, but, after traveling to Central Asia many times since the mid-1990s, I have a sense of place. I pity those world leaders doing the airport tarmac press conferences on the ten-Asian-countries-in-ten-days tours. It's Tuesday, so this must be Tajikistan.

It's similar to the geographical confusion brought on by the end of European colonialism in Africa a half century ago. It wasn't enough for the imperial powers to surrender their political and economic dominance. They also had to learn postcolonial geographical vocabulary. It's not Upper Volta any more. It's Burkina Faso, and its capital is—get ready to roll those vowels—Ouagadougou.

"As a generality," writes the Central Asia scholar Karl E. Meyer, "Americans think of the world in terms of seaports and airports, whereas Central Asians and their neighbors look inwardly to a vast realm tied together by caravan routes, rails, mountain passes, rivers and nowadays oil pipelines. Americans commonly dwell in a perpetual present, while inhabitants of the Asian heartland and their imperial former masters inhabit a gallery where whispering voices never cease recalling past triumphs or prior humiliations."[4] To travel writer Colin Thubron, one of the first Westerners to travel in the region after the breakup of the Soviet Union, it was intangible, a historical and geographical paradox:

> Even on the map it was ill-defined, and in history only vaguely named: 'Turkestan', 'Central Asia', 'The Land Beyond the River'. Somewhere north of Iran and Afghanistan, west of the Chinese deserts, east of the Caspian Sea … this enormous secret country had turned on itself. Its glacier-fed rivers … never reached the ocean, but vanished in landlocked seas or died across the desert. The Himalaya cut off its mountains from any life-giving monsoon where the Pamirs rose in a naked glitter of plateau, so high, wrote Marco Polo, that no bird flew there and fire burnt with a pale flame in which you could rest your hand.[5]

We all construct mental maps of essential information, and our maps are shaped as much by culture and pragmatism as by physical features and political boundaries. Of course, we all know about other places, but they don't appear in our mental maps, not even on the fringes, unless they seem relevant. Even though Afghanistan has been embroiled in conflict since the Soviet invasion of 1979—or, to take a longer historical perspective, since the first Anglo-Afghan War of 1839–42—it was not on most Americans' mental maps before September 11, 2001.

As long as Afghanistan and Pakistan were the only "stans" we had to remember, the map was reasonably manageable. Then Mikhail Gorbachev came along. The collapse of the Soviet Union gave us fourteen new countries (plus Russia) including the five "stans" of Central Asia—Kazakhstan, Kyrgyzstan, Tajikistan, Turkmenistan, and Uzbekistan. We can be grateful the Soviet Union did not break up any further, or we would have to deal with Bashkortostan, Dagestan, and Tatarstan (now Russian republics). Or that Armenia did not adopt its native name, Hayastan. Or that the Central Asian republics themselves did not splinter, with Karakalpakstan breaking away from Uzbekistan.

If we struggle to remember the "stans," is it more helpful to think about "Central Asia"? It depends. In terms of geopolitics, it's a more elastic region, partly because it is (apart from the Caspian Sea)

MAP 1.1 Central Asian republics (map by Brian Edward Balsley, GISP)

landlocked, so has no coastline for demarcation. Since September 11, Afghanistan has often been classified as Central Asia. The north of the country, bordering Uzbekistan, has a large ethnic Uzbek population; in the east, Tajiks are a significant minority. By religion, culture, and language, the Uighurs of China's Xinjiang Autonomous Region have more in common with the Kazakhs and Kyrgyz than with the rest of China, and Uighur nationalists dream of reuniting with their neighbors in a Greater Turkestan region. The Caspian Sea clearly divides the Caucasus republics of Armenia, Azerbaijan, and Georgia, and the Russian republics of Dagestan, Chechnya, and Ingushetia, from Kazakhstan, Uzbekistan, and Turkmenistan, although some policy experts lump them together as "Central Asia and the Caucasus." What about Mongolia? Ethnically, Kazakhs and Kyrgyz are Mongols. Unlike other regions that can be neatly subdivided, Central Asia is amorphous, expanding and contracting as it is viewed through different political, social, economic, and cultural lenses.

In this book, I use the narrow political definition of Central Asia to refer to these five former Soviet republics—Kazakhstan, Kyrgystan, Tajikistan, Turkmenistan, and Uzbekistan. Since 1995, I have faced the challenge of trying to explain the region to colleagues, students, and friends. After one trip to Kyrgyzstan, a colleague insisted I had been in Kurdistan (which does not yet exist, except in Northern Iraq and in the maps of Kurdish separatist movements).

"No, K-oe-rg-oe-zstan," I replied, trying to wrap my tongue around the challenging Russian vowel "ы" in the first and second syllables. I gave the ten-second profile. "Poor country, former Soviet Union, borders China, beautiful mountains and lakes, nomadic herders with sheep and horses, lots of meat in the diet, bad hotels, slow Internet, very hospitable people."

You would have thought the conflict in Afghanistan would have focused the attention of Westerners on the countries next door, but unfortunately it hasn't. Just as medieval European maps tagged vast regions of Africa, Asia, and America as *terra incognita*, the five Central Asian republics are a geographical blank between Afghanistan and Pakistan to the west and China to the east. To many Westerners, my travels in Kazakhstan, Kyrgyzstan, Tajikistan, and Uzbekistan might as well have been on another planet. I had simply been in "Stanland."

It's difficult to know why we have so much trouble with the "stans." The suffix, derived from a Persian word meaning "place of," is similar in meaning to "land" in English, German, or Dutch. We have no problem distinguishing England, Scotland, Ireland, Iceland, Finland, Poland, and Switzerland, and maybe even Greenland, Friesland, Rhineland, and Lapland. So why can't we find Turkmenistan, let alone Balochistan, the largest of Pakistan's four provinces?

Maybe it's because we're not as globally minded as we suppose. American ignorance—or perhaps ignore-ance better describes it—of the geography of Central Asia was famously lampooned on the cover of the December 10, 2001, edition of the *New Yorker* magazine, three months after September 11 (see page 10). The "New Yorkistan" cover satirically depicted the five boroughs and individual neighborhoods, mixing local and Yiddish names with suffixes common in Central Asia and the Middle East. Starting from their original idea, Bronxistan, the creators Maira Kalman and Rick Meyerowitz took readers on a stroll in Manhattan's Central Parkistan, hailed a cab at Taxistan (LaGuardia Airport), speculated in real estate at (Donald) Trumpistan, celebrated cultural diversity in Lubavistan (named for a branch of the Hasidic Jews) and Gaymenistan, and then ventured to the outer suburbs of Coldturkeystan and Extra Stan (traveling through Hiphopabad, passing by the Flatbushtuns and the district of Khandibar).[6]

Why are the "stans" important? In a 1904 paper, "The Geographical Pivot of History," delivered at Britain's Royal Geographical Society, the Oxford geographer Sir Halford Mackinder, now recognized as one of the doyens of geopolitics, argued that interior Asia and Eastern Europe, the so-called Eurasian heartland, was the strategic center of the "World Island." For more than a century, imperial Britannia had ruled the waves, but Mackinder, despite his imperialist views, warned of the decline of sea power in the twentieth century. As the heartland rose, Britain would become part of the subordinate "maritime lands." Since the first millennium BCE, the landlocked steppes of Eurasia have provided the staging ground for horse-borne invasions. Shielded by the Arctic Ocean to the north and mountain ranges to the south, armies from the heartland could strike east to China, west to Europe, and southwest to the Middle East.[7]

Developing his theory after World War I and drawing on his experiences trying to unite White Russian forces in the civil war that followed the Bolshevik Revolution, Mackinder warned of the dangers of German or Russian domination, and foresaw the NATO alliance by calling on North America and Western Europe to offset the power of the Eurasian

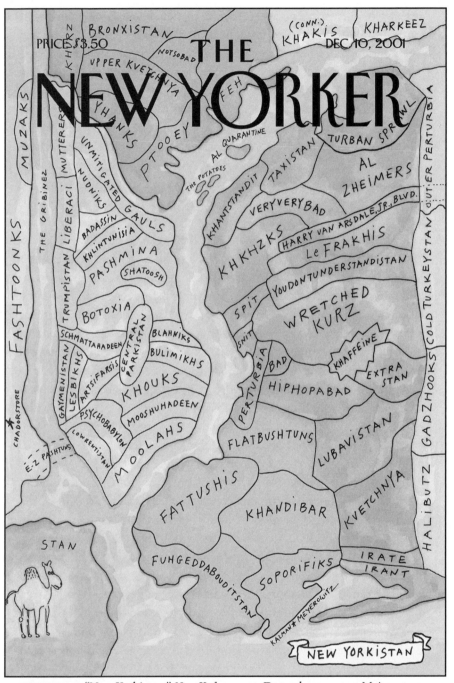

FIGURE 1.1 "New Yorkistan," *New Yorker* cover, December 10, 2001, Maira Kalman and Rick Meyerowitz (Condé Nast collection)

heartland. Although the "geographical pivot" theory is well known to academics and policy wonks, it has not percolated into popular understanding. Many Westerners are still lost in Stanland.

So are some of the citizens of these republics, which, more than a quarter of a century after independence, are still struggling to establish national identities. The problem is that, despite recent nationalist revisionist historiography, the five republics, each named for an ethnic group, are new countries created by Soviet cartographers in the mid-1920s. Stalin's policy of divide and rule, intended to suppress ethnic unrest and militant Islam, created a crazy-quilt pattern of borders between ethnically mixed Soviet Socialist Republics. These became de facto political borders in 1991.

Those who still yearn for the social and ideological certainties of the Soviet Union and curse Gorbachev for messing up their lives may never accept their "stan." But for those born after independence the Soviet era is now just a heavily edited chapter in the school history textbook. The new generation that will dominate politics, business, and intellectual life has a stronger sense of national identity and history.

That means that the West needs to better understand the "stans." I still have much to understand myself. Despite traveling and working in the region for many years, I can never expect to have the same understanding, particularly on cultural issues, as those who were born, brought up, and live in Central Asia. By the same token, I may be better prepared than they are to explain the "stans" to Westerners precisely because I *am* an outsider. What seems normal or unexceptional to people in Central Asia often strikes me as interesting and worth noting. It goes both ways. For twenty years, Stephanie and I lived in a nineteenth-century farmhouse in the rolling hills south of Athens, Ohio. Academic colleagues from Central Asia who visited were puzzled. "Is this your home or your dacha?" they asked. Most Central Asians live in apartments, and some have a modest dacha where they grow fruit and vegetables. But you don't *live* at the dacha. Our visitors also wondered why we spent several hours a week mowing the grass. What seemed normal to us surprised them.

A Map Is Worth a Thousand Words

That cultural conundrum—how we look at other people and their cultures, and how they look at us—has always fascinated me. In elementary school in the mid-1950s, I innocently asked my teacher why so much of the map of the world was colored pink. The question surprised him. "It's the British Empire, of course," he said, stiffening his back (and maybe also his upper lip) as if he were going to salute and break into "God Save the Queen." Instead, he told me I should be proud to be a subject of an empire on which the sun never set. I soon began to doubt his faith. The BBC was reporting trouble on the Malay peninsula, the Mau Mau insurrection in Kenya, civil war in Cyprus. Obviously, not everyone was proud to be a subject of the empire. The sun set more quickly on the Soviet than on the British empire, but for more than seventy years Soviet citizens were also told—by teachers, politicians, and the media—that they should be happy to live in a country free of the evils of Western capitalism.

On my first trip to Kyrgyzstan in 1995, I bought several Soviet-era maps, the heavy-duty glossy cloth-backed versions used in schools, at a bookstore in Bishkek. One is a historical map of the United States from the end of the nineteenth century to the beginning of the twentieth century. Its most prominent features are red flags scattered across the northern United States. I didn't know much Russian at the time, so could not read the scale, but I figured out the significance of the flags from the dates beside them. Pittsburgh, Buffalo, Louisville, St. Louis, Chicago, and other cities in 1877—the great railroad workers' strike. Chicago in 1886—the Haymarket Affair. Near Pittsburgh in 1892—the Homestead steelworkers' strike. Colorado in 1913—the miners' strike and the Ludlow Massacre. And so on.

US history and geography were presented to Soviet schoolchildren as a series of bloody labor disputes, the proletariat rising against the oppressive mine and factory owners. An inset map depicts "Imperialist Aggression, late 19th to early 20th Centuries," a cluster of black arrows in the Caribbean thrusting toward Mexico, Cuba, Guatemala, Panama, Puerto Rico, and Colombia, in the Pacific toward Hawaii, Western Samoa, Guam, and the Philippines.

The history of the United States told through red flags and black arrows. I imagined that the Cold War period was similarly depicted with black arrows targeting Cuba, Chile, Venezuela, and Nicaragua and red flags marking the racial conflicts of the civil rights era—Montgomery, Selma, Watts. No wonder many Soviet citizens feared and loathed the West, even as they bartered for Levis and listened to the Rolling Stones.

And then, almost abruptly in 1991, it was all over. The Soviet Union collapsed, and the republics of Central Asia were now numbered among the so-called Newly Independent States. It was a convenient, if misleading, label because they lacked both economic independence and political institutions. The ideology of Marxist-Leninism was replaced by a new civil religion whose creed included "democracy," "the free market," "structural reform," and "civil society." The old school maps came off the walls to be replaced by more positive cartography, courtesy of "democracy building" NGOs funded by the United States and other foreign governments.

Changing the name of a country, the maps, and school textbooks does not change culture, even with heavy doses of foreign aid, the privatization of property, and an army of foreign consultants with advice on elections, the rule of law, and capital markets. It takes many years for people who grew up, lived, and worked in a system to start looking at the world and themselves in new ways. In many respects, Kyrgyzstan in December 1995 still seemed stuck in a Soviet time warp, cut adrift from Moscow's economic and social safety net yet not willing to embrace an uncertain future.

Although some people in Central Asia continue to cling to the past, it's been clear for many years that change is the new norm. The Soviet Union, or anything like it, is not coming back, and the certainties that underpinned its society have disappeared. This book is about this process of change.

My relationship with Central Asia is a personal one. And, like any relationship, it's complicated. There is much that I love and admire about the region and its peoples, and, at the same time, much that I find troubling. It's that tension between the positive and negative that makes Central Asia worth writing about. My goal is to add the "stans" in all their complexity to the mental maps of readers. This has been my personal mission since December 1995. And it all began on the fabled Silk Road in the medieval city of Osh.

two

Sacred Mountain and Silly Borders

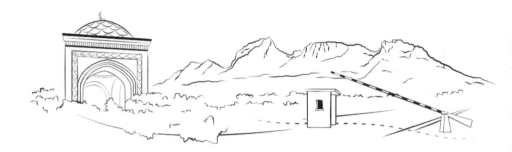

Deconstructing Lenin

Statues of Lenin, although not yet on the endangered species list, are not as common in the former Soviet Union or Communist bloc as they once were. As the Soviet political and economic system fell apart, reformers made sure that its founder took a symbolic fall too. In central squares from Tallinn to Tbilisi, crowds cheered as statues of Lenin were unceremoniously pulled down and bulldozed.

However, Lenin still stands tall in what was once a distant outpost of the Soviet empire—the city of Osh in southern Kyrgyzstan. In the broad, fertile Fergana Valley, between two great mountain ranges, the Fergana and the Pamir Alay, Lenin looks out on a sprawling, multiethnic city still struggling to adjust to the post-Soviet world.

Like Stalin, Vladimir Ilyich Ulyanov (Lenin was his nom de plume) remains a controversial historical figure. Indeed, the presence or absence of a Lenin statue tells us something about how ready a country or a people is to shake off cultural and ideological links to the Soviet era. In Eastern Europe, the Baltic States, and the Caucasus, the break came quickly and decisively, and the Lenin statues fell almost as fast—in 1989 in Krakow, in 1990 in Bucharest, in 1991 in Tbilisi and Yerevan, and so on. Yet in Russia, Belarus, eastern Ukraine, and some Central Asian republics, Lenin statues still stand in many public squares and parks.

In 2012, Russian lawmakers proposed relocating Lenin monuments to museums or side streets, or selling them to collectors, ostensibly to reduce vandalism and maintenance costs. But the debate in the parliament (Duma) revealed an ideological agenda. One deputy claimed that the presence of Lenin statues in most Russian cities and towns meant the revolutionary leader still exercised a stranglehold on history, and that was unfair to other Russian historical figures. Didn't Ivan the Terrible or Catherine the Great deserve equal historical billing? Predictably, the Communist Party did not like the idea. As one senior party member put it: "Lenin is the founding father of the Russian Federation. Same as George Washington in America."[1]

Kyrgyzstan, like other Central Asian republics, has a schizophrenic relationship with its Russian and Soviet past—a mix of resentment against military conquest and repression, political and economic control, and nostalgia for a time when everyone had housing, education, medical care, and a job, even if pay was low, the lines at the shops were long, and there wasn't much on the shelves once you got inside.

In 1984, to mark the sixtieth anniversary of the creation of the Kyrgyz Autonomous Soviet Socialist Republic (ASSR), a new Lenin Square was built in the capital, Bishkek, along the main east-west street, Leninsky Prospekt. Its focal point, in front of the new historical museum, was a statue of Lenin in one of his more dramatic poses, his right arm raised in the direction of the Kyrgyz Ala Too mountains to the south.

At independence, Leninsky Prospekt became Chuy Prospekt, and Lenin Square Ala Too Square, but Lenin remained, his arm outstretched. Locals jested that he was trying to direct traffic or hail a taxi on one of the city's busiest streets. In August 2003, the authorities moved the statue to a more discreet location—a park on the other side of the historical museum. To mark what the government described, in something of a historical stretch, as "2,200 years of Kyrgyz statehood," the statue of Lenin was replaced by a statue of Erkindik (Liberty)—a winged female figure on top of a globe, holding a tunduk, the circular frame that forms the top of the traditional Kyrgyz nomadic dwelling, the yurt. As the Lenin statue was dismantled, protesters filed a lawsuit and marched with "Hands Off Lenin!" banners. The Communist party leader and parliamentary deputy Absamat Masaliev claimed officials wanted to convert a bomb shelter under the statue into an underground retail complex. "Who gave the small nation of Kyrgyzstan its statehood? Lenin!" said another opponent.[2]

The removal was supported by a coalition of NGOs. "Lenin did not offer anything except violence and dictatorship," its leader, Edil Baisalov, said. He claimed that there were about four thousand Lenin statues in towns and villages in Kyrgyzstan. "Isn't that rather too many for a person who never even visited Kyrgyzstan, and didn't say a word about our country anywhere in his works? For Kyrgyzstan to still have so many monuments to Lenin is like Germany preserving statues of Hitler. If we really want to build a democracy and a new civil society, we must tear such things down." Other commentators were more cynical. "If the authorities don't like Lenin anymore, why don't they just remove the statue's head?" asked one parliamentary deputy. "That way, each new leader could simply screw a model of his head onto Lenin's body. Just think of the money that could be saved."[3] The government ended up spending more money. In 2011, reportedly because some Kyrgyz believed that a woman holding a tunduk was a bad omen, Erkindik was supplanted by Manas, the national folk hero.

Although some Kyrgyz nationalists in Osh would support the removal of the Lenin statue, the city has escaped a public spat on the issue, probably because it faces more pressing challenges—a stagnant economy, declining social services, a high crime rate, and periodic bloody conflicts between ethnic Kyrgyz and Uzbeks, the most recent in 2010 when more than 470 people were killed and 2,800 properties damaged. However, the statue's reprieve does not denote nostalgia for Soviet rule; it's simply (and Lenin would understand this) a matter of economics. The city does not have the money to tear down or move the statue, let alone put up something more politically correct in its place. Today, it's a local landmark, a place where visitors pose for snapshots, kids ride skateboards, and lovers scrawl their names. If Lenin stays, it will be for that best capitalist reason—because he's good for business.

Lenin statues come in many varieties. There's Lenin with his head raised, looking to the skies or stars, Lenin the action figure rallying the masses, Lenin deep in thought, Lenin looking resolute. There's even a Lenin looking rather uneasy outside a taco joint in Seattle. Kyrgyzstan's two most prominent Lenins do look different. Bishkek Lenin, with his right arm outstretched towards the mountains, is the dynamic leader, pointing towards some mystic, communist, egalitarian future. Osh Lenin holds out his arms as if to greet people. He seems kinder, gentler, more human. Considering Osh's troubled history, maybe the Lenin statue is a symbol worth keeping.

Mountain Barriers

From the so-called Pamir Knot in Tajikistan, the great mountain ranges of Asia extend in all directions—the Himalayas and the Karakoram to the southeast, the Hindu Kush to the southwest, the Kunlun to the east, and the Tian Shan to the northeast. In Kyrgyzstan, the Central Tian Shan range forms a natural border with China's Xinjiang Province, rising to Pik Pobedy (Victory), at 24,111 feet the second-highest point in the former Soviet Union. South of Bishkek, the Kyrgyz Ala Too range runs east-west to the deep mountain lake of Issyk Kul; the Kungey Ala Too range north of the lake forms the border with Kazakhstan; the Fergana range straddles the middle of the country; the Pamir Alay range dominates the south. More than 90 percent of Kyrgyzstan's land area—the size of Austria and Hungary combined, or the US state of Montana—consists of mountains, with 40 percent higher than 3,000 feet.

The mountains are both a blessing and a curse. Their natural beauty offers potential for tourism, but "Switzerland of Asia" campaigns have so far failed to contribute significantly to the economy, mainly because of the remoteness of the country and poor roads and tourist facilities. It's great trekking terrain, but the so-called resorts—most of them former summer camps for Soviet industrial workers—are short on both modern facilities and après-ski ambience. There are mineral deposits, many of them unexploited because of the cost and difficulty of mining in remote regions. Hydroelectric plants have the potential to provide all the country's electricity supply, with some left over for export. However, as the glaciers continue to recede, scientists worry about the sustainability of the country's water resources. For centuries, the mountains have provided summer pastures for herds of sheep, goats, and horses, but most of the land cannot be cultivated.

Few roads cross the mountains, and they are often blocked by avalanches and mudslides; cash-strapped local authorities struggle to maintain or improve them. Building new roads to improve commerce and boost the economy in rural areas means moving massive quantities of earth and rock and constructing bridges and tunnels—a major investment that usually requires help from foreign donors. It is difficult and expensive to transport goods, deliver the mail, or provide medical services; in winter, a trip to the town market or the hospital may be impossible. At higher elevations, the first snows come in October; some settlements are cut off from November to May.

The mountains are as much a cultural and political as a physical barrier. The major concentrations of population are in two large valleys— the Chuy in the north, with the capital Bishkek, and the Fergana in the south, with Osh and Djalalabad, the second and third largest cities. About half the country's population of 5.3 million live in the south. The Ala Too and Fergana ranges separate the valleys, splitting the country and its major urban centers into two distinct regions. In Kyrgyz society, where identity and loyalty are still defined by family, clan, and village, the government in Bishkek can seem very distant. The north is more industrialized and secular, oriented to Kyrgyzstan's larger and more

MAP 2.1 Kyrgyzstan and the Fergana Valley (map by Brian Edward Balsley, GISP)

prosperous Central Asian neighbor, Kazakhstan, and to Russia and the West. The south is more agricultural, conservative, and Islamic, looking to Uzbekistan and further west to Iran. Some northerners fear separatism, Islamic fundamentalism, and the influence of Uzbekistan in the south; some southerners believe the government in Bishkek exploits their region, while shortchanging it on tax revenue and social services. Polls show that most people in Kyrgyzstan consider the differences between the north and south to be the major challenge to national unity.

Landing in Osh

It's a one-hour flight from Bishkek to Osh over a rugged landscape of rocky, treeless mountain slopes, with fast-running rivers, patches of green pasture, and the occasional settlement. Even in summer, there's snow on the mountain peaks. On my first flight in early December 1995, snow covered most of the valleys. From the window of the Soviet-era, twin-prop Yak-40, I felt as if I could almost step out onto a summit. The pilot flew low to avoid the cloud cover, trusting his view from the cockpit more than his navigation instruments. Flying into the wind, the plane shook and rattled but held its course. My traveling companion, Kuban Tabaldiev, assured me we would be safe. He said he had taken this flight many times. The plane might be old, but the pilots were well trained. They had experience flying in bad weather across all kinds of terrain, taking off and landing at small airports throughout Central Asia and Siberia.

Kuban was the media specialist for the United States Information Service (USIS), the agency which in the 1990s administered US-funded educational and cultural programs. In 1995, USIS partnered with the UNESCO regional office to provide training and resources for journalists in Kyrgyzstan. A media center was planned at the National Library in Bishkek. My assignment was to establish a center in Osh for Kyrgyz, Uzbek, and Russian-language journalists in the south.

USIS and UNESCO staff assured me that they had successfully negotiated space for the center at the oblast (provincial) library. My job was to meet with local journalists and media owners to assess training needs, hire a manager, compile a list of equipment, and write a report. The tasks were enumerated in the usual bureaucratic language. On the ground in Osh, it didn't work out quite as smoothly.

Kuban and I checked into the Hotel Intourist (post-independence, it was renamed the Hotel Osh, but no one seemed to use the new name) for three nights until I found an apartment for the three weeks I was to spend in the city. Like all Soviet-era hotels, the Intourist was centrally located, but that was about its only competitive advantage. When we arrived, the lobby was dark, and the elevators weren't working; the clerk said that the electricity would come on at 5:30 p.m. It did, but the elevators still didn't work, and there was no heat or hot water that night. The first edition of the Lonely Planet guide to Central Asia, published a few months later, warned travelers to stay away from the hotel restaurant with its "ear-splitting music and no customers beyond a few pinstriped thugs."[4] Fortunately, when dinnertime arrived, it was closed. We went out to buy bread, cheese, and fruit, ordered tea and extra blankets from the cheerful *dezhurnaya* (the floor lady who was a fixture in all Soviet-era hotels), and made it an early night. After 10:00 p.m., the second-largest city in Kyrgyzstan was dark and quiet. The only nightlife was the occasional car on the main drag, Kurmanjan Dakta, a few barking dogs, and some Russians down the hallway complaining about the economy over a bottle of vodka.

Ethnic Tension on the Silk Road

At least from the fifth century BCE, Osh has been a crossroads city, a trading center attracting people of many races, religions, and cultures. It lies in the east of the largest and richest agricultural region in Central Asia, the Fergana Valley, where the Ak Burra River, flowing out of the Pamir Alay, emerges from its gorge and flows into the once-mighty Syr Darya, on its way to the Aral Sea. Osh was on a branch of the Silk Road that ran east along the Fergana Valley, crossing the Pamir Alay to Kashgar in China. From as early as the eighth century, Osh was known as a center for silk production and for its huge bazaar. According to archaeological data, the city with its citadel and mosque was surrounded by a fortified wall with three gates. The Mongols razed the city in the thirteenth century, but because of its strategic location Osh soon revived. By the sixteenth century, it was a religious and trading center with mosques and madrassas, markets and wealthy merchant homes. As the tsar's armies advanced through Central Asia, Osh was annexed in 1876. In the Soviet era, it was the administrative center of an oblast (province) in the Kyrgyz Soviet Socialist Republic (SSR), and its demographics began to change. Like other trading cities in the Fergana Valley, most of its population was ethnically Uzbek. From the 1960s, as the Soviet Union began building textile and other industrial plants in the south, authorities encouraged ethnic Kyrgyz to move from the countryside to take factory jobs. The growth in the Kyrgyz population contributed to social tension with the Uzbeks. As long the Soviet authorities maintained tight control over the region, tensions remained largely dormant. When the empire began falling apart, they exploded.

By the late 1980s, economic disparities between the Uzbek and Kyrgyz populations were becoming sharper. The Uzbeks, traditionally traders and arable farmers, benefited from the market conditions of Mikhail Gorbachev's perestroika. The Kyrgyz, most of whom were animal herders, suffered as the collective farms were broken up and they lost their jobs and housing. Uzbeks feared for their future in an independent Kyrgyzstan where ethnic Kyrgyz would dominate politics; although Uzbeks accounted for over a quarter of the population of southern Kyrgyzstan in 1990 (and about half the population of Osh), they held only 4 percent of official posts. In the spring of 1990, an Uzbek nationalist group petitioned the oblast government for greater representation and freedom for Uzbek-language schools, publications, and culture. Meanwhile, a Kyrgyz nationalist group called for the redistribution of land from an Uzbek collective farm. The authorities decided to reallocate most of the land to Kyrgyz farmers with little compensation to the Uzbeks.

Clashes between gangs of Kyrgyz and Uzbeks, many of them young and some intoxicated, began on June 4, 1990, in the town of Uzgen, and soon spread to Osh, thirty-five miles away. The local militsiya (police) stepped in, sometimes with excessive force; some policemen supported their own ethnic group by taking part in the riots. In the countryside, Kyrgyz herders on horseback terrorized Uzbek farmers and attacked chaikhanas, the traditional Uzbek teahouses. Under orders from Gorbachev, army units moved in to Osh and Uzgen, and closed the border with the Uzbek SSR to stop Uzbeks joining the conflict. Official estimates from the three days of fighting put the death toll at more than 300, although unofficial estimates claim it was closer to 1,000. In 1991, the government of newly independent Kyrgyzstan held trials for 48 accused, most of them ethnic Kyrgyz, on charges of murder, rape, arson, destruction of property, and other crimes; 46 were convicted and sentenced.

Despite their symbolism, the trials did not mark a new phase in ethnic relations in the south. Under President Askar Akayev, ethnic Kyrgyz dominated both the national government in Bishkek and the regional and local administrations in the south, including the police and the tax authorities. Although Uzbeks remained dominant in business and trade, they suffered along with the Kyrgyz and other ethnic groups in the economic collapse of the 1990s. In such a volatile situation, government-owned and private media outlets had a crucial role to play. If they succumbed to nationalist or ethnic rhetoric, they could exacerbate tensions. If they served as a voice of reason, they could help build bridges between the ethnic groups. The 1990 riots had unnerved Western governments who feared that Central Asia could descend into the kind of ethnic and religious conflict that wracked the former Yugoslavia. Foreign aid came flowing in to Kyrgyzstan—to develop a market economy, to privatize state-owned property, to draft laws and train legislators and judges, to build civil society, and to support media and raise professional standards in journalism. The Osh Media Resource Center was one of these initiatives.

Let's Make a Deal

Kuban and I spent two days visiting newspapers and TV stations. The media owners were concerned about staying in business: the economy was in a slump, businesses were not buying advertising, and local government officials and the mafia were squeezing them for payoffs. The journalists were concerned about poor pay and working conditions. Most earned less than $50 a month, and needed two or three jobs to put food on the table. Both groups welcomed opportunities for training, agreeing that standards in the profession needed to be raised. Everyone said it was important for Kyrgyz, Uzbek, and Russian media to work harmoniously together. Memories of the June 1990 clashes were still vivid.

After Kuban left, I hired a student from Osh State University as my interpreter and began planning for the center. The library director, Ismailova Ibragimovna, was proving to be a tough negotiator. The library's budget had been slashed, and she was struggling to pay the staff and maintain the building. There was no money for books and newspaper and magazine subscriptions. A new center with computers, radio equipment, satellite TV and—perhaps most exciting of all in 1995—an

Internet connection, promised to bring in new patrons and raise the profile of the library with the oblast administration. UNESCO and USIS had agreed to fund the newspaper and magazine subscriptions. I expected Ibragimovna to enthusiastically support the project.

Instead, she held out for more. Perhaps she thought the donors had deep pockets; perhaps she thought she could play hardball with a green Westerner on his first job in Central Asia. The agreement with USIS and UNESCO was not in writing, and did not specify the size or location of the room for the center. Ibragimovna started by showing me a windowless second-floor room, not much larger than a broom closet. She claimed all other rooms in the library were occupied. Even a casual visitor would have concluded otherwise because several rooms were, if not exactly unoccupied, at least underused. When you opened the door, a couple of staff members invited you to join them for tea; there were no shelves, typewriters, and certainly no books in the room. I decided to call Ibragimovna's bluff and said that the room she offered was unsatisfactory. The center had to be located in a larger room with windows on the first floor. The donors would pay for repairs and painting, new desks and furniture, and install a security system.

Ibragimova thought for a moment. "Maybe I can find such a room," she said. "But it will not be easy. I know you need to hire a manager for the center. My daughter needs a job."

I suppose I should not have been shocked, but this was the first time I had come face-to-face with an attempt to parlay influence into a job. And the request needs to be put into cultural context. In Kyrgyz society, kinship ties are the ones that really bind. Your family comes first, then your tribe or clan. In a traditional nomadic society, there's a duty to help a family member who falls sick or loses livestock in a winter storm. However, when this value system moves from the yurts and mountain pastures to the city, to government agencies, universities, and private companies, it can breed corruption and nepotism—jobs, government contracts, and sweet business deals for relatives, bribes for university admission and diplomas, and payoffs to officials and the police. In the city, the extended family grows to include political supporters and business associates.

Politicians in Central Asia are regularly accused of corruption for using their positions to enrich themselves and their relatives. Often their response, at least in private, is that they are upholding traditional values. Because they had the ability or good fortune to attain power and wealth, it is now their responsibility to help less fortunate family members. How far this responsibility goes is another matter. Is it a moral duty to find a job for a family member who lacks the basic qualifications? To bribe a judge to get your brother off on a drug-trafficking charge? To award a government contract or a commercial network TV license to your daughter? Still, the conflict in value systems is real enough. Conduct that in the West would be considered corrupt or at least ethically questionable may be regarded as a moral duty in Central Asia. In other words, not doing whatever you can to help relatives may be unethical.

I agreed to meet Ibragimovna's daughter. She was a second-year university student with no background in journalism and no interest in the field. I gave her as much advice as I could muster on a career in retail fashion. I promised to revise her résumé and have it translated into English. She told her mother how helpful I had been and said she wasn't interested in the manager job after all. The next day, Ibragimovna was able to find a spacious first-floor room with windows for the center.

I then proposed that we draft a job description for the manager, translate it into Kyrgyz, Russian, and Uzbek, distribute it to media outlets, NGOs, and government offices, and run an advertisement in the local newspapers. Ibragimovna seemed surprised. "That's not the way we do things here," she said. "Why don't you just go ahead and pick someone you like? That's how I choose my staff." I said that I was dealing with donor funds, and we had to follow the rules—an open search process, with written applications and interviews. With a mild protest, but also with a sense of curiosity, Ibragimovna joined me and a UNESCO representative in interviewing eight of the twelve applicants. The unanimous choice was Renat Khusainov, a twenty-eight-year-old university teacher with a background in journalism and computers, who was fluent in Russian, Kyrgyz, and English. He was a Tatar, a member of an ethnic minority. At the end of the discussion, Ibragimovna looked me straight in the eye. "Is ethnic origin an issue in this appointment?" she asked. "Well, it's not an issue for me if it's not one for you," I shot back. She smiled. "This is a very good day for the library," she said.

On the Road to the Sacred Mountain

After three nights at the grim Hotel Intourist, I moved into an apartment a few blocks south on Kurmanjan Dakta. The apartment was sparsely furnished but within easy walking distance of the library. Most important, the heating was working. In almost every Soviet city, a central thermal plant supplied heated water to radiators in houses, apartments, businesses, and public buildings. Or at least it was supposed to. Lack of fuel, maintenance, or some combination of the two meant that the system was notoriously unreliable. In winter, parts of Osh were without heat for days because of frozen pipes and equipment breakdowns. Most government officials lived in the city center where the system was better maintained. I was lucky to be in the right neighborhood.

Unfortunately, the heat never came on in the restaurants, where the few diners huddled in overcoats and fur hats. Even though soup and a main course cost as little as $1.50, and it was difficult to pay more than $4, few could afford to eat out. Apart from the occasional wedding reception, the restaurants were almost deserted. At the Ak-Burra Restaurant, a lonely attendant sat by the huge empty cloakroom. The cavernous upstairs dining room probably hadn't changed much since the Soviet era when the local party brass went out to celebrate—ornate pillars, heavy red drapes, chandeliers, long mirrors, and paintings in fake gold frames. At 8:30 p.m. on Friday, only one other table was occupied. A sad-faced waiter handed me a five-page menu, but when I tried to order he told me that the kitchen could serve only kotelet (ground meat) with noodles, flat lipioshki bread, and green tea. On other nights, there was beef stroganoff with mashed potatoes and garnish and, sometimes soup and funchosa, a cold, spicy noodle salad. Most restaurant patrons came to drink and dance. Almost every restaurant had a stage for a live band, which belted out pop tunes at a decibel level that made conversation almost impossible. Because there was no heat, patrons danced in overcoats, boots, and fur hats. The music was a cross-cultural mix—a soulful Turkish pop ballad segueing into an American oldie, rendered in a thick accent, and usually without the definite articles: "Heavy bo-dee in whole-sale block, wuz dancin' to jailhuz rock."

After a week or so, I had learned enough Russian to greet the neighbors, shop for food at the bazaar, and tell a cab driver my destination. In 1995, communication and travel in Osh were daily challenges. The telephone switching system was antiquated and overloaded. You could usually get a local call through on the second or third attempt, but to call another city meant dialing a complex series of digits; making an international call required a trip to the city telephone exchange where you waited in line to book the call. The major challenge was finding the number. The library staff, journalists, and media owners (and anyone else who had to make calls on a regular basis) kept numbers in well-worn pocket organizers. Osh, the second largest city in the country, did not have a telephone directory.

There was also no city map—or at least no one I asked could remember ever having seen one. Even if it had existed, it would have likely featured Soviet-era street names that were fast disappearing as the city authorities dug into history and changed them to the politically correct names of Kyrgyz leaders and literary figures. Ulitsa Pionerskaya (Pioneers' Street) was renamed for the painter Gapar Aytiev, Ulitsa 25 Oktyabrya (October 25th Street), marking the date of the Bolshevik Revolution, for the writer Kasym Bayalinov. The main one-way south street, Ulitsa Lenina (Lenin Street) became Kurmanjan Dakta kuchasi, named for the Queen of the South, the tribal chief who ruled the region after her husband was murdered in a palace coup in Khokand in 1862.

Even for fervent Kyrgyz nationalists, the name changes were confusing, and many people continued to use the old Russian names long after they disappeared from the street signs. Lenin was a particular source of confusion. Even though he was usurped by the Queen of the South on the main one-way south street, he simply moved one block east to take over the main one-way north street, pushing aside his one-time Bolshevik comrade-in-arms Yakov Sverdlov, as Ulitsa Sverdlova officially disappeared into street-sign history.

The city buses and marshrutkas (private minibuses) plied both the old and new Lenin Streets, but I did not know the city well enough to know where they would take me, so I took cabs for most trips. In Central Asian cities, the taxi business is still the most visible part of the informal economy. Although there are commercial taxi services, many drivers in private cars pick up passengers on the street. There's a brief negotiation over the fare, although experienced passengers know the going rate between most points.

Apart from the occasional Mercedes, Audi, or BMW driven by a government official or crime boss, there were few vehicles in Osh in December 1995 that should have been on the road at all. The problem wasn't just the bare tires and noisy mufflers. It was the streets, which had received little maintenance from a cash-strapped city government since independence. Cold winters and sizzling hot summers had buckled the road surfaces and created huge potholes. To avoid them, vehicles weaved and swerved, statistically increasing the chance of accidents. The Soviet-era Moskvichs, Volgas, and Ladas with their dented doors and shattered windshields looked like casualties of a fender-bender war, and a few were flamboyantly out of alignment. There were few auto repair shops, and parts were in short supply. If you needed a radiator or a distributor, you headed for the bazaar to scour the used parts laid out on tarpaulins and old blankets. A shortage of auto parts can spur innovation, and drivers routinely made repairs with scraps of metal and wire or a part salvaged from a different type of car. In 1995, gasoline cost about the same as in the United States (making it expensive by local standards), but there was no quality control. Because there were few gas stations, most drivers filled up at the roadside from roving tanker trucks called benavoz that sometimes dispensed a mechanically injurious blend of diesel and gasoline.

On days when I had to visit several newspapers or TV stations, I hired a car and driver for about $30 a day. My regular driver Babur, a broad-shouldered grinning Uzbek with a perfect set of gold teeth, fearlessly gunned his Volga through the rutted side streets, dodging pedestrians and farm animals, shouting (in English) "No problem!" It turned out that he was a police driver who took time off work because I paid more than the police did. Whenever we got stuck behind other vehicles he put a flashing light on top of the car and bellowed orders through a small speaker mounted on the hood. The cars magically parted in front of us.

Babur's favorite, but absolutely unverifiable, claim was that he was a lineal descendant of King Zahiruddin Babur (1483–1530). Official histories describe Babur as a great poet and prose-writer, but he didn't get to be head of the most powerful Moghul state in the world by penning rhyming couplets; he did a lot of fighting along the way. Babur (the name means "lion") had both the lineage and role models to become a warrior king; he was a direct descendant of Tamerlane (Timur) through his father and of Genghis Khan through his mother. In 1497, as the newly crowned king of Fergana, he built a shelter and private mosque on the eastern promontory of Suleiman's Mountain, the rocky outcrop that rises above the city of Osh. In 1504, his small army entered what today is Afghanistan and captured Kabul, where he established himself as ruler. In 1525, he set out to conquer India, using heavy guns to defeat the numerically superior forces of Sultan Ibrahim Lodi and capture Delhi. He went on to defeat other armies and by his death in 1530 had established the Moghul dynasty in India.

It's a steep thirty-minute climb to Dom Babura, the rebuilt version of the small house on Suleiman's Mountain where Babur came to pray. The formation, with its five peaks, is the result of glacial movement, but it is easy to see why travelers believed the mountain, rising majestically from the middle of the wide, flat valley, was the work of God. For centuries, it has been a place of pilgrimage for Muslims. It is said that the Prophet Muhammad once prayed there and that a shrine marks the grave of Suleiman (Solomon), a prophet in the Qur'an. Women who ascend to the shrine and crawl through an opening will, according to legend, give birth to healthy children. As in other parts of Central Asia, Islam is casually mixed with older belief systems, particularly animism—the belief that natural physical entities including animals and plants, and often inanimate objects such as rocks, possess a spiritual essence. The trees and bushes on the mountain are draped with prayer flags. UNESCO, which added Suleiman's Mountain to its list of World Heritage Sites in 2009, has recorded more than 100 sites with petroglyphs representing humans and animals, and 17 sites of worship, linked by a network of ancient paths. Each is reputed to have a medical specialty—to cure barrenness, headaches, or back pain, and even to give the blessing of longevity. According to UNESCO, the mountain is "the most complete example of a sacred mountain anywhere in Central Asia, worshipped over several millennia."[5]

The Russians Are Coming

The Russian push into Central Asia began in the early 1700s with the first of several costly missions to subdue Khiva, the most western of the khanates. In 1735, having defeated the three major Kazakh tribal groups (the Great, Middle, and Little Hordes), the Russians built a forward base at Orenburg in the southern Urals. From the 1850s, in a close parallel to the advance of the American frontier (although in the opposite direction), Russia's armies and railroad builders, followed by settlers seeking farmland, relentlessly pushed east from the industrial cities of the Urals into Siberia and southeast into Central Asia.

What motivated Russian expansion or, as Karl E. Meyer and Shareen Blair Brysac eloquently put it, "the prodigious projection of power over an interminable solitude"? Was it the fear of a revived Mongol empire that could threaten Europe or an impulse for historical revenge? Or a strategic calculation, almost two centuries before Sir Halford Mackinder advanced his theory that the Eurasian heartland was the geographical pivot of history? Meyer and Brysac suggest there were several reasons.

> For an empire lacking natural boundaries, space itself formed a wall. The Yale scholar Firuz Kazemzadeh has pointed to Russia's abiding *horror vacui,* the fear that a hostile power might populate the empty steppe. Nor can one ignore the Russian ambition to secure an overland passage to India, for purposes of commerce and possible conquest—the abiding British nightmare. Other analysts, judging these explanations inadequate, claimed the key lay in the recesses of the Slavic soul. "Russia was as much compelled to go forward," Lord Curzon [the Viceroy of India] maintained, "as the earth is to go around the sun."[6]

The more prosaic explanation is economic. In 1861, the Civil War in the United States cut off exports of American cotton, forcing Russia to turn to other regions to supply its growing textile industry. The climate and soil of the Fergana Valley were considered ideal for cotton growing. Russia also looked to the region for other raw materials and mineral resources, and as a new market for its manufactured goods.

As Russia pushed southward, the British in India were pushing—or rather probing—northward. For half a century, the two colonial empires competed for influence and trade in a vast region stretching from Afghanistan to Tibet in what became known to historians as the "Great Game." The term came from a letter by a British army officer, Captain Arthur Conolly, serving in Afghanistan. Conolly was an extreme example of the Victorian Christian soldier, melding imperialism with humanitarian and missionary zeal. He believed his destiny was to unite the khanates of Central Asia under British protection to stem Russian expansionism and promote commerce with India, persuade their rulers to abandon slavery, and spread Christianity. In 1841, he set off for Bukhara where the emir had imprisoned and tortured another British officer, Colonel Charles Stoddart. The mission failed, with the emir having both officers executed, so Conolly's main legacy was to name the contest between the two great powers. He wrote that he wanted to play a leading role in "a great game, a *noble* game" in Central Asia. The military historian Sir John Kaye, quoting from Conolly's letters, was the first to use the term. It was popularized by Rudyard Kipling in his 1901 novel *Kim* about Kimball O'Hara, the orphaned, street-smart vagabond who foils a Russian plot in British India.

The pawns in the Great Game were the khanates. Conolly's nemesis, the emir of Bukhara, and the khans of Khiva and Khokand were throwbacks to medieval despots, with lavish palaces and courts, harems and slave markets. More important, the khanates controlled trade routes, agricultural lands, and natural resources, and could send large armies into the field. Fortunately for the Russians, they were almost always fighting each other. One by one, they were conquered, annexed, or co-opted by the tsar's generals. Between 1839 and 1895, Russia annexed approximately 1.5 million square miles of territory in Central Asia. It was, writes the historian Alexander Morrison, "an example of European expansion that in speed and scale is matched only by the 'Scramble for Africa' or the British annexation of India."[7] By World War I, the Russian Empire encompassed all of what today are the five republics of Central Asia.

By 1850, the Kazakhs, who had reluctantly agreed to Russian "protection" in the mid-eighteenth century, were subdued after a short-lived revolt to prevent Tatar and Cossack farmers from taking over their

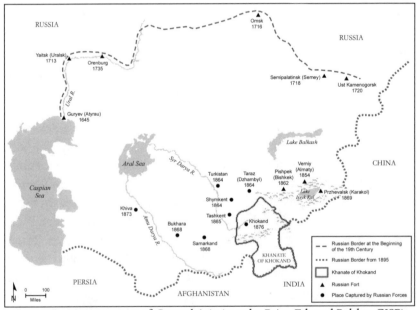

MAP 2.2 Russian conquest of Central Asia (map by Brian Edward Balsley, GISP)

pasture lands. The khans of the three Kazakh hordes became puppet rulers in a Russian colony. To the south, Kyrgyz tribes, descendants of herders from the Upper Yenisey basin of what today is southern Siberia, were scattered throughout the mountains. From the thirteenth century to the seventeenth, successive waves of Mongol invaders had pushed them south, first into the Tian Shan and then to the Fergana and Pamir Alay. Although the khanate of Khokand was still the dominant regional power, the more serious threat came from the Russian armies advancing from the north. To protect their tribes, chiefs such as Kurmanjan Dakta decided to back the Russians. In 1862, a Russian army with support from Kyrgyz irregulars captured the Khokand fortress of Pishpek (now Bishkek); the fortresses of Turkistan, Zhambyl, and Shymkent fell in 1864, Tashkent in 1865, Samarkand in 1868, and finally Khokand in 1876. With the conquest of the khanates, the northern mountains became part of the Russian imperial province of Semireche (Seven Rivers) while the south, including Osh, was absorbed into the province of Fergana.

For almost a century, Russia's southern frontier attracted a gallery of heroes and villains—rogue army commanders who willfully ignored orders from St. Petersburg and whose adventures ended in famous victories or utter disasters, intrepid explorers, railroad builders, entrepreneurs, missionaries, exiled writers, spies, and adventure-seekers on the run from the law, their families, or society in general. The frontier was the place where fame and fortune was won or lost. Central Asia offered the same mix of danger, adventure, and opportunity as the American West in roughly the same period, prompting some scholars to apply Frederick Jackson Turner's frontier thesis to the region.

Russia's hold on the region was always precarious, because its strength depended largely on forts and armies, not on commerce, history, language, or culture. Even though the khans had ruled despotically, sending armies to plunder neighboring kingdoms, extorting tolls and taxes, torturing and executing opponents, and maintaining a lucrative slave trade, at least they were local despots who spoke the language of their peoples and understood Islam and tradition. Russia was the invader, the colonial power. The lands of Central Asia were always on the borderlands of empire and their allegiance to the central power fragile and suspect.

Resentment against Russian rule rose during World War I. Cattle were requisitioned from herders in Semireche, food and cotton from Fergana. In 1916, the authorities began conscripting men into noncombatant labor battalions. An armed uprising that began in Tashkent was joined by Kazakhs and Kyrgyz, exasperated by the loss of their lands and heavy taxation. Although the intended targets were Russian military and government installations, roving bands on horseback attacked Russian colonists and burned their villages. Russian troops retaliated, razing Kazakh and Kyrgyz settlements, killing the inhabitants or forcing them to flee. In the middle of winter, an estimated 50,000 tried to escape over the Tian Shan to China, but many froze or starved to death on the journey.

In the turmoil that followed the Bolshevik Revolution, with civil war raging between the White and Red Armies from the Urals to the Far East, political leaders took advantage of the power vacuum and declared independent republics in Central Asia. Most revolts were short-lived and brutally suppressed by the Red Army. In early 1922, the charismatic Ottoman Turkish soldier Enver Pasha launched a "holy war" to establish a new pan-Turkic caliphate. The revolt attracted thousands of recruits, including bands of *basmachi* guerrillas. After a string of successes in which his army took Dushanbe and recaptured most of the former emirate of Bukhara (whose ruler, exiled in Afghanistan, was bankrolling the campaign), the self-styled "Commander in Chief of All the Armies of Islam" saw his support wane. The Bolsheviks adopted a carrot-and-stick strategy: Moscow cut taxes and returned confiscated land while sending 100,000 more troops to the region. Pasha died in August 1922, just nine months after his revolt began, reportedly cut down by Red Army machine guns while leading a suicidal cavalry charge.

Soviet Gerrymandering

When the Soviet cartographers sliced and diced Central Asia in the 1920s, someone must have said, "The Kyrgyz. Aren't they all nomads? Let's give them the mountains."

Before the Soviet era, there were no national borders between the peoples of the region, and identity was defined by religion, family, clan, and place. The Soviets feared that such muddled loyalties could help Islamic, social, or political movements gain popular support, as Pasha's rebellion had shown. Educated Central Asians and religious leaders still talked privately of a Greater Turkestan or a Central Asian caliphate. The Soviets attempted to counter pan-Islamic and pan-Turkic tendencies by constructing nationalities, giving each a defined territory with national borders, along with a ready-made history, language, culture, and ethnic profile. Your loyalty was no longer to your tribe, village, or faith, but to your nationality as a Kazakh, Kyrgyz, Tajik, Turkmen, or Uzbek and to its Soviet Socialist Republic (SSR).

The Uzbek and Turkmen SSRs were created in 1924, the Tajik SSR in 1929. It took the Russians longer to sort out the Kazakhs and the Kyrgyz, who share similar physical features, traditions, and language. Indeed, in the nineteenth century, they were all referred to as Kyrgyz. As ethnographic research began to reveal differences, the mountain tribes became known as Kara-Kyrgyz (black Kyrgyz) to distinguish them from the steppe-dwelling Kazakhs, who were called simply Kyrgyz because "Kazakh" sounded too much like the name of another group, the Cossacks. Although the Russians seemed confused, the Kazakhs knew perfectly well who they were, and that they were not Kyrgyz. They were members of a tribe that was part of either the Great, Middle, or Little Horde, each of which had its own khan. In 1926, most of present-day Kyrgyzstan became the Kara-Kyrgyz Autonomous Soviet Socialist Republic (ASSR) and a full Kyrgyz SSR in 1936. In the same year, the Kazakh SSR was formed. And so, through the miracle of Soviet ethnic engineering, the Kara-Kyrgyz were no longer black but true Kyrgyz, while the people who had been called Kyrgyz for over a century turned out to be Kazakhs after all.

While promoting new national loyalties, the Soviets realized that too much nationalism could be dangerous. In a parallel effort to solidify control, they shifted around ethnic groups to ensure that none was dominant in a specific area. Thousands of Central Asians were moved to other parts of the Soviet Union. Russian and Ukrainian farm workers and factory workers were settled in Central Asia, while Volga Germans, Chechens, Koreans, and other ethnicities were deported to the region. The policy of divide and rule, intended to suppress ethnic unrest and militant Islam, created artificial borders between ethnically mixed SSRs. The medieval cities of Samarkand and Bukhara, historically major centers of Tajik culture and with large ethnic Tajik populations, ended up in the Uzbek SSR. Osh was a classic case of ethnic gerrymandering. As the Central Asia scholar Madeleine Reeves points out, if the Soviets had drawn boundaries exclusively along national lines, the nomadic Kyrgyz would "end up with a Kyrgyz republic that had no cities of its own: a worrying prospect for a state preoccupied with thrusting 'backward' populations into Soviet modernity."[8] Their solution was to make Osh, with its predominantly Uzbek population of traders and arable farmers, the republic's southern city.

Independence came suddenly to all Soviet republics. Unlike liberation struggles in Asia or Africa, there was no army emerging from the mountains or jungles to be cheered by flag-waving crowds, no government in exile, no heroes or martyrs to freedom. Citizens of each SSR suddenly found themselves citizens of an independent country. As the journalist Ahmed Rashid recalls, the five future Central Asian presidents who met at Ashkhabat in Turkmenistan on December 12, 1991, were reluctant to assume leadership of independent nations:

> Four days earlier Boris Yeltsin, president of Russia, and the leaders of Ukraine and Belarus had signed a treaty dissolving the Soviet Union. The five republics were now suddenly independent but nobody had consulted the Central Asian leaders themselves. Angry, frustrated, fearful, feeling abandoned by their "mother Russia," and terrified about the consequences, the leaders sat up all night to discuss their future. It was strange to see the heirs of conquerors of the world—Genghis Khan, Tamerlane, and Babur—so cowered. They were tied to Moscow in thousands of ways, from electricity grids to road, rail, and telephone networks. Central Asia had become a vast colony producing raw materials—cotton, wheat, metals, oil, and gas—for the Soviet industrial machine based in western Russia. They feared an economic and social collapse as Yeltsin cast them out of the empire. That night a deputy Turkmen foreign minister told me, "We are not celebrating—we are mourning our independence."[9]

The next day, the leaders agreed to join Russia and other former SSRs in the newly formed Commonwealth of Independent States (CIS). That was pretty much the last time they agreed on anything. Despite periodic summits and high-minded talk of regional integration, more issues divide than unite the Central Asian republics. They've disagreed over borders, trade and tariffs, water, gas and oil resources, environmental issues, religion, terrorism, and drug traffickers.

Achieving independence is one thing; creating national identity is another. At independence, ethnic Kazakhs were a minority (albeit the largest one) in Kazakhstan, making up about 41 percent of the population. At the same time, almost one quarter of Tajikistan's population was ethnically Uzbek. With the possible exception of Turkmenistan, all republics have a rich, but potentially volatile, ethnic mix. The region, noted the *New York Times,* looked like "a medieval map" where power is defined by ethnicities and clans, not by borders. Former US National Security Advisor Zbigniew Brzezinski famously referred to Central Asia as "the Eurasian Balkans."

The balkanization is illustrated by the Fergana Valley. Although most of the valley is in Uzbekistan, the northern panhandle of Tajikistan (Sughd province, with a population of over two million) juts into the valley, physically, economically, and culturally separated from the rest of the country by the Pamir Alay. Uzbekistan literally bisects southern Kyrgyzstan, the frontier zigzagging in and out of the foothills of the Fergana and the Pamir Alay; most of the route from Osh to Djalalabad, Kyrgyzstan's third largest city, lies in Uzbekistan. The frontier cuts through the middle of villages and the market town of Kara Soo near Osh. Uzbekistan has five territorial enclaves within Kyrgyzstan, Tajikistan one in Kyrgyzstan and one in Uzbekistan, Kyrgyzstan one in Uzbekistan. When tensions between Kyrgyzstan and Uzbekistan run high (as they often are over water, gas, electricity, and politics) frontier guards sometimes shift their posts a few yards up the road, symbolically extending national territory. In January 2000, Uzbekistan unilaterally seized a thirty-eight-mile stretch of Kyrgyzstan; it also laid mines along its borders with Kyrgyzstan and Tajikistan, ostensibly to keep out Islamic extremists. The *Economist* described Uzbekistan's Islam Karimov as "the regional bully" and noted that "good neighbourliness is in short supply in Central Asia."[10]

Cursing the Future

A man waits in line outside a food shop in Moscow. Finally, he's had enough and tells his friend: "That's it. I'm going over to the Kremlin to kill that Gorbachev." Two hours later he comes back. "Well," says the friend, "did you do it?" "No," he replies, "there was an even longer line over there."

Through the 1990s, in cities, towns, and villages throughout the former Soviet Union, industrial workers gathered in bars, restaurants, chaikhanas, and bazaars to "curse the future." I credit the phrase to my friend Asqat

Yerkimbay, describing growing up in the central Kazakhstan mining town of Zhezdy. But I had heard a similar story from many other people.

For seventh-five years, industrial workers were folk heroes, lauded in speeches, newspapers, books, movies, and wall posters for their efforts to make the Soviet Union a world power. Although agricultural production was vital, Soviet industry seemed more glamorous, and definitely more photogenic. Newsreels and propaganda films recorded the whirring machines of the factory assembly line, the intense heat of the steel furnace, the jagged face of the coal seam, the electricity pylons stretching into the distance. Each product coming off the line, each steel ingot, ton of coal, or megawatt of electricity represented the growing strength of the USSR, the fulfillment of the great socialist dream. And the dream makers were Lenin's proletariat—the engineers, coal miners, steelworkers, engine drivers. Industrial jobs paid better than most professions, and often came with perks such as apartments and vacations to summer resorts in the Kyrgyz SSR. They also helped reinforce the status of women in society. The Soviet Union never needed a Roza the Riveter because women were always in the industrial workforce.

And then it all ended. Despite Gorbachev's policies of perestroika (literally restructuring or rebuilding), most citizens had no idea of what was coming or how it would change their lives forever. With the collapse of the Soviet Union, the central planning system that had supported the economy collapsed too. In every sector, production had been determined by targets and quotas, which usually had little or no relationship to demand. Factories, mines, and collective farms had to meet targets, even if what they produced was not needed and piled up in rail cars or rotted in warehouses. Managers were rewarded for exceeding targets, fired or demoted for falling short—a system that provided ample incentive for cooking the books on cotton or steel production.

In the factories of Central Asia, workers continued to show up, but the targets and subsidies from Moscow had ended, and there were few new customers. Some factories tried to adapt to the market economy, but most lacked the money to invest in new equipment and compete for quality and price with industries in other countries. Compared with other Soviet republics, the industrial base of the Kyrgyz SSR was small because Moscow considered the region too remote to become a major industrial producer. However, factories for agricultural processing, textiles, and household goods employed thousands in the Chuy and Fergana Valleys.

By the mid-1990s, most had closed. Almost all the canned goods, clothes, shoes, and pots and pans at the bazaar were imported from China and other Asian countries.

Kyrgyzstan struggled to adopt the reforms that donor countries and the International Monetary Fund said were needed to qualify for loans and aid and to build a market economy. The government abandoned subsidies and price controls, and replaced the Russian ruble with a new currency, the som. The pace of reform caused massive economic dislocation; in one year, inflation ran close to 1,000 percent, devastating people on pensions and fixed incomes. With international support, the government eventually stabilized the currency and brought inflation down to manageable levels, but economic recovery remained slow, and poverty rates increased.

Official reports tell the story of Kyrgyzstan's economic collapse in sanitized, bureaucratic terms—the language of economists, policymakers, and development experts. The calculations were at the macro level—cold measurements of Gross Domestic Product, consumer price indexes, output by economic sector, government debt, foreign direct investment. These were often coupled with Pollyanna-like projections about foreign direct investment, government bond auctions and the reform of the financial services sector. In the mid-1990s, it was questionable whether Kyrgyzstan even had a financial services sector to reform. The som had been devalued, inflation remained high, and almost no one trusted the banks to keep their money safe. With few deposits, banks had little money to lend, and when they made loans, it was at ruinous 30 percent interest rates. If you wanted to start a new business, you asked your family to lend or give you the money. Even the loan sharks at the bazaar charged less interest than the banks.

The economic statistics were sometimes based on questionable data. One year the government, in an attempt to convince foreign donors and investors that the economy was picking up, declared that the unemployment rate had dropped below 10 percent for the first time since independence. Even government supporters were incredulous. It turned out that in its sample the statistical agency had included every tout hawking cigarettes, pirated cassettes, and homebrew on the streets as a "self-employed market vendor." The real rate was probably at least 40 percent.

None of the reports and statistics told the human stories of dislocation, especially for industrial workers. Their skills were not needed in the new economy, and there were few opportunities for retraining. Some left for Russia, hoping to find jobs, but the situation in many Russian regions was as bad as in Central Asia. A few started private businesses or worked as drivers. Some just gave up. It was not only the loss of income, devastating though that was. It was the loss of purpose, dignity, and respect. They had been the breadwinners for their families; now they had no jobs and no prospects. In some families, women became the main wage earners, which led some husbands to feel their loss of status more intensely. Back in the good old days, industrial workers could afford a bottle of vodka or cognac for a party or holiday celebration. Now some turned to the bottle to try to forget their plight. Official reports on the economy do not figure in the social costs of alcoholism, depression, broken marriages, domestic violence, and suicides. It is not surprising that the engineers, miners, and steelworkers denounced Gorbachev as a traitor and cursed a future that seemed to offer them nothing.

At the Osh Bazaar

A man walks into a shop and asks, "Don't you have any fish?" The shop assistant replies, "You've got it wrong. This is a butcher's—we don't have any meat. They don't have any fish in the fish shop across the street!"

In the Soviet era, all shops—from the Tsum central department store to the small corner store—were state-owned and -operated and numbered, with fixed prices and limited selection. Shoppers complained of long lines and surly customer service. In some areas, seasonal shortages of basic foodstuffs—bread, meat, dairy products, fruits, and vegetables—were common.

An underground retail sector existed alongside the state-run shops. Prices were higher, but the quality was better, and some items were simply not sold in state-run stores. For Levis or Marlboros, you needed to talk to the guy in the leather jacket who hung around behind the Palace of Culture. In agricultural regions such as the Fergana Valley, some city dwellers had dachas where they grew apples, apricots, peaches, and cherries, and raised vegetables; they canned for the winter months and sold surplus to neighbors and friends. The police periodically cracked down on the underground economy, especially when it involved large shipments of alcohol, cigarettes, or consumer electronics. But it was not worth the effort to stop a babushka selling tomatoes or strawberry jam to her neighbors in the apartment block, or even to stop the production and sale of moonshine called *samogon* (translated literally as "self-run"), the homemade distilled alcoholic concoction usually made from sugar, beets, potatoes, bread, or fruit.

In many ways, the state shops were a Potemkin Village—impressive facades, with empty shelves inside. And so the Soviets quietly allowed business in the informal economy to keep running, especially at the bazaars. In Osh, the massive Jayma bazaar which sprawls along the western bank of the Ak-Burra River, winding up dozens of side streets and alleys, had been one of the great markets on the Silk Road since medieval times. Today, it is open seven days a week, and thronged on Friday and Sunday, the traditional market days. It is still primarily an agricultural market, with slaughterhouses and warehouses. One section is piled high with bales of hay; in another, live chickens are sold; in another, raw cotton and wool; nearby, blacksmiths forge horseshoes, nails, stovepipes, cooking pots, and traditional Uzbek ornamental knives. In the summer, the market bulges with fresh produce—peaches, apricots, oranges, cherries, grapes, melons, and vegetables. Even in winter, apples, pears, figs, pomegranates, potatoes, onions, and carrots are abundant, and dried apricots, raisins, pistachios, almonds, and walnuts are sold year round. Uzgen rice—the main ingredient of the Uzbek national dish *plov*, a lamb pilaf with carrots, onions, and hot peppers—is sold from open bags. *Lipioshki* (flatbread) is baked in tandoori ovens. Butter comes by the slab, sugar in huge yellow crystalline lumps. *Shashlyk* (marinated mutton or beef kebabs, served with vinegary onions), *laghman* (a Uighur spicy noodle and vegetable soup), *manti* (dumplings stuffed with diced lamb and onion), and *samsa* (pastry filled with spicy meat or vegetables) are sold from stalls.

Even for a seasoned traveler, the sights, sounds, and crush of people can be overwhelming. Ear-splitting commercials for local businesses blast out over the tinny speakers of the public address system, forcing the bootleg music vendors to crank up the volume on their boom boxes, playing the latest Turkish and Chinese pop hits. In the auto section, there's a brisk trade in used alternators, batteries, worn belts and tires; engine oil, sold in mason jars, looks as if it's already serviced a fleet of diesel buses. Although traditional silk, wool, and cotton fabrics are sold, the garment district has largely been taken over by vendors hawking cheap imports from India, Pakistan, Iran, and Turkey with fake (and often misspelled) designer labels. The unofficial money exchanges do brisk business. For the brave investor, there was even a financial services sector, of sorts—a group of burly men with shaven heads dressed in trainers hawking share certificates for newly privatized companies.

Leaving Kyrgyzstan

Three days before Christmas in 1995, I took the flight north from Osh to Bishkek to report in to USIS, and then fly back to the United States. After three weeks, I left the city with mixed feelings. I looked forward to spending the holidays with Stephanie, but worried about the future of the Osh Media Resource Center. And I felt a bond with the people with whom I had worked, who had helped me begin to understand their country and culture and the challenges they faced. I had no idea of whether I would ever see Kyrgyzstan again. Little did I know that, less than a year later, I would be returning to Osh. This time it was not on a Yak-40, but in a beat-up Lada with a case of vodka in the trunk.

three

How Do You Say "Rump Roast"?

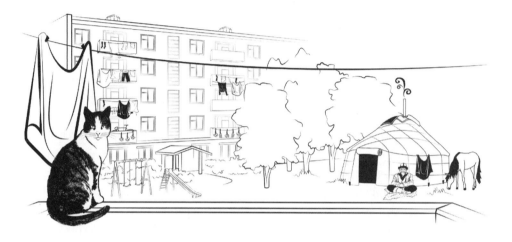

The Twelve Suitcases

In June 1996, the news I had been waiting for finally came. I would be going back to Kyrgyzstan in September for a one-year Fulbright Fellowship to teach journalism and mass communication at the state university in Bishkek, guest-lecture at other universities, and work with journalists and the new commercial TV stations that were starting up. Stephanie gamely agreed to join me for the year.

Fulbright scholar awards are typically made in the spring. That leaves enough time to apply for an academic leave, find a renter and pet-sitter, sort out the bills and bank accounts, and figure out what to pack. Unfortunately in 1996, politics intervened. I really can't blame House Speaker Newt Gingrich, the Republican Congress, or President Bill Clinton. They were fighting over the federal budget and funding for Medicare, education, and the environment. Sending me to Kyrgyzstan did not require raising the federal debt limit. Nevertheless, the two government shutdowns (six days in November 1995 and twenty-two days in December 1995–January 1996) had a knock-on effect as spending bills and appropriations were delayed. Among the casualties was the Council for the International Exchange of Scholars (CIES), which administers the Fulbright Program. My Fulbright had been approved, the program officer assured me, but CIES did not yet have the money. I should certainly not do anything foolish, such as rent the house or buy an air ticket, until funding was confirmed.

When it was, CIES hurriedly arranged an orientation session in Washington, DC, for scholars and student awardees heading for Asia. It was standing-room only for India and China but less than a dozen gathered for the Central Asia briefing. It had taken a couple of years for the Fulbright program to get going in Central Asia, so few scholars and students had been there. An anthropologist who had done research in Kyrgyzstan presented a slide show of ancient sites and talked about nomadic culture and oral traditions. A nursing professor who had been in Uzbekistan talked about her attempts to educate her students about bad cholesterol. Her teaching included public health movies; the students' favorite was called *Killer Fat*. No one discussed the higher education system, told us what to pack, or what we could buy at the bazaar in January.

In the mid-1990s, there were few resources for Westerners who were going to live in Central Asia for an extended period. For historical background, I could read about the Great Game with evocative descriptions of mountains and steppe by British and Russian explorers and military envoys. However, I was planning to arrive in Bishkek by plane, not on horseback from Delhi with wagons, porters, and formal greetings from the viceroy to the local khan. There were books on the Soviet era, but in the early 1990s, before the blossoming of Central Asia scholarship, there were few studies of the region in the post-Soviet era. Today, it seems that every Peace Corps volunteer teaching English in a Kyrgyz village blogs about the experience, but there were no such tales in 1996. Thankfully, the first edition of the *Lonely Planet Guide* came out in summer 1996, just in time to help us plan the trip.

Because new luggage is a target for thieves, we decided to travel with beat-up, yet sturdy, suitcases. We added to our collection of well-worn travel pieces with some thrift store $2 specials. Then we worked on packing lists. We simply didn't know what to expect, so it all went in—winter and summer clothes, books and papers, aspirins and antibiotics, Ziploc bags, duct tape, a pressure cooker, cookbooks, and the contents of the kitchen spice rack. Someone had told Stephanie there was no basil in Kyrgyzstan; instead, it was one of the first things she saw at the bazaar. The Fulbright grant included a generous excess baggage allowance. It is almost embarrassing to admit, but we exceeded it. When everything was assembled, we had twelve suitcases—a total of 490 pounds.

Our flight from Washington to Frankfurt was delayed, and the Delta agent said we would not make the connection in Istanbul for the Turkish Airlines flight to Bishkek; we would have to wait two days for the next flight. The only option was to fly via Moscow to Almaty in Kazakhstan, and make the last part of the trip by road. The agent booked us on Transaero, a new Russian private airline.

We staggered up to the Transaero check-in in Frankfurt, our bodies sagging from the five heavy carry-on bags. "That looks like more than five kilos," said the agent. "Oh, they're not heavy, I'm just weak," said Stephanie in her excellent German, trying to disguise her panting. A dispute was averted by the news that we had been bumped up to business class where there was no carry-on limit. We settled down for a glass of champagne, and wondered how we'd make the transfer to the Almaty flight in Moscow.

Moscow's Sheremetyevo is, in my experience, one of the least welcoming airports in the world (unless you're Edward Snowden, and you have to hole up in the transit area) with overpriced (even by airport standards) shops and restaurants, and few seats for transit passengers. In 1996, the arrivals hall was a soulless room with faded Soviet-era decor. Because we were taking another Transaero flight, we expected our luggage to be transferred. Our hearts sank when the first of our twelve bags emerged on the carousel. As we heaved them off the belt, other passengers stepped in to help. One pulled another bag off the carousel and added it to our stack. "Not ours," said Stephanie. "Oh, we thought they were *all* yours," the passenger replied with a wry smile.

There were no luggage carts, but Stephanie spotted a man with a dolly. "U menya dvenatsat' chemodanov (I have twelve suitcases)," she announced. He broke into a smile; I was half expecting cartoon-like dollar signs to pop up in his eyes. Somehow, he loaded all twelve cases onto the dolly. It was a short walk to the terminal, but we felt he well deserved his $20. The Transaero agent was not welcoming. "You must pay $500 for excess luggage," she said. We showed her the receipt from Delta. "That was in Washington. Now you are in Moscow. You must pay," she insisted. We refused. Supervisors were called. The Delta paperwork was scrutinized, discussed, held up to the light, photocopied. Eventually, the agent gave up. "Have a nice trip," she said, handing us our boarding cards.

In Almaty, we emerged from the arrivals hall into a clutch of tough-looking characters shouting "taxi, taxi." The words "dvenatsat' chemodanov'" and "Bishkek" gave us instant celebrity status, with drivers competing for what would definitely be the best-paying fare of the day. We needed two cars and decided to travel separately so that we could keep an eye on the luggage; we had been counting bags at each transit point. I rode in a comfortable, dented Mercedes; Stephanie had a more challenging trip in a right-hand-drive Toyota. No one has ever explained to me how right-hand-drive Japanese cars manufactured for the domestic market ended up in Central Asia in the 1990s, but they were pretty common, and among the more dangerous vehicles on the road. The two cars weaved through the midday city traffic, avoiding collisions by important inches. At one stoplight, the Toyota pulled up on the right side of the Mercedes. Stephanie and I wound down the windows, held hands for a moment, and glanced nervously at each other. "Have a safe trip, darling," I said, without any sense of irony. Out on the two-lane highway to Bishkek, her driver kept pulling out to pass trucks and buses. "Nyet, nyet," shouted Stephanie, who was always the first to see the approaching vehicle. The Toyota swerved back into the right-hand lane before the driver attempted his next suicidal maneuver.

The highway parallels the northern slope of the Zailiysky Ala Too range, a branch of the Tian Shan, running southwest along the treeless plain before dipping south through a serpentine pass to the Chuy Valley and Bishkek. Bathed in the late afternoon sun, the mountains, some with snow-capped peaks, were spectacular. Our adventure had begun.

The Mountains Are Always South

The first permanent settlement on the Chuy River at the site of present-day Bishkek was a clay fort built by the khan of Khokand in 1825 along one of the Silk Road routes across the Tian Shan. By the 1860s, the khanate was facing a double threat—the tsar's armies advancing from the north and west, and Kyrgyz tribes who resented Khokand's taxes and military conscription. The fort was in a strategic location on the road from Verniy (now Almaty) to Tashkent. In 1860, it fell to a Russian force after a seven-day siege, but the Russians inexplicably returned to Verniy, leaving the location undefended, and Khokand sent troops to rebuild the fort. In 1862, Kyrgyz horsemen joined a Russian force of 1,400 troops with cannon to retake the fort. After a ten-day siege, it fell again. This time, the Russians stayed, and the town of Pishpek was founded sixteen years later. The fertile soil of the Chuy Valley attracted Russian and Ukrainian settlers, swelling the population of the region.

As with many places in Central Asia, the name of the city changed with the prevailing ideological winds. There's an unresolved debate over the origin of Pishpek, its first name. In Kyrgyz, *pishpek* or *bishkek* describes the wooden instrument used to churn fermented mare's milk (*kumys*). As *Lonely Planet* remarks, "Numerous legends—some quaint, some rude—explain how a town came to be named for a wooden plunger." A more prosaic version has it that pishpek is a corruption of a more ancient name that means the "place below the mountains."[1] The issue became moot in 1926 when the Soviets changed the name to Frunze, in honor of the Red Army commander, Mikhail Vasilevich Frunze, who was born there in 1885. After the 1917 revolution, Frunze led forces in the civil war, eventually being given command of the Eastern Front. In Central Asia, he recaptured Khiva and Bukhara, driving the White Army out of the region and the basmachi guerrillas into the mountains. Although his death in 1925—from an excessive dose of chloroform during routine surgery—was suspicious, raising speculation that Stalin was involved, Frunze retained his place in Soviet iconography, with a military academy, rifle division, two metro stations (in Moscow and St. Petersburg), and a battleship named for him, as well as the town of his birth.

Kyrgyzstan's casual tolerance of its Soviet past—as demonstrated by the longevity of the Lenin statues—is illustrated by the preservation of Frunze's legacy. Around the thatched cottage where he was born, the Soviets constructed a two-story museum with military artifacts and memorabilia. In this historical narrative, Frunze is a brave military leader and loving father and husband, not the ruthless commander who suppressed nationalist movements in Central Asia. Although the Soviet names of many streets in Bishkek were changed to politically correct Kyrgyz names after independence, Frunze's name remains on one of the main east-west streets. There's a bronze statue of Frunze on a horse opposite the railroad station. And airline passengers cannot avoid Frunze because the International Air Transport Association (IATA) retains the code FRU for Bishkek. That can be confusing for first-time travelers who wonder if their baggage is going to a different city. In terms of acronyms, FRU is perilously close to airports in Botswana, Chile, Guatemala, and Papua New Guinea.

Bishkek was laid out on a grid pattern, with broad north-south and east-west streets. Orienting yourself is easy as long as you remember the cardinal rule: the mountains are always south. In Almaty, where the same rule applies, it's of limited use in some areas because tall buildings block the view, but Bishkek is still a low-rise city. Water from two mountain rivers, the Ala-Archa and Alamedin, flows in channels to a canal north of the city, and on to the Chuy River. In mid-September, Bishkek felt more like a sleepy country town than the capital of a country. Compared to Almaty, the traffic was light. People strolled along the tree-lined streets, stopping to buy an ice cream or *gazirovka* (gas water), a syrup-based carbonated drink, from sidewalk vendors. Children played and rode bicycles around the Lenin statue in Ala Too Square. Police directing traffic at the main intersections smiled as they ineffectually waved their arms in the air. Horse-drawn wagons slowed down traffic near the Osh bazaar, the large market on the west side of the city. Babushkas squatted on the sidewalk, selling apples, tomatoes, cherries, and raspberries from their dachas. On a patch of land next to the National Library on Sovietskaya, one of the main north-south streets, sheep were grazing.

We rented a spacious though sparsely furnished apartment on Pervomayskaya (1st of May Street) in the city center. Officially, the street was called Razzakova, renamed for Ishak Razzakov who briefly headed the government of the Kyrgyz SSR in the mid-1940s. Razzakov was hardly a well-known historical figure, and no one we met (including the neighbors) used the new name. Taxi drivers had certainly never heard of it, so we sacrificed political correctness for convenience and stuck with Pervomayskaya. In Soviet real estate parlance, the apartment was a *khrushchevka*, named for the Soviet premier, Nikita Khrushchev. Faced with a severe housing shortage after World War II, the government encouraged technologies to provide low-cost, easy-to-assemble housing. Unlike the earlier *stalinkas,* which were built on site and sometimes even boasted neoclassical details, the prefabricated concrete panels of the khrushchevkas were mass produced and shipped by truck. Elevators were considered too costly and time consuming to build so almost all khrushchevkas had five stories—the maximum height of a building without an elevator under Soviet health and safety standards. Ours was a standard, three-room apartment with a small kitchen and bathroom in a block of thirty units. It was in a prime location—about a twenty-minute walk to the university and two blocks from the USIS office, where I reported to the Public Affairs Officer. It was one block from the central Panfilov Park, close to a market on Jibek Jolu (Silk Road) and a short walk from Ala Too Square. Today, this is the high-rent district where government officials, business people, and foreign contractors pay top som for an apartment. In 1996, we rented it for $300 a month (plus modestly priced utilities). We put up with minor inconveniences—the small refrigerator, the lack of working electrical outlets, and the rickety furniture. We bought a VCR, a toaster, and kitchen utensils. And we started going to the bazaar to buy fruits and vegetables. We knew that by November fresh produce would be scarce so we joined other apartment-dwellers in the annual ritual of canning.

In mid-September, the Osh bazaar was groaning with fresh produce, and prices were low. We filled a box with over five kilos of Roma tomatoes for a couple of dollars. A large bucket of raspberries was $4.80, a bucket of plums $1.20, and about seven kilos of apricots $5.20. A Kyrgyz

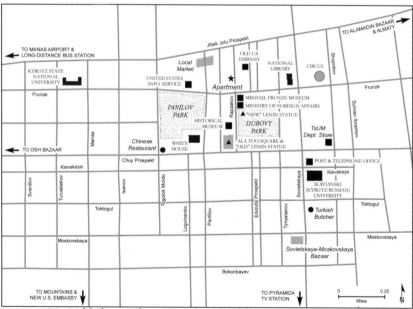

MAP 3.1 My Bishkek (map by Brian Edward Balsley, GISP)

colleague came over to the apartment, armed with pots, pans, and canning recipes. The system—or the technology, as she called it—was different from the one Stephanie had used in the United States and we struggled to fit the lids on the jars with a device that worked like a reverse-action can opener. Still, by the end of the day, we had canned several jars of tomatoes and plum jam and two jars of *adjika*—a relish made from tomatoes, carrots, peppers, apples, hot chili peppers, vinegar, oil, salt, and sugar. Our colleague said the recipe came from a Bulgarian version of *Good Housekeeping* that circulated in Bishkek in Soviet times.

A Walking City

It was a 1½-som (9-cent) ride home on the bus from the Osh bazaar with our buckets of fruit and box of tomatoes. Bishkek residents, especially those who live in the outer suburbs (*microraions*), depend on public transportation—the buses, trolley buses, and *marshrutkas* (minibuses). The buses varied in size, age, and mechanical condition; most of the older ones sounded as if they needed a clutch job. The newer buses were visible examples of foreign aid. They were German-made, with German-language ads on the side, and apparently still heading for destinations in Berlin, Essen, or Wiesbaden. You learned not to pay attention to destinations such as the Hauptbahnhof or Goetheplatz; if the bus was heading west on Kievskaya, you could be pretty sure it was going to the Osh bazaar.

Public transportation was cheap but often crowded, so we developed tactics, as well as elbow muscles, to deal with the crush. If the bus or trolley was full, we started pushing to the front a couple of stops before we wanted to get off. On the trolleys, the only advantage to crowding was the soft human padding. When the driver took a corner too tightly, the conducting rods detached from the overhead cables; the trolley immediately lost power and stopped abruptly, throwing everyone around. Then you were glad the trolley was packed. There was a short delay while the driver climbed up a ladder to the roof of the bus, lifted the rods and restored the current.

The marshrutka (short for *marshrutnoye taksi* which literally means "routed taxi"), common throughout the former Soviet Union, costs a few som more than the bus or trolley but is much faster. Like the African "bush taxi," it follows a route, picking up and dropping off passengers anywhere along the way. A marshrutka has twelve to fourteen seats, but on local routes it sometimes takes as many as twenty passengers. There's no schedule—a marshrutka leaves when it's full of passengers and luggage, or when the driver figures he has enough fares to make the journey viable.

Most of the time, we walked. To the university, the local bazaar, to shops and restaurants—most of the places we needed to reach were within ten to fifteen minutes by foot along tree-lined sidewalks, boulevards, and parks. Apart from the traffic, the main hazards were the uneven sidewalks. In places, they were even missing. By "missing," I do not mean that there was no sidewalk, as is often the case in US cities. It was there, but you had to step around a gaping hole in the ground. Although some were the result of seasonal cracking and expansion of the concrete, most appeared where a manhole cover should have been, since many had been stolen and melted down for scrap. In daylight and good weather, you could avoid the holes. At night, walking became riskier. Walking in winter, you learned to keep an eye out for geometrically shaped depressions in the snow; if it was a circle or rectangle, you could be pretty sure there was no sidewalk under it.

One of our favorite local walks was to the US embassy, which was housed in a modestly sized but elegant nineteenth-century Russian-style house on leafy Prospekt Erkindik (Freedom), about two blocks from our apartment. Most of the time, we did not have official business but stopped by to read week-old newspapers and magazines, borrow a video or book from the ambassador's collection, or check on expat social events. The office of the ambassador, Eileen Malloy, was just off the main entrance, and she would stop to chat in breaks between meetings. The place bustled with visitors. Security was thorough, but unobtrusive.

Today, the US embassy is located on a flat, open area of land on Prospekt Mira in the south of the city with no other construction permitted nearby. Its thick, high walls are topped with spikes and monitored by security cameras. It's a long bus ride from downtown, so no one just stops by any more. It looks like a prison, not a diplomatic mission.

Supply Thread

Business people and economists like to talk about the *supply chain,* the intricate, interlinked system of organizations, people, information, and resources that it takes to move a product or service from supplier to customer. In Kyrgyzstan in the mid-1990s, there wasn't so much a supply chain as a supply *thread;* at best it was tangled and frayed, and sometimes it just broke until someone knotted it together again.

The Soviet economy, although based on the artificial creation of supply and demand, at least had a supply chain of sorts. The cotton, wheat, or mutton from your collective farm or tractor tires from your factory were shipped somewhere else. You received a modest salary, free housing, medical care, and education. The cotton or tires might sit in a warehouse or railroad siding because they were not needed, but that didn't matter as long as Moscow kept sending the money. The collapse of the Soviet economy shattered the supply chain because no one was going to pay for cotton or tires they didn't need. Now the challenge for all the Central Asian republics was to produce goods and services that people would pay for and get them to market—in other words, to create a supply chain.

To take the economic pulse of Kyrgyzstan in the mid-1990s, you didn't go to the government ministries where they'd give you the dubious statistics they compiled to keep the foreign donors happy. Instead, you went to the bazaar where most of the economic activity took place. Although there were small street bazaars all over the city, Bishkek had three large daily markets—the Osh bazaar on the west side, Alamedin in the northeast, and Ortosay in the south. About six miles north of the city center—a twenty-minute bus or trolley ride—was Tolchok (which means "push" in Kyrgyz), a sprawling, crowded weekend market with imported consumer goods, and a livestock bazaar, where horses, sheep, cattle, and goats were bought and sold, and traditional Kyrgyz horseback games held. Close by was the auto bazaar, where you could buy a used Lada, Niva, Volga, or Moskvich and maybe also the parts to keep it running.

Stephanie and I frequented the Osh and Alamedin bazaars. They illustrated, better than any statistics, Kyrgyzstan's uneven progress toward a market economy. Let's start in the geographic center, in the covered market halls where meat, dairy goods, and dried fruits and nuts were sold. Here, the vendors had established business relationships with farmers. There were separate sections for mutton, beef, and horse. The Volga Germans sold pork. You could buy a fresh chicken (and pluck it yourself if you knew how), but by 1996 frozen chicken had arrived, reportedly from the United States and Europe. We were told the breast meat went to domestic markets, so all we could buy were legs, backs, and thighs. Dairy vendors had regular supplies of milk, butter, cream, yogurt, *smetana* (sour cream), kumys (fermented mare's milk), the yogurt-like kefir or *airan,* and local cheese. Dried fruit (apricots, red and white raisins, cherries) and nuts (walnuts, pistachios, almonds, apricot pits, sunflower seeds) were available year round, most shipped by truck from the Fergana Valley. You could go to the market halls any day of the year, and be pretty sure of finding what you needed. Here, the supply thread was at its strongest.

As you moved outside the covered halls, the bazaar became more chaotic and the thread weaker. There were stalls with fruits and vegetables, alongside others selling lipioshki, fresh eggs, cigarettes and candy, household goods, cleaning products, paper and school supplies, electrical parts, and imported clothes. Most of the clothes came from India, Pakistan, Bangladesh, and Turkey, with fake, misspelled, sewn-in designer labels—the Calvert Kleins and the Tommy Hilsburgers. Cheap electronics came from China and Southeast Asia. Although some goods were shipped by road, most high-priced items were purchased on so-called shopping trips to Moscow, Krasnoyarsk in Siberia, Urumchi in Western China, Istanbul, or Bangkok. Here the supply thread became tangled, and often broken; whether or not a particular item was available depended on whether someone had made a recent shopping trip.

This section of the bazaar was also the service area with barbers, money exchangers, shoe and watch (and today mobile phone) repair shops, food stalls and fortune-tellers squatting at small tables with tarot cards and magical stones. It was where the official and informal economies met with itinerant vendors selling plastic shopping bags, cigarettes, sunglasses, fake Rolexes, and pens. You didn't want to inquire too closely about *their* supply chain.

In the open areas outside the bazaar proper, trucks and vans were parked, their owners selling goods directly from the tailgate. One day, you could find truckloads of potatoes, onions, or cabbages; on another, cases of beer, wine, or vodka. The inventory was unpredictable, depending on what had been shipped. This was the supply thread at its simplest and weakest.

On the fringes of the bazaar and in the streets leading to it, people squatted on the sidewalks, selling home-canned goods and fruits and vegetables grown at their dachas. Saddest of all were the families or babushkas with their household belongings spread out on blankets. They were literally selling what they owned—clothes, pots, pans, kitchen utensils, personal memorabilia—to survive. This was the supply thread at its most desperate.

FIGURE 3.1 (*above*) Uzbek bread stand in Osh

FIGURE 3.2 (*left*) Kyrgyz *komuz* player at Osh bazaar, Bishkek

FIGURE 3.3
Consumer
electronics aisle
at Osh bazaar,
Bishkek

FIGURE 3.4
Decanting
cooking oil into
soda bottles
at Osh bazaar,
Bishkek

FIGURE 3.5
Shirdaks for
sale at Osh
bazaar, Bishkek

Stephanie and I adopted a simple shopping rule: if we saw an item and we either needed or liked it, we bought it because we might never see it again. One Sunday (the main market day) in November 1996 at the Alamedin bazaar illustrates the buy-it-when-you-see-it principle. We began outside the bazaar proper in the hardware section where people lay out sheets, blankets, and newspapers with new and used car tires, batteries, radiators, alternators, bicycles, hand tools, electrical, plumbing and gas fittings, nuts, bolts, screws, and nails. We bought a drain hose for our arthritic washing machine, which had been dripping on the bathroom floor for two months, then a pair of slippers, some chopsticks, and a small, sharp, hand-forged cleaver. We made one babushka happy by buying her entire inventory—three small rag rugs. She immediately packed up and headed home, presumably to make some more. The catch of the day was a collection of commemorative lapel pins. I'd seen people selling these pins, issued in the Soviet era to mark many occasions, including holidays and sporting events. With the Soviet Union gone, I figured they were worth collecting. One woman had a large collection pinned to two worn red wall hangings with a faded picture of Lenin. She was asking one som (5 cents) for each pin. It was going to take too long to select those I wanted, so I went for a bulk purchase. How much for the whole collection of almost three hundred pins, plus the wall hangings? Although it's traditional to bargain, the price was so low that it seemed mean-spirited to haggle.

The supply thread included recycling. Bishkek did not have a city recycling program, and any public appeals to reduce waste and protect the environment would have likely fallen on deaf ears. People recycled because it saved money, and because there was often no alternative. You couldn't buy some items such as milk and cream at the bazaar or on the street unless you brought your own container. Beer, soda, and milk bottles were returned for a refund. Empty glass and plastic bottles, some retrieved from dumpsters, were resold at the bazaars. Tin cans were used as planters. Fast food such as *samsa, piroshki,* and roasted sunflower seeds came wrapped in scrap paper torn from a ledger or an old textbook. Once we were rewarded for our volunteer editing for the *Kyrgyzstan Chronicle,* the weekly English-language newspaper, with 30 kilos of onions. One of the newspaper's advertisers was going through a liquidity crisis and had settled the bill with half a truckload of onions. We wondered how to store them. Our Russian teacher, Galina, said that Russian women keep old stockings around for such contingencies. Stephanie pulled out some old runny pantyhose; we filled them full of onions and hung them from a line on the balcony. Galina was impressed. "You're a good Russian woman," she told Stephanie.

It's almost a cliché to say that you can buy anything at the bazaar, including a few things that probably should not be for sale, such as hard drugs, Kalashnikovs, and samogon, the Russian moonshine, which, depending on the vintage, chemical composition, and distilling process can give you a warm and fuzzy feeling, leave you with a nasty hangover, or kill you. Unregulated, questionable or illegal activities usually took place on the fringes of the bazaar. At weekends, an informal *sobachiy* (dog) bazaar was held in a field by a creek, a couple of blocks from the Osh bazaar. Dogs of all breeds and sizes were on sale, no questions asked about pedigree or shots. There were litters of puppies in the trunks of cars; others peeped out from under the coats of their owners. The seamy side of the sobachiy bazaar was down on the creek bed where dog fights were held; crowds gathered along the creek wall to watch and place their bets. Dogfighting was illegal, but the police and market officials quietly let the fights go on.

Sign Language

Stephanie and I had taken two Russian classes to prepare for our stay, but for the first three months we struggled to communicate. We could exchange simple greetings, ask for directions, shop at the bazaar, and read street and bus signs, but not much more. One problem with being able to speak a little in any language is that people think you know more, and try to start a conversation. Stephanie was often targeted; with her friendly, outgoing manner, she looked like a willing conversation partner. Besides, with her shoulder-length red hair, she *looked* Russian. "Ya Sibiryachka [I'm a Siberian woman]," she joked, a reference to the fact that her grandparents had once lived in Krasnoyarsk in Siberia before fleeing to Manchuria ahead of the advancing Red Army.

A dubious Russian heritage and a few basic Russian phrases were of less use to Stephanie than her experience in amateur dramatics and improvisational comedy classes. When she didn't know how to say something, she acted it out. For the first week, we didn't have any dishwashing detergent and had no idea which cleaning product to use. Stephanie put on an elaborate performance (without props but with sound effects) for a vendor; she finished off a meal, licked her fingers, put down her knife and fork, carried the dishes and utensils to the sink, and turned on the faucet. Then she reached for an imaginary bottle of detergent and looked puzzled. The vendor applauded, showed her the product, and knocked a few som off the price for the free show.

Buying meat was another challenge. Parts of carcasses hung from hooks at market stalls, and customers ordered in quantities of 100 grams. Unless you knew animal anatomy, you were never sure which part of the animal you were buying. This was not good enough for Stephanie, who had recipes for different cuts. How could she buy a rump roast? She started by holding her hands to her ears, pointing her index fingers forward, and making a "Moooo!" sound. It would have been easier to learn the Russian word for beef, *govyadina,* but that would have ruined the first act. "OK, so what part do you want?" asked the butcher. He led her into the freezer room where the carcasses were hanging. She repeated her impression of the head and then traced her hand along the back of the imaginary steer, pretending to wiggle the tail. The butcher seized one carcass and wiggled a real tail. "Tochno! [exactly!]," said Stephanie.

A Turkish friend, Mustafa, recommended a Turkish butcher's shop on Sovietskaya. It was more expensive than the bazaar, but it was clean and the quality reliable. The first time, Stephanie went through her usual routine; when she came in again, one of the butchers would lean over the counter, put his index fingers to his ears, and go "Mooo," to the amusement of his colleagues. Stephanie added props to her routine and showed up with a cookbook. "Look here," she said, pointing to one of the diagrams that showed the cuts from cattle and sheep. "I'm doing a rib roast. This is what I need." The language barrier disappeared; she and the butchers were talking meat. After a couple more visits, the butchers borrowed the book, made copies of the diagrams, laminated them and put them on the counter so other customers could order cuts. One small step toward a market economy where the customer comes first.

The $2.50 Phone Bill

Even for those with good language skills, getting things done in Kyrgyzstan in the mid-1990s was a challenge. A seemingly straightforward task, such as banking or paying a utility bill, often turned out to be a complex, time-consuming activity that required visiting several offices, filling out forms and slips of paper, and obtaining signatures and stamps. Sometimes, it involved waiting around for the only person authorized to conduct the transaction to return from lunch. A case in point was our phone bill.

Living in the central district, our phone number began with the number 26. We were told we were fortunate to have that number. Bishkek's Soviet-era telephone system was more reliable than most, but some exchanges in the city were notorious for dropped calls and crackly lines; by contrast, the 26 exchange usually worked. It's all relative, because there was always noise on the line, occasionally interrupted by mysterious clicking sounds; it could have been the secret police checking on our dinner plans, but more likely it was simply the creaking and groaning of the arthritic switching system.

Although claiming we had a working phone seemed a stretch, we still had to pay for it. The phone had already been cut off once because the bill hadn't been paid, but the landlord took care of it. We had just received a recorded phone message and figured it was a reminder to pay the phone bill, so we brushed up on bill-paying phrases and headed off to the main post office. To pay the bill, you first need to know how much you owe, and that's recorded on a printout on a table. We scanned through it but could not find our number; apparently, another customer had removed that page rather than make a note of the bill. The post office staff said they did not have another printout; they just took money and gave receipts, but had no records. We were directed to the building next door where the records were kept, but the office was closed for lunch. We came back later, went up to the window for our station (number 26), and had the clerk enter the amount. Then we went back to the post office to pay and get a receipt and the obligatory official stamps. We had spent almost two hours to pay a 41 som ($2.50) bill.

Where Does All the Money Go?

Perhaps we could have shortened the wait time at the post office by offering a clerk a few som to look up our bill. In Central Asia in the mid-1990s, the line between tipping and low-level bribery to have people do what they were paid to do was a fine one. Of course, most of those who took small bribes—police, officials in government offices, university and school teachers, judges, lawyers, doctors, journalists—did so not because they were

innately corrupt but out of sheer economic necessity. Many people working in the public sector earned less than $100 a month; even with a couple of
part-time jobs, it was a struggle to put food on the table, and the occasional
bribe to avoid a traffic ticket or to buy a grade made a difference.

The problem was that corruption occurred at all levels of society.
The most corrupt were among the wealthiest and most powerful people
in politics and business who didn't need the money to feed their families.
The government launched periodic anticorruption campaigns, partly
to impress foreign donors. In a sweep in late 1996, President Akayev's
new anticorruption task force took action against officials accused of
shady deals, plundering tax revenues and foreign grants, and soliciting
bribes; one minister, two provincial governors, several members of the
parliament, and several low-level officials lost their jobs, although only a
couple ended up in prison. The more interesting question was whether
the clampdown was partly political, with the government going after
crooked political opponents and ignoring corruption in its own party
and the president's staff.

What concerned me was the hypocrisy of international organizations and foreign governments that publicly denounced corruption but
privately connived in perpetuating it. In the early 1990s, Kyrgyzstan,
more than any other republic in Central Asia, had embraced the economic and political reforms favored by the West. The donors responded
by pouring in aid. Some was well spent on development projects, and
some was simply wasted or stolen. Unfortunately, some donors, including UN agencies, regarded corruption as the cost of doing business, and
found ways to conceal payoffs in the "Administrative Services" or "Logistical Support" line items in their budgets. I was told that the markup
for graft ranged from 10 to 25 percent, depending on the project and
which ministry or agency was the implementing partner. Fortunately,
some donors—including, as far as I could tell, US government agencies
and USAID—worked hard to monitor where the money went, even if
they drove their grantees crazy with excessive reporting requirements.

Despite official denials, everyone knew that corruption went on.
However, diplomatic niceties had to be observed. The United States had
dubbed Kyrgyzstan an "island of democracy" in Central Asia, and no one
in the US embassy was going to undermine the image by asking President
Akayev where he got the money to buy his villa in Switzerland. Instead,
Ambassador Eileen Malloy, a competent diplomat who understood Kyrgyz

FIGURE 3.6 Chess game in park, Bishkek

society and politics better than most of her successors, talked about "slippage." In a speech to a conference held to mark five years of Kyrgyz-US cooperation, she said: "I cannot sit here and tell you that every cent of every dollar or every grain of wheat contributed by the United States has gone where it should. Inevitably, there is slippage." She was brave to say as much, but the word glossed over the extent of corruption. So the university rector spent part of his US travel grant on a new wardrobe? Not to worry—it's only slippage. So the agriculture minister who supervised the USAID-funded privatization campaign is driving a new BMW? It's only slippage. Too many slippages turn into a slippery slope.

Life in the Dvor

Most Soviet-era apartment blocks were built around a *dvor* (courtyard). This patch of land—dusty in summer, snow-covered in winter, muddy in spring—is a public space, a commons for apartment dwellers. In most complexes, apartment entrances are on the dvor, not the street side; you enter the dvor through a tunnel or driveway from the street. When you give directions, especially to a large block, it's not enough to provide the *dom* (house) and *kvartira* (apartment) number, because there may be half a dozen separate entrances (*podyezd*), each with a staircase and, if you're lucky, a working elevator. Unless you know the block, you'll try a couple of entrances before figuring out which one leads to the apartment.

The layout of apartment complexes means that all traffic—people, vehicles, stray animals—passes through the dvor. There are swings and slides for the children, and benches under the trees where, on warm days, neighbors sit and chat. Car owners park on the roadway outside their podyezd, unless they're fortunate enough to have a small garage at the back of the dvor. Residents cross the dvor to take garbage to the communal dumpsters. Although there's sometimes litter, many residents take pride in keeping the dvor clean, sweeping the area outside their podyezd. Often, there's a small grocery or convenience store, and sometimes a hairdresser or shoe repair shop. In our dvor, we knew it was time to get out of bed when we heard the call of the dairyman who sold milk, cream, and eggs from the trunk of his Lada; we went down with our *banki* (large glass jars), joining the short line of neighbors and children. In the depths of winter, it was a relief to put your coat on over your pajamas and spend a few minutes in the cold, rather than hiking through the snow to the market or store.

Like everyone else, Stephanie and I used the balcony on the dvor side to hang out our washing. The climate of the region is continental, with no rain most days in summer, fall, and early winter; clothes hung out in the evening are dry by the next morning. One morning in late December 1996, as we took down the laundry, we noticed a group of men assembling two yurts in the dvor. The traditional Kyrgyz nomadic dwelling is a round, tent-like structure, about fifteen feet across; sheepskins or canvas are stretched over a wooden frame, and the floors and walls are covered with shirdaks, brightly colored felt rugs. Then the group began chopping wood and building a fire. On our way out to the university, we passed a horse tethered to the fence; when we returned, the carcass was roasting on the spit. We thought it was too early for a New Year celebration so Stephanie asked Ainura, a young neighbor girl who was watching, what they were celebrating. Her face fell, and she started crying. "My grandfather died," she sobbed. The extended family had come to Bishkek to mourn and to bury the patriarch. By tradition the women of the family sit with the body inside the yurt and wail, while the men sit outside and talk about the life of the deceased. The whole affair lasts a couple of days, and then they bury the body. It is easy to see how this tradition evolved when the Kyrgyz were nomads, moving from winter to summer pastures with their flocks of sheep and horses, and living in yurts year-round. But it was now transposed to an urban setting; the ceremony took place just off a busy main street near shops, markets, and government ministries. It was another sign that although about one-third of the population lived in cities and towns, in some ways they hadn't moved too far from their rural roots. The mourners likely informed the police of their plans in advance, but in 1996 a wake with open fires and slaughtered horses in the middle of the capital city seemed a normal occurrence. No one was going to tell a Kyrgyz where he could pitch his yurt.

Stephanie got to know the children who played in the dvor, including Dima who lived in the apartment above us and was about nine years old. He would often appear to be talking to himself; when we inquired, he said that in school he had to recite verses by the Russian literary greats, and he was practicing his Pushkin. One day in early October, Stephanie heard a child talking in English (with a Texas accent) in the dvor. "Can I hold your kitten?" asked six-year-old Laura Marie. Dima was holding up a scrawny tabby male kitten he had found. A group of children had gathered, and were passing the kitten around. Stephanie assumed it was Dima's kitten, and said that he should take it back to his apartment to its mother. Dima said he had found it in the dvor. When he indicated he might wring its neck, Laura Marie burst out crying: "I'm going to ask my mother if we can keep the little kitty." The answer was no: the family already had two cats and two puppies. "We'll take the kitten for the night until we can find its owner," Stephanie volunteered. Of course, no one was going to claim the poor creature, so he stayed in our apartment, happy to have warm food and milk and to curl up under the covers with Stephanie. We made half-hearted attempts to give him away. We placed a small ad in the embassy newsletter which got exactly the same number of responses as most of those "lovely kittens free to good home" ads: none. After a couple of weeks, we realized that the cat was here to stay, and we had better give him a name. We wanted it be culturally appropriate but short and memorable. Partly in honor of his nemesis Dima, we decided to call him Pushkin. When we told Dima, he thought it was the funniest thing in the world. He would ask "Kak Pushkin? [How's Pushkin?]" and howl with laughter. Fortunately, we did not adopt any other cats or we would have felt obliged to use the names of other Russian literary greats. "Dostoyevsky, stop scratching the sofa." "Chekov, it's time for your flea medicine."

Over the next few months, Pushkin grew healthy, strong, and good-natured. Some cats are lap pets, but Pushkin preferred shoulders. He climbed up Stephanie's back and hung over her neck and shoulders, even when she was cooking. He would sit on my shoulders as I worked on the computer. Our Russian teacher, Galina, got the same treatment; our friend Nicholas who took care of Pushkin for a few weeks said that he hung around his neck while he played his drum set.

Nine months later, as Stephanie was preparing to leave Kyrgyzstan (I was to stay on for four more months) we faced a difficult decision: what would happen to Pushkin? We decided to bring him home, hoping he'd get along with our other cats. We contacted the embassy and asked what we needed to do to export a cat. This caused a minor bureaucratic crisis: apparently, we were the first Americans to take a cat out of Kyrgyzstan, so no one knew what regulations applied. The embassy made a few calls to government officials who were equally perplexed but decided that giving Pushkin a feline exit visa would not jeopardize national security. We signed a document attesting that the cat was not an endangered species or a valuable commercial commodity. A vet came to the apartment to give him shots and a medical examination. His clean bill of health was translated into English.

At the airport Stephanie faced down a Turkish Airlines agent who was insisting she pay $1,300 in excess baggage charges. Eventually, the agent relented. "But you must pay for the cat," she said. Stephanie agreed, and Pushkin, who was unhappily constrained in his carrier and was crying, was duly weighed. "That will be $60," said the agent. Stephanie handed her a $50 and a $10 bill. "I cannot accept this $10 bill, it's too old," said the agent, and handed it back. Stephanie didn't offer any more bills, so the cat ended up traveling for $50. The agent asked whether the cat should travel in the cabin or in the baggage hold. "In the cabin, of course," said Stephanie, as if taking cats on international flights was the sort of thing she did every day. The steward asked a passenger to move to another seat so that Pushkin and Stephanie could sit together. After a two-night stay in Frankfurt, both made it safely home, and Pushkin settled into life with our other cats at our home in rural southeastern Ohio.

Pushkin died from kidney failure on August 8, 2013, in Charleston, West Virginia. He was seventeen years old and had outlived all but one of our other cats. As far as we know, he never missed the dvor.

four

Kasha, Honor, Dignity, and Revolution

Back in the USSR

My first meeting with the dean of the journalism faculty at Kyrgyz State National University (KSNU) in Bishkek did not go well. I had met Anisa Borubayeva in November 1995 while she was on a six-week trip to the United States to visit journalism and communications schools. She said that if I was awarded a Fulbright, KSNU would be happy to host me.

I was excited about the prospect of teaching and working with new colleagues, but I wanted to avoid the mistake many Westerners working in developing countries make—telling people what they need. I planned to listen and be sensitive. After a few minutes of polite conversation, I asked through the interpreter what I thought was the appropriate question.

"As dean, what do you think the main needs of the journalism faculty are?"

Anisa looked uncomfortable. "I really don't know," she said. "I was hoping you could tell us what we need."

And so the conversation went. I asked about the curriculum. The qualifications of the teachers. The facilities and equipment. On almost every topic, Anisa said that she would rely on my expert judgment. As I left her office, she told me how proud she was to have a Fulbright scholar on the faculty. The rector, Sovietbek Toktomushev, the university's chief academic and administrative officer, had sent her a letter of congratulations. Her star was rising.

After independence, Kyrgyzstan needed all the help it could find in almost every sector of society, including higher education. Western governments and international agencies provided scholarships to teachers for postgraduate study and dispatched a motley crew of teaching help—from Fulbright scholars to Peace Corps volunteers—to the universities. My Fulbright colleague Martha Merrill, who has worked on higher education reform in Kyrgyzstan since the mid-1990s, says the country has welcomed almost every donor-funded initiative, not only because it lacks resources but because it has been open to new ideas. Each donor has its own idea of what Kyrgyzstan needs, and efforts to standardize and maintain quality have been ineffective. University education, she writes, includes "three-year bachelor's degrees, four-year bachelor's degrees, five-year diplomas . . . programs based on contact hours, programs using credit hours (some US-style, some European), and universities teaching in Kyrgyz, Russian, English, and Turkish." The net result, as Martha puts it, is "kasha—literally [in Russian] porridge, with a little of this and a little of that added in, but in slang, a mess."[1]

In the field of journalism education, I could not blame Anisa for a lack of vision and ideas. Historically, journalism in the Soviet Union was a subfield of literature, so education was conducted in faculties of philology (language and literature). Curricula were heavy on theory, stylistics, and literature, with few practical courses. Most teachers, like Anisa, had degrees in philology but little or no professional experience in media. She worked hard, hired young and promising teachers, and aggressively pursued grants and linkages with foreign institutions. As dean, she was one of a new breed of academic entrepreneurs in Central Asia and was credited with reviving a moribund faculty. However, her relations with the university administration were always precarious. The rector had hired her and could fire her if she displeased him.

In the 1990s, Kyrgyzstan more or less merited its "island of democracy" label. In contrast to the other Central Asian republics where

Moscow's rule had been replaced by a new authoritarian regime, Kyrgyzstan held elections that were generally considered fair and transparent. Its president, Askar Akayev, was a political outsider. He had worked as a physicist in the Soviet era, the only Central Asian leader who had not been a Soviet apparatchik. There appeared to be a balance of power between the executive and legislative branches. Politically, if not economically, Kyrgyzstan was making the right moves.

Unfortunately, universities were still floating in an authoritarian Soviet sea. Rectors were political appointees, lording it over their fiefdoms like Soviet commissars, khans, or emirs. Poorly paid teachers had little or no job security and little motivation to do more than show up for class. The old joke—"We pretend to work and you pretend to pay us"—seemed even more apt than in Soviet times, because some had not been paid for months. Students had almost no say in what was going on. Martha was frustrated that the Ministry of Education, to which she was assigned, did not seem much interested in university reform. Administrators and faculty said they could not understand how US universities were free to develop curricula and award their own degrees, rather than follow a national curriculum. The notion of student choice seemed even more outlandish. When Martha told one group that the number of hours a week a student spends in class depends on the major and classes chosen, one vice-rector bristled at the interpreter: "I know you translated that wrong because that can't be what she said, it can't be the student's choice."

The KSNU journalism faculty occupied one second-floor wing of the main university building (*glavni corpus*). Like most Soviet-era public buildings, the building looked impressive from the outside—a three-story block with two wings and a large portico, set in grounds facing Frunze Street. Once you got past the bored-looking guard at the front door, the signs of neglect were everywhere. Plaster and paint peeled from the walls, and the bathrooms smelled of urine. Students sat in rows behind fixed wooden desks. In summer, the heat was stifling; in winter, it was so cold that everyone, including the teachers, wore coats and hats. You had to take off your gloves to write on the chalkboard.

Each week brought a new challenge. One was predicting whether or not the students would be there, because the semester calendar was punctuated by numerous holidays. After independence, the government, in a popular attempt to combine traditions, introduced new holidays, but retained or renamed most of the Soviet ones. The New

Year was celebrated twice—on January 1 and for three days in March to mark Nooruz (Islamic New Year). Nooruz was followed by the Day of National Revolution (March 24), effectively creating a one-week holiday. There was Eastern Orthodox Christmas in January, Fatherland Defenders' Day in February to mark the formation of the Red Army, and International Women's Day in March. May began with International Workers' Day (May 1), which in post-Soviet political adjustment became Kyrgyzstan People's Unity Day, followed by Constitution Day (May 5), Remembrance Day (May 8), and the (Great Patriotic War Against Fascism) Victory Day (May 9). Eid al-Fitr (Breaking of the Fast) marked the end of Ramadan, and there were other Muslim holidays adjusted to the lunar calendar. KSNU added its own holidays and *subbotniks,* days when classes were canceled so that students could pitch in with cleaning, trash pickup, and grounds maintenance at the university.

Sometimes I learned about a holiday in advance, but often it was too late. I showed up for class, and the students were not there. Most internal communication seemed to be oral. There was no bulletin board to post notices about meetings or other matters, and there were no faculty mailboxes; if you needed to contact colleagues, you had to go and find them. The journalism faculty did not have a copying machine (or an overhead projector, the main classroom teaching aid in the mid-1990s) and only one telephone that sometimes didn't work. It was in Anisa's office and people were constantly walking in and out to make calls.

Furniture was scanty, but one fixture in most offices was a heavy metal safe. This appeared to be a hangover from Soviet times, when sensitive documents such as the class schedule or the reading list for Journalism 101 were closely guarded secrets. Anisa was constantly locking and unlocking her safe, although all she usually pulled out were file folders of correspondence. Apparently, the most valuable item in the safe was the faculty's official ink stamp which had to be affixed to all documents to attest to their authenticity.

Security extended to the classrooms, which were locked when not in use, as if someone was going to sneak in and steal the chalk. Some class periods began with a frantic search for the key while the students milled around in the corridor or wandered off. The attempt to keep people honest by locking everything up seemed ironic, given the rampant academic dishonesty afoot. Corruption exists at every level of education in Central Asia, but is probably worst at universities where students or their parents pay bribes for university places, to pass exams, and for grades. On one level, such practices are unethical, but on another they are, if not forgivable, at least understandable. Most university teachers received a pitifully low salary and had to put in many classroom hours to earn it; most taught at other universities or had part-time jobs to scrape out a living. Some had not been paid for months but still showed up for work. Of course, the culture of bribery undermines the fundamental principles of education. Why bother studying if you are going to have to buy the grade anyway? As educational standards plummet, employers question the value of a diploma that may have been bought. As a study by Vanderbilt University of academic corruption in six former Soviet republics including Kazakhstan and Kyrgyzstan concluded: "By design, one function of education is to purposefully teach the young how to behave in the future. If the education system is corrupt, one can expect future citizens to be corrupt as well."[2]

As for cheating, it was so much a part of classroom culture that students performed skits about it at their talent shows. And it had roots in a set of traditional values where your first duty is to your immediate and extended family. When students enter the university, they are assigned to a group; they attend all or most of their classes with the same group of fifteen to twenty students, and often socialize outside class. Away from your biological family, the group becomes your new family; you help group members who are struggling with their studies, sharing notes or the answers to test questions. Even class attendance is a group responsibility. When my Fulbright colleague Harvey Flad, a geography professor, passed out an attendance sheet at the American University in Kyrgyzstan, it came back with twenty signatures, even though only a dozen students were in the room.

I Don't Read Lectures!

The one issue settled at my first meeting with Anisa was the three courses I would teach in Fall semester. But not without some initial confusion.

"Kakiye lektsii voe chitayete?" Anisa asked. The interpreter translated literally. "Which lectures will you be reading?"

I bristled, and launched into a self-righteous diatribe about how I did not *read lectures*. As a teacher, my role was to provide students with basic information and resources, and then challenge them to think, ask questions, and conduct their own independent research. There would be in-class activities, open discussions, and debates.

Anisa listened patiently, and told me that of course I was free to conduct my classes in whatever way I saw fit. The phrase *chitat' lektsii* (to read lectures), the interpreter added, was simply how you described the courses you were teaching.

I wasn't so sure. I had already seen teachers in action, and most of the time they were standing at lecterns reading their lectures. The students sat quietly at long wooden desks and took notes. Occasionally, a student would ask a question, but it was almost always to clarify something the teacher had said. The material presented was never disputed. There was no class discussion because there was nothing to discuss. The teacher had said it, so it must be true. Teaching became the process of delivering knowledge, and memorizing it. On tests and oral examinations, students repeated what they had heard, without thinking much about it.

Rote learning has its place if, like our neighbor Dima, you need to recite Pushkin. I told my students that, beyond some basic concepts, I didn't care what they remembered from my brief lectures; it was their ability to analyze and apply the knowledge and conduct research that was important. Still, it was difficult to combat the passivity that the chitat' lektsii tradition engendered. In the second semester, I taught a course titled "Contemporary Issues in Journalism" for fourth-year students. I encouraged them to debate ethical issues such as conflict of interest, faking and staging, and invasion of privacy. Some asked questions and offered thoughtful opinions, but at least half of the class seemed bewildered when I asked them what they thought. They felt uncomfortable discussing issues about which apparently there were no correct and clearly defined answers to be regurgitated on a test. These students were in their final year, and all said they wanted to be journalists, but most seemed remarkably unreflective, lacking in intellectual curiosity.

There Will Be Tea

With dismal pay and working conditions, the teachers and administrative staff were ready to celebrate almost any occasion. Two or three times a month, they gathered in the common room to mark a public, university, or family occasion. There were snacks—*manti, samsa,* horse-meat, fresh fruit, dried apricots (*kuragi*), raisins, pistachios, almonds, cakes, candy, fruit juice, and tea. And a series of toasts to the faculty, the university, Krygyzstan's independence, better times ahead, friendship, peace in the world and, occasionally, to President Clinton (but not Russian president Yeltsin). In another vestige of Soviet culture in a nominally Islamic country, alcohol was always available. No social function at a university was complete without a few bottles on the table, but consumption was modest, and I never saw anyone get drunk. The toasts came at fifteen- to twenty-minute intervals with the oldest men toasting first. Foreigners came next, and, although I always feigned surprise at being invited to toast, I learned to anticipate when my turn would come. My first toasts were in English, but over the year I learned enough Russian phrases to do a reasonably intelligible toast, albeit with mangled syntax and incorrect word endings.

Although social occasions were planned, I rarely had advance warning. I politely asked if I could have more than ten minutes' notice. From that time on, the studio engineer, Kochkun, took it upon himself to keep me informed. He would come up to me in the corridor or pop his head around the classroom door. "Budet chai [there will be tea]," he said, with a broad wink. Chai, of course, was the code for vodka.

The President's Bathroom

The most eagerly anticipated event of the academic year was the visit of President Akayev to the journalism faculty. The reason for the visit was never entirely clear to me, but I was told I had a key role. I was to show the president the new radio production studio built and equipped with UNESCO funds, and explain how radio could build civil society and the market economy. In Kyrgyzstan in the 1990s, there was a good argument to be made for radio as a mass medium, given the scattered population, the mountainous terrain, difficulties of newspaper distribution, and the high cost of TV transmission. Whether it could change society was more debatable, but as an academic I knew I could come up with something that sounded plausible, even if there was no research to support it.

Preparations for the visit began weeks earlier with a work crew fixing the holes in the walls, painting the classrooms and installing red carpet along the corridor. Office furniture and equipment were purchased, drapes hung, and new signs installed on the doors. Even the metal safes got a new coat of paint, although they looked more authentic in the old Soviet battleship gray. Most important, the crew rebuilt the men's bathroom, replacing broken toilets, urinals, and sinks, fixing the leaky plumbing and applying a fresh coat of paint. The odds of Akayev popping in for a pee during his short visit were pretty low, but I didn't complain. If it took a presidential visit to fix up the bathroom, all the male teachers would benefit.

Agitated administrators hurried hither and thither, locking and unlocking doors. A detailed, minute-by-minute schedule was issued. The day before the visit, everyone was summoned for a dress rehearsal. The rector's staff went from room to room, timing the prepared speeches of teachers and staff, and ordering cuts to keep the visit on schedule. On the day, nothing went to plan. Akayev lingered in one room, chatting with teachers. He walked right past another room where a group had gathered to brief him on the curriculum, but no one was going to tell him where to go.

I waited in the radio studio, along with one of the president's bodyguards. Akayev showed up fifteen minutes late, accompanied by the entourage of administrators and deans. In halting Russian, I explained the studio setup and asked Akayev to formally open the facility by pushing up faders on the audio console and hitting record on the tape machine. He asked how I enjoyed teaching on the faculty. I told him what I knew the entourage wanted him to hear and then made my prepared speech about the role of radio in the new Kyrgyzstan. Akayev left, and I went off to commiserate with the group of bypassed teachers. At least I did not have to take part in the charade in the TV studio. Actually, the faculty did not have a TV studio. What it had was a recently redecorated and carpeted room, with a control booth, ancient studio lights (most without bulbs), and an old Soviet lighting board that took up half of one wall. UNESCO had approved a grant for studio equipment, but the money was not to be released for several months, and the gear would not arrive before summer. Unfortunately, someone had told Akayev's staff that the faculty had a TV studio. Appearances had to be maintained, so they borrowed TV equipment from another facility for the day. It would have made more sense to brief the president about what the faculty needed, rather than show him equipment it didn't have, but it was all about appearances.

As far as I know, Akayev never used the bathroom. Everyone seemed happy the visit had gone off without incident. The rector apparently promised everyone on the journalism faculty a pay bonus. We were summoned to the common room. "Budet chai," said Kochkun, with a larger-than-usual wink.

There's No Money in Poetry

For most of my students, the novelty of having their first Western teacher was enough. It didn't matter what I was teaching. They said they liked my interactive style, a contrast to the chitat' leksii method. Still, in my first semester, I was disappointed that third- and fourth-year students seemed to know so little about media and journalism. What on earth had they been studying the first two years?

Students learning English liked to chat with me in the corridor on class breaks, and the mystery was solved when one of them plucked up the courage to ask me a direct question: "When are you going to teach my journalism group?"

I was puzzled. "I thought I *was* teaching the journalism group," I replied. "No, the university decided you should teach the literature group," he said. "They all want to be poets."

Anisa said she understood my concerns but there was nothing she could do about it. The decision, like so many others, had been made *na verkhu* (above). I asked for an appointment with the rector, who was presumably as "above" as it goes. His secretary said that he did not take appointments. I gave up, and resolved to do what I could to turn budding poets into journalists. I doubt I had much success. I certainly could not use the "There's no money in poetry" argument, because everyone knew there wasn't much money in journalism either.

Godfather Rector

The rector of KSNU looked as if he had stepped off the set of one of *The Godfather* movies. At over three hundred pounds, with a ruddy face and the build of a professional wrestler, he could have passed for one of the thugs with a New Jersey accent who hung out in the shadows waiting for a quiet order from Don Corleone to make a rival crime boss disappear to the bottom of the East River. The only difference was that at KSNU the rector *was* the godfather. Everyone bowed to his will, and did their best to please him. Like a mafia boss, he had a reputation for good-naturedly slapping you on the back to congratulate you one day and stabbing you in the back the next.

His name was Sovietbek Toktomushev, and he was a former apparatchik, who, as an ethnic Kyrgyz, had seen his career take off after independence. Like many born in the Soviet era, his parents had given him an appropriately socialist first name with a Kyrgyz *bek* (a Turkic word meaning noble or chief). There was also Soyuzbek (Union), Stalinbek, and even Melisbek (the acronym MELIS is for "Marx, Engels, Lenin, and Stalin"). For those who worked on collective farms, Traktorbek was a favorite. In Russian, *soviet* literally means advice or counsel, but Toktomushev was not into participatory management or communication. The Soviet Union may have ended, but he was doing his best to preserve top-down administration.

I tried to stay out of his way, which wasn't too difficult because he was rarely seen in the corridors of the glavni corpus. Indeed, he was often gone for days. In what would be a clear conflict of interest in some societies, but was accepted as perfectly normal in Kyrgyzstan, he was also a member of parliament, presumably voting on education policy and budgets.

Toktomushev's administrative style was ruthless but efficient. His main weapon was the schedule, because the only appointments he kept were the ones he made. Every day, deans and administrators showed up at his office, hoping for a few minutes of his time. His secretary would ask them to wait. And so they did, often for hours, neglecting their own duties. Then the secretary would appear to announce that Toktomushev had been unexpectedly called to the parliament for a meeting and would not be returning to the office that day. Those waiting were invited to return tomorrow and try their luck. By the time deans and administrators finally got in to see Toktomushev, they were exhausted, dispirited, and ready to agree to whatever he wanted. Hundreds of hours were wasted sitting around waiting for an audience with the Godfather, and most who kissed the ring left his office empty-handed. But no one complained, because they all served at his pleasure.

Anisa, riding high on the credit from the successful Akayev visit, kept trying to keep Toktomushev happy. A couple of times a week, she brought visitors to the showpiece radio studio, usually in the middle of my class. I'd see them coming down the corridor through the studio glass window and groan, "Here comes another international delegation." But such visits were the coin of the realm, and Anisa was playing the game successfully. Then it all went badly wrong.

Anisa's Fall

The day after Nooruz, the Islamic New Year celebrated on March 21, students from all over Bishkek staged a demonstration outside the presidential residence, the White House. They were protesting a proposal by the city's mayor to raise revenue by dropping the subsidy for student bus passes; instead of paying 11 som a month, a student would have to pay over 90 som ($5). Students were already feeling the pinch. In the Soviet era, higher education was free of charge; by 1997, about half the students in Bishkek were paying modest tuition fees. The average family income in Kyrgyzstan was $600 a year, and students received a monthly living stipend of only 50 som (just over $3) a month. Certainly, the cost of living was low—a loaf of bread cost 3 som and a filling if carbohydrate- heavy meal in the student cafeteria 7 or 8 som. But raising the price of a bus pass to almost twice the monthly stipend was too much, particularly since police, soldiers, and, incredibly, parliamentary deputies (including Toktomushev) could travel for free. The demonstration was effective, and the city administration backed down, opting for more modest fare increases (the single trip fare was raised from 1.50 to 2 som).

During the demonstration, a KSNU journalism student buttonholed the prime minister and gave a less-than-flattering assessment of Toktomushev, citing his lack of concern for students, classroom facilities, and higher education in general. Word got back to Toktomushev, who fired Anisa on the spot. The dean of foreign languages and literature who, unlike other toe-the-line deans, had not instructed her students to stay away from the demonstration, was also canned.

I stopped by Anisa's office to express my sympathies. I asked why she had accepted the rector's decision without protest. Surely a dean cannot be held responsible for something a student, rightly or wrongly, has said? Anisa told me that perhaps she had "not brought up my students well enough." "Are you meant to be their mother?" I asked. The question did not seem rhetorical to her. She had failed to control her students and had paid the penalty. I was shocked by Toktomushev's actions, but was even more surprised by Anisa's contrition. At a time when we were encouraging students to think independently in a country that claimed to be the most democratic in Central Asia, Soviet-era attitudes persisted.

Word of the firings spread quickly. Most journalism students boycotted classes for a day. On the foreign languages and literature faculty, students collected signatures on a petition calling for the dean's reinstatement. The leaders were threatened with expulsion and forced to circulate another petition apologizing for their insubordination. Anisa kept quiet, hoping the storm would blow over, and that she would get her job back. Within a week, a new dean, Bolot Mamatsariev, was appointed. Within a few days, he showed his colors by firing the efficient and well-liked departmental secretary, hiring two of his associates to teach, and sending everyone else scurrying for cover. Like Toktomushev and the old-style politicians, Mamatsariev was trying to protect his own position by hiring people who would owe their jobs only to him, and firing anyone whose loyalty might be questionable. If he had experience in journalism or media, perhaps his appointment could have been justified, but his academic background (like Anisa's) was in Russian literature. At a meeting with visiting journalism students from Norway, he looked frankly bemused when the discussion turned to news coverage.

All Deals Are Off

Academic politics can be nasty, but this was brutal. And innocent people were suffering, including my interpreter. Under the agreement with the embassy, the university was to provide my interpreter. I was not thrilled when Anisa appointed her sister, Gulkhan, but she turned out to be an excellent choice; diligent and efficient, she quickly grasped concepts and related well to the students. The problem was that she had not been paid since she started work. Anisa was always promising to see Toktomushev about it, but nothing was worked out. Now Anisa was out of a job and, according to Mamatsariev, all deals were off. However, the embassy had a letter stating that the university would provide me with an interpreter (it also promised an office, telephone, and fax machine, none of which materialized.) It emerged that a deputy rector had agreed to this, only to be fired himself a week later.

Kelly Keiderling, the public affairs officer, and I decided to insist on institutional responsibility, and gave Toktomushev an ultimatum: give

Gulkhan her back pay and a contract through June, or I would walk out. We knew appearances were important: even if Toktomushev did not value my teaching, the university would not want to suffer the embarrassment of losing a Fulbrighter. For a few days, the university played the bureaucratic game. They could not find the letter Kelly had sent. They had composed a response but Toktomushev was busy at the parliament and had not had time to review it. A public holiday was coming up, and the university offices were closed. Eventually, a letter arrived apologizing for the "minor misunderstanding" and saying that Gulkhan would be paid. When she went to collect her $250 in back pay, the cashier said that the office would not have any money until the next month. This was actually not unusual; teachers sometimes had to wait for months because government funds had not been transferred.

Although Gulkhan was eventually paid, the damage had been done. Under Godfather Toktomushev, the rule seemed to be that if you fired an administrator, anything she or he had agreed to no longer applied. The issue was not so much about the money as about trust, about the university meeting its obligations. The saddest thing was that I was the only one with the luxury of standing on principle, because I did not depend on KSNU for my job and income. The other teachers were scared of losing their jobs and could say nothing. Meanwhile, the international delegations kept coming, and Toktomushev kept boasting of his fine institution and hitting them up for money.

A few months later, the government rewarded Toktomushev for his academic leadership by naming him Minister of Education. He immediately fired almost every other university rector, and appointed his cronies. It was little consolation that Toktomushev later lost his job; like all political appointees, his shelf life was only as long as that of the prime minister who appointed him. Since the mid-1990s, the average tenure of a minister of education has been under two years, making it almost impossible for the country to pursue a consistent policy. Higher education in Kyrgyzstan seemed to be drifting away from the island of democracy into a sea of kasha.

Transmission Problems

At independence, Krygyzstan inherited the Soviet-built infrastructure on its territory—the roads, bridges, tunnels, factories, mines, hydroelectric stations, and central heating plants. And all the equipment—from city buses to farm tractors and threshing machines. The new flag of the republic was raised, and the name "Kyrgyz Republic" replaced "USSR" on signs at public facilities. Maintaining the infrastructure and equipment proved a more daunting challenge.

The government knew that communication was essential to nation-building—to creating a sense of unity, history, and common purpose among the population. Under the communist system, media had specific functions—to inform citizens of policies and programs, celebrate the achievements of the state, denounce opponents and detractors, and build a society that embodied Marxist-Leninist ideology and placed the collective above the individual. To achieve these goals, the Soviets invested heavily in media, publishing newspapers, magazines, and books and building an extensive network of radio and television transmitters. Because it was essential to reach every citizen, there was no cost-benefit analysis: the state subsidized minority-language newspapers with tiny circulations and built radio and TV towers in remote, thinly populated areas. In principle, a yurt-dwelling Kyrgyz herder should have the same media access as a Moscow apartment-dweller.

In the economic crisis that followed independence, the government slashed the budget for the rebranded national broadcasting system, the Kyrgyz State Radio and Television Company (KRT). Transmitters broke down, and radio and TV reception became patchy in some rural areas. Back at KRT headquarters in Bishkek, most TV studio equipment was vintage 1970s—massive video switchers and clunky studio cameras with aging tubes that often made studio guests look green around the edges. There was no money for new studio lights or even to replace the bulbs in the old ones. The wooden studio sets were chipped and faded, and the presenters sitting behind them didn't look much brighter—some had not been paid for months. Over in the radio studios, engineers were salvaging parts from discarded audio consoles and analog tape machines to try to keep others running. Fortunately, much of the Soviet-era equipment was standard issue, so if you didn't have a part, you called a colleague in Tashkent or Tbilisi. "Yuri, it's Ullukbek, in Bishkek. I really need four tape guides and VU meters for the Hungarian recorders. How about I send you a pair of studio speakers in exchange? OK, I'll throw in a couple of relays too."

Fixing transmitters and equipment was one thing; fixing the programming was another. In the island of democracy, the Akayev regime still regarded KRT as the voice of government. Its purpose, as in the Soviet era, was not to respond to the interests of viewers and listeners, but to serve the state, building support for the regime and its policies. Although censorship was halted, KRT was under the supervision of the Ministry of Information, which monitored content and made the key managerial appointments. Radio and TV newscasts focused on official news, the comings and goings of President Akayev and his ministers, economic reforms and privatization programs, Kyrgyzstan's relations with other Central Asian republics, Russia, and the West. Government journalists were accustomed to taking orders on what to cover and how to cover it: the only difference now was that the orders came from the White House in Bishkek, not from Moscow.

The government regarded TV as a medium to revive Kyrgyz language and culture, so the order came down to produce more Kyrgyz-language programs. Unfortunately, it did not come with a production budget, so the only way KRT could increase Kyrgyz-language programming was to do it on the cheap, producing in-studio talk shows with artists, writers, musicians and academics. More popular, but more expensive, were multicamera, live-audience spectaculars with tuxedoed hosts, traditional musicians soulfully playing the *komuz* and singing verses from the national epic, the *Manas,* and boy bands in matching white suits belting out Kyrgyz pop hits as dancers in national costumes performed synchronized routines.

Bad News from Central Asia

Despite its efforts to promote Kyrgyz language and culture, the government was smart enough not to turn off Russian TV. The main state channels, ORT and RTR, were broadcast on government transmitters. And new commercial TV stations in Bishkek and Osh were relaying programs from nongovernment channels and program syndicators. Russian TV offered classic and new movies, live sports, action-adventure, drama, sitcoms, American, Mexican, and Brazilian soaps, late-night talk shows, and (at least for a few years) relatively independent news coverage. The programs were visually appealing and fast-paced. Even the commercials looked better than most of what KRT was showing. The Russian channels paid the government for the rights to rebroadcast. In turn, the government had leverage it could use if it didn't like the programming; it could raise the rates, limit the number of daily broadcast hours, or cut off the broadcasts altogether.

Entertainment shows were rarely an issue, despite a few clerics complaining that partial nudity undermined Islamic values. The fuss was always over the news. Central Asian governments claimed that Russian media painted a distorted picture of the region, focusing on civil disorder, ethnic conflict, poverty, economic chaos, and official corruption. It's a common postcolonial complaint; in similar fashion, the governments of former European colonies in Africa claim that the Western media depict their countries as strife-torn, corrupt, and beset with disease and famine. Whether in Africa or Central Asia, the perceived subtext in the images of coups, refugees, and emaciated children is the same: maybe you shouldn't have been so quick to kick us out because you've made a real mess of your country.

Negative coverage of economic, social, or political problems was often deemed as an affront to national pride or, worse, as subversive or destabilizing. In 1997, Russian television caused an uproar with a story about a children's home near Bishkek. The footage, aired on the three main networks, ORT, RTR, and NTV, showed naked, emaciated, and sickly children living in filthy conditions, with minimal adult supervision. For the government of Kyrgyzstan, the broadcast was highly embarrassing, straining Kyrgyz-Russian relations and coming on the eve of a high-profile visit by American First Lady Hillary Clinton. Officials claimed that conditions at this home were no worse than those at others in other former Soviet republics. Why then did the networks not use footage from a Russian children's home? Clearly, Russia was deliberately tarnishing Kyrgyzstan's international reputation. President Akayev called it a "planned" political action, and his deputy prime minister denounced the reports as a "prefabricated sensation."

A Meeting Was Held Today . . .

A few weeks after I arrived in Bishkek, Turat Makanbayev, the media assistant at USIS, introduced me to Andrey Tsvetkov, the news director at Piramida TV. The commercial station was the first to open in Bishkek, although it wasn't the first in the country; that honor went to the (now closed) Uzbek-language Osh TV. But Bishkek was a larger market than

Osh with more advertisers, and Piramida, founded by a couple of ex-KRT managers, had been doing well.

Andrey, who had visited local TV stations in Russia, knew it could be doing better, especially on its newscasts. He had hired young, enthusiastic reporters, photographers, and producers, but most were doing TV news for the first time and had no formal training. There were no senior TV journalists to serve as role models. Could I help them improve their professional standards? I agreed, and over the next nine months visited the station almost every week to conduct informal training sessions, go out with reporters on stories and discuss news values and legal and ethical issues with the staff.

The main challenge was an overreliance on official news. As we left a dull press conference one morning, I asked the reporter why Piramida was covering it. "We have to," he said. "This is a small city. Not much happens here. We have to do the meetings and press conferences." I disagreed. Bishkek, with a population of almost three-quarters of a million, was the nation's capital and the commercial and transportation center of the Chuy Valley. In the United States, cities half this size had three or four TV stations, each running at least ninety minutes of news each evening. The issue here was the definition of news, and whether the station was simply reactive—taking what government, business, or other institutions offered—or proactive, producing news of concern and interest to its audience.

At KRT, where journalists were still government servants, every presidential action, ministry press conference, and official visit by a foreign dignitary was covered. But Piramida's journalists had no excuse for doing the government's bidding. Too many items began with "A press conference was held at the Ministry of Agriculture," "Delegates from Osh attended a conference at the Kyrgyz Technical University," "A European Union seminar on structural reform took place at the Ministry of Finance," and "The deputy foreign minister of Botswana visited the White House today." The images were always the same. Speakers at a lectern or behind a long table, covered with a white cloth with a row of plastic water bottles. Conference delegates looking interested or bored out of their minds. Participants earnestly taking notes. Officials signing documents. Officials shaking hands. Officials receiving bouquets of flowers from young women in national costume.

As I reviewed the items with the reporters and videographers, I posed two questions: What's the story? And why should your viewers care? The story was not that a meeting, press conference, or seminar had been held. Sometimes, such events were newsworthy, but they should not be covered simply because they were scheduled. To do so put the journalists in a subordinate position, because officials were determining what was news. I asked them to think about issues that mattered to their viewers. They quickly came up with a list—jobs, housing, city services, inflation, taxes, health services, pensions, education, litter, dangerous drivers. "Maybe those are the stories you should be covering," I suggested. If the starting point for deciding what's news is not "Which meetings and press conferences and official functions are scheduled today?" but "What are people at the bazaars, at the bus stops, in their apartments talking about?" you end up with a different news program, one that is likely to resonate with viewers. Of course, these stories are not as easy to cover because they require research, interviews, and analysis, but that's what makes the difference.

A few months later, I wrote a report summarizing suggestions for news coverage, as well as recommendations on the scheduling of newscasts and technical issues. I didn't know how management would react to a report that was critical of the station's performance and feared it would be filed and forgotten. Instead, in a rare departure from the top-down management style I'd observed in other organizations, Andrey and the company president decided to ask the staff what they thought. The translated version was distributed to staff members (about fifty in all) at a meeting where decisions about expanding facilities and coverage were made.

Searching for Independent TV Stations

I'd like to report that Piramida was an independent TV station, free of political influence, but I can't. Certainly, it had more freedom than KRT, but it still had to tread carefully on hot topic issues, such as ethnic relations, and refrain from criticizing leading political figures who had the power to withdraw its license, send the tax police to scrutinize the books, or lean on advertisers. Piramida President Adylbek Binazarov readily recognized the limits of freedom when he described his company's policy to me: "Our first priority. No politics. Only information and entertainment programs."

In the murky world of media and politics in Kyrgyzstan in the mid-1990s, I never put much stock in labels. Foreign donors were always trying to classify media outlets as "government," "nongovernment," or "independent" so that they could decide which to support. The USAID contractor Internews claimed to work only with "independent, nongovernment journalists." In principle, this sounded fine but in practice it didn't work because journalists changed jobs, moving between government and commercial media. I argued that we should be trying to raise the professional standards of all journalists, no matter where they worked.

Certainly, the government controlled newspapers and KRT's radio and TV networks, but to claim that commercial media outlets were independent simply because they were not owned and operated by the government failed to grasp the complexities of the media landscape. Political parties, ministers, members of parliament, and wealthy individuals with political ambitions invested heavily in media to have a public forum for their views, especially at election time. One Bishkek commercial TV station was owned by a furniture magnate active in politics, another by the president of the state gold-mining concern. Even when political figures had no direct financial interest in a station, alliances were formed. Both parties stood to gain from the arrangement; the politician offered the station protection against interference from agencies such as the tax police or building inspectors; in return, the station provided the politician with a bully pulpit. Some station owners were open about their political agendas. Erkin Ala-Too, one of the two Kyrgyz-language stations in Osh, was closely allied with the city's mayor. The station's objective was "to ensure the election of a president from the south," according to its director, Nurdin Isakov. "The TV station is a political instrument," he said.

Despite evidence that most media outlets had political ties, donors kept classifying and counting, trying to measure the growth of Kyrgyzstan's "independent media sector." In such calculations, scale or reach were rarely considered. It was assumed that the greater the number of "independent" TV stations, the greater the media freedom and access to information. Which brings me to a vexing question: What is a TV station? The question is not as silly as it sounds. Obviously, a TV station must broadcast over the air or by cable or satellite to an audience to qualify as a TV station. But that's about the only criterion.

In October 1997, I joined a Russian consultant, Lena Fomina, in Djalalabad, the third-largest city, to compile data on the four "independent"

TV stations that were presumably producing critical news coverage of local issues and disseminating positive messages about democracy and free enterprise. How did we know there were four stations? The number was on a PowerPoint presentation compiled for USAID, so it must be correct, although the source was not cited.

Lena and I found the first two stations, but the results were disappointing. Both boasted a "news and information block" but all the "stories" were sponsored, paid for by local businesses and government or nongovernment organizations. Our search for the third station took longer, but eventually we were directed to an apartment block on the outskirts of the city. There we found two students playing pirated movies they had bought at the bazaar and selling simple graphic ads. We never found the fourth station. The three we visited each broadcast for a few hours a week on government transmitters and had no full-time staff.

To count these as "independent" stations, in the same category as Piramida with its fifty-plus staff and twelve-hour daily schedule, including newscasts—or even other stations with a smaller staff and fewer broadcast hours—was to grossly distort the media landscape of Kyrgyzstan. Yet such statistics, usually unverified, kept popping up in reports to donors, reinforcing the illusion of independent media in the island of democracy.

The stations in Djalalabad were not the only ones hawking news. Faced with declining government subsidies or competing for scarce advertising revenue, some media outlets came to regard "news" as simply another commodity to be bought, sold, or bartered. The line between news and advertising was always blurred. Newspapers contained hidden advertisements for businesses, organizations, and individuals, while TV stations ran sponsored programs masquerading as news. There were occasional cases of editorial blackmail. A newspaper would threaten to publish a critical or unflattering story on an individual or institution; the only way to avoid publication was to buy a (presumably flattering) advertisement.

Journalists in Kyrgyzstan faced direct and indirect pressures that limited their reporting. And so they learned to set their own boundaries. These boundaries were by no means stable or universally accepted; indeed, they shifted according to the political climate, economic conditions, or the attitudes of media managers and owners. But they were always there; almost every journalist I talked to could provide a list of taboo topics, or those, such as ethnic relations, that could be covered only with great caution. If they went ahead, they might receive a "telephone order." Sometimes, it came from a government official, requesting that the station drop a story or tone it down; sometimes it came from an advertiser with political ties; sometimes from a manager and editor. But most of the time, it was self-censorship. Journalists simply did not cover certain issues and avoided criticism of the rich and powerful. Those who did not conform might end up in court—or in jail.

Honor, Dignity, and Truth

Question to Armenian radio: What is the difference between the constitutions of the USA and the USSR? Both guarantee freedom of speech.

Answer: Yes, but the constitution of the USA also guarantees freedom *after* the speech.

—Soviet-era joke

I met Ryspek Omurzakov in June 1997 at a reception at the US embassy to mark his release from prison. In his late thirties, Omurzakov was tall, studious-looking, and conservatively dressed. He could have been a teacher, a scientist, or a civil servant. He didn't look like a crusading journalist, a prisoner of conscience. Indeed, he looked a bit uncomfortable as embassy staff and journalists buzzed around asking him about his experiences.

Omurzakov's crime was to "tell it like it is." A journalist for the weekly *Res Publika*, he had written an article about conditions at a factory hostel in Bishkek where workers lived in cramped, unheated rooms infested with vermin. Omurzakov's report was based on firsthand observations, interviews, and a petition signed by 108 employees, complaining about substandard conditions. In the mid-1990s, Kyrgyzstan remained one of the few countries in the world where libel was punishable as a criminal offense, with fines and prison sentences up to three years. The factory manager, Mikhail Paryshkura, filed a criminal libel suit against the journalist and *Res Publika*; Omurzakov was arrested in late March and held in prison until the case went to trial in May. Two factory workers who testified that the article was accurate were in turn charged with "disseminating deliberately false information" and named as codefendants. When the trial reopened, their testimony had mysteriously vanished from the record. Fearful of losing their jobs, no new workers came to testify on Omurzakov's behalf.

The trial did not focus on conditions at the hostel, in other words, on the accuracy of the report. Instead, the central issue was the "honor and dignity" of the factory manager; even if he was responsible for housing workers in appalling conditions, his public reputation had been impugned, and Omurzakov had crossed the line by criticizing him. The case demonstrated that in libel cases provable truth was not a defense, and that officials could use the threat of libel actions to silence critics. "The facts have nothing to do with it," said Omurzakov. "The authorities want to teach independent journalists a lesson in this country, and I'm going to be their latest whipping boy."[3]

Amnesty International accused the authorities of "using criminal legislation in a bogus manner to punish and silence a prominent government critic." In a letter to President Akayev, the New York–based Committee to Protect Journalists (CPJ) said: "While we recognize the right of individuals to file libel suits to protect their reputations, we deplore the use of such statutes by public officials to shield themselves from public scrutiny."[4] The government was surprised by the international reaction. Akayev's press secretary, Kanybek Imanaliev, asked me to come over to the White House to explain what was going on. "Why are we getting letters from these advocacy groups?" he asked. "This is a domestic issue. People in New York should not be telling us what to do." I told him, as politely as I could, that as long as Kyrgyzstan kept throwing journalists in jail, the government would keep hearing from human rights and journalism advocacy groups, and that the reports would circulate in international media through e-mail and listservs. "There's no way that you can stop this," I said. "Maybe the parliament should be thinking about changing the law."

Omurzakov was released in June after almost three months in jail. In September, he was sentenced to two and a half years in prison but released under an amnesty law. The Supreme Court upheld his conviction but ruled that he was guilty of libel under the civil, not the criminal code—a creative legal interpretation. Although Akayev publicly supported decriminalization, parliamentary deputies consistently voted to keep libel as a criminal offense, arguing that "without this provision there would be anarchy . . . politicians and public officials would be left unprotected from the lies printed by the media." In April 1998, deputies voted to sue Kyrgyzstan's most widely read newspaper, *Vecherniy Bishkek* (Evening Bishkek) for an article featuring a photo of five deputies, in which an interviewee called the parliament a corrupt and mafia-run organization. Another article accused one of the deputies, Omurbek Tekebayev, of illegal efforts to free his brother from prison. "As long as I am a deputy in parliament," said Tekebayev, "libel will not be taken out of the criminal code." His comments carried weight, for he chaired the Committee on State Structure and Judicial and Legal Reform. "The media use their power irresponsibly," he said. "If I have to choose between freedom of speech and a stable government, I will always choose stability." A new media bill introduced a raft of restrictions—from pornography to reporting on people under criminal indictment. As one newspaper put it, the prohibitions ranged from "tax evasion by politicians to Kim Basinger's legs." It was clearly a self-serving measure, because 117 deputies were under indictment for various crimes.[5]

The debate over libel dragged on, with local journalists, media advocacy organizations, Western embassies and some politicians advocating for decriminalization, and parliamentary deputies opposing any change. Every couple of years, there would be a flurry of activity—a conference on media and the law, a petition to the parliament, a draft bill. Hopes were raised for a few months until more pressing political issues pushed libel off the agenda. It was not until April 2011, fourteen years after Omurzakov had gone to prison and after other journalists had spent time inside, that parliament voted to make libel a civil offense. Western governments and journalists' advocacy groups hailed the decision as a landmark in Kyrgyzstan's progress toward democracy. They should have known better because what the politicians give, they can also take away. In 2014, parliament reversed itself, passing by a vote of 85–6 a "False Accusation Law," ostensibly to prevent the publication of libelous reports about people under criminal investigation. President Almazbek Atambayev dithered for a few weeks before signing it. The law makes "intentional defamation" a criminal offense, punishable by up to three years in prison. While some argued that the law will stop journalists using hearsay in reports on criminal matters, most observers saw it as a setback for freedom of speech, saying it could be used selectively to stifle investigative reports.

Hillary's Boxes

It was November 12, 1997, and I was standing on a flatbed truck with a clutch of photographers and videographers, waiting for Hillary Clinton's plane to arrive at Bishkek's Manas Airport. My job, as explained to me by the USIS public affairs officer, Kelly Keiderling, was to hold a good camera position for ABC News, which was providing pool coverage for the US networks. I felt slightly overqualified to be a media bouncer, but held my ground as the plane dipped out of the clouds and the photographers pushed and shoved to find a good angle.

The members of the American press corps came running from the plane to the press area that Kelly, two USIS staff members, and I were policing. A few minutes later, Mrs. Clinton got her cue and walked down the gangway to be greeted by the president's wife, Mayram Akayeva, the US ambassador, and government dignitaries, before walking to a stage to make a brief speech. It occurred to me that only two types of plane park on the tarmac, with passengers descending by steps—those operated by cut-price airlines and those carrying political leaders. The first park out on the tarmac because they do not have gate privileges; the second use the steps as a photo opportunity.

For days, USIS staff had been working to prepare for the whirlwind five-and-a-half-hour visit. The schedule was planned, reviewed, revised, translated into Russian and Kyrgyz, and revised again. Press kits were compiled; they included "Visit of First Lady Hillary Clinton to the Kyrgyz Republic" notepads. Every newspaper and every TV and radio station in Bishkek wanted to cover the visit, so a press pool system had to be devised. Eleven US journalists were accompanying Mrs. Clinton on her six-cities-in-six-days tour—to Lviv (Ukraine), Yekaterinburg (Russia), Tashkent (Uzbekistan), Bishkek (Kyrgyzstan), Almaty (Kazakhstan), and Novosibirsk (Russia)—so to maintain balance eleven local journalists were selected to join them in the airport press area and at other events. The idea of a press pool was a novelty in Kyrgyzstan, and everyone expected disputes over who should be included. The government wanted more slots for KTR, and tried to drop Piramida. Kelly protested, and the government backed off.

Preparations at the airport had begun the previous day. We had the driver pull the flatbed into different positions so that we could calculate the best position for shots of the gangway and stage, given the angle of the sun and the amount of backlight. Meanwhile, government officials were carefully positioning the small crowd enclosure. There were the questions about whom Mrs. Clinton was going to meet and in what order. Will Madame Akayeva step up to the podium from the left or right? Do we need twenty-five flag-waving children, or will twenty be enough? The airport event was held to mark the donation of two truck-loads of medical supplies by the United States to a charity run by Madame Akayeva. This called for a backdrop of boxes, and officials shuffled them around to frame exactly the right image behind the podium. "OK, let's try it with five across the bottom, and let's get the welcome banner two inches to the right."

From the airport, Mrs. Clinton was driven in a motorcade to the city to speak at the formal inauguration of the new Kyrgyz-American University, visit a women's poverty alleviation project at the Osh bazaar, and have lunch with the first couple at their summer residence in the mountains. The heavily choreographed visit ended with a meeting with the "American community" in the airport VIP lounge. It lasted only fifteen minutes. Mrs. Clinton and Madame Akayeva spoke, and posed for pictures with children, including Pushkin's protector from the dvor, Laura-Marie. Then Mrs. Clinton was off again. In Almaty, they were already lining up the flatbed truck, and arranging the backdrop.

Back to Bishkek and Osh

I've been back to Kyrgyzstan six times since my Fulbright ended in 1997. After living in Bishkek for almost a year and a half, I know my way around. I joked that if my academic career didn't work out, I could always make a living as a taxi driver. I knew most of the street names in the center, and could find my way to several of the microraions.

Like any city, Bishkek seemed both familiar and unfamiliar when I returned. Our apartment block on Pervomayskaya had been spruced up and the rents raised; it was now considered a "prestige district," with apartments for government officials, bankers, and international contract staff. New restaurants and bars, including several expat hangouts, had opened. In 2001, the United States had concluded a lease agreement for the old Soviet air base at Manas Airport to serve as supply and refueling hub for forces in Afghanistan. For several years, military personnel were welcome in Bishkek, mostly because they were spending their dollars at shops, bars, and restaurants. The mood began to change after servicemen got into bar fights and were accused of harassing local women. There were alcohol-related crashes on the airport road. A serviceman who shot and killed a Russian driver at a truck checkpoint was whisked out of the country to stand trial in a US military court. The most bizarre case was that of US Air Force Major Jill Metzger, who mysteriously disappeared while shopping in the Tsum department store in September 2006. Back in the United States, yellow ribbons were tied to trees, prayers were uttered for her safety, and family members made the rounds of the TV talk shows. She turned up three days later at a farmhouse, within sight of the Russian air base at Kant, with her blonde hair dyed dark and a story about being kidnapped by terrorists who forced her into a car by claiming to have planted an explosive device in her pocket. She claimed she escaped after overpowering a guard and running barefoot, thirty miles, to freedom. Traces of dye on her hands indicated that she probably had more to do with her own disappearance than she was letting on, but an Air Force inquiry released six years later concluded that she had been kidnapped. After these incidents, few US personnel ventured outside the base (where they could enjoy fast food, watch movies and sports, and feel as if they never left the United States).

The familiar city streets served as the stage for two revolutions in five years. In March 2005, in the so-called Tulip Revolution, protesters broke into the White House, hurled stones at the parliament building, looted shops, and burned cars. Akayev and his family were forced to flee, seeking refuge in Russia. Although the revolution began in Bishkek, resentment was strongest in the south, which had long felt that a northern, Akayev clan–dominated government was doing little to alleviate poverty, improve infrastructure, and social services, or deal with energy shortages. The new administration, headed by a southerner, Kurmanbek Bakiyev, promised a new era of clean government accountable to the people.

Many citizens soon realized that things hadn't changed: they had simply replaced the corrupt Akayev clan with the even more corrupt Bakiyev clan. The president centralized power, putting the Ministries of Interior and Defense and the National Security Service directly under his authority. His son Maksim headed the agency that controlled all foreign financial inflows, including aid and credits, and the national hydroelectric and gold companies. Economic and social conditions did not improve. When I visited Bishkek in July 2009, a week before the presidential election, colleagues who had supported the Tulip Revolution seemed disillusioned. "I was a leader in the student movement," said one. "Our hopes, our dreams, were so high. I never thought I'd say this, but things are worse now than under Akayev. Bakiyev and his son are stealing our country."

Although Bakiyev lacked support in the north and among the urban middle class, his populist positions still won votes in the south and rural areas. His campaign posted billboards on major streets in Bishkek, featuring the earnest (and sometimes smiling) faces of a demographic and ethnic mix of "ordinary people" with slogans such as "Bakiyev—Of Course," "Bakiyev—A Real President" and (simply) "Bakiyev Is Good" (I'm sure the phrase resonates more in Kyrgyz than in English). In a country where literacy levels had actually declined since independence, simple sloganeering was the name of the political game. Bakiyev won handily, with around 78 percent of the vote; on election day, his nearest rival withdrew from the contest, claiming extensive fraud. Observers from the Organization for Security and Cooperation in Europe (OSCE) agreed, documenting vote rigging and saying that media coverage had overwhelmingly favored Bakiyev. Voters had the option of casting a ballot "against all of the above." More than 100,000 (4.66 percent) did so, indicating their disgust with all the country's politicians.

One election issue was the future of the Manas air base. In February 2009, the parliament, dominated by Bakiyev's Ak Zhol party, had voted to end the lease agreement, ostensibly to protect national sovereignty but more likely in response to Russian pressure. President Dmitry Medvedev had announced that Russia would invest $1.7 billion in infrastructure projects, provide $450 million to help balance the budget, and cancel a $180 million debt. A bidding war ensued. Kyrgyzstan tripled the rent (from $17.4 to $60 million a year) and the United States agreed to pay; in addition, the United States pledged more than $66 million for airport improvements, $20 million for economic development, $21 million for counternarcotics efforts, and $10 million for counterterrorism efforts—a total of $117 million in aid on top of the rent. Poor countries like Kyrgyzstan need to make money any way they can, and renting out airfields to superpowers is a good source of steady income. But that was soon over. With NATO's pullout from Afghanistan, the United States withdrew from the base, and it was formally handed over to Kyrgyzstan's military in June 2014.

Two months after the 2009 election, I was back in Bishkek for an OSCE-sponsored conference on Central Asia media. Reelection had done nothing to temper the authoritarian tendencies of the Bakiyev regime or its pressure on media. The deputy foreign minister formally opened the conference with a stiff speech on how his government was committed to press freedom, access to information, and political transparency. The delegates listened in stunned silence. The months that followed were marked by attacks on opposition figures, journalists, and NGO activists. The journalist Gennadiy Pavlyuk, who had exposed high-level corruption and was planning to establish an opposition newspaper, was lured to a sixth-floor apartment in Almaty and thrown from the balcony, his hands and feet bound with tape; he died six days later in hospital. Another journalist who reported on his murder was stabbed to death a week later. Investigators named three members of Kyrgyzstan's National Security Service as the chief suspects in Pavlyuk's murder, but no arrests were made.

Opposition to the Bakiyev regime intensified in the winter of 2009–10 as the economic situation deteriorated, utility costs rose, and media reported on official corruption and nepotism. Bakiyev's decision to accept Russian aid but renew the US lease on the Manas airbase had angered the Russian government, which launched a media campaign against him. In April, Russia imposed duties on energy exports to Kyrgyzstan, resulting in an increase in fuel prices. On April 6 in the city of Talas, a demonstration called by opposition leaders to protest corruption and living costs turned violent when protesters stormed a government building and took officials hostage. The demonstrations spread to Bishkek. Riot police used tear gas, rubber bullets, and stun grenades in an attempt to disperse protesters. When they drove two trucks into the gates of the White House, the police opened fire with live ammunition. At least 86 were killed. Protesters stormed the parliament building and the headquarters of KRT. Meanwhile, rallies and protests took place in other cities and towns. By the evening on April 7, opposition leaders announced the formation of an interim government and issued warrants for the arrest of Bakiyev and his family and associates.

Under pressure from Russia, Kazakhstan, and the West, Bakiyev resigned, but a week later, from his safe haven in Belarus, he retracted the resignation and called on the international community to reject the "bandits" who had illegitimately seized power. Pro-Bakiyev rallies were held throughout the south, with supporters seizing government offices. Clashes between government forces and Bakiyev supporters in Djalalabad on May 14 left at least eight dead and 65 injured.

The conflict escalated on June 9 when crowds of Kyrgyz and Uzbeks clashed in Osh. The violence spread to other towns as groups looted and set fire to homes and businesses in ethnic neighborhoods. Military units were deployed, and Uzbekistan moved troops to its border to stop the clashes spilling over. The scale and cruelty of the violence eclipsed the interethnic clashes of 1990. Some victims were raped and burned alive. In Djalalabad, crowds attacked the hospital where the wounded were being treated. Official figures put the death toll at more than 470, but these figures included only those whose deaths were recorded. In accordance with Islamic custom, many people buried their dead relatives immediately without registering them. Uzbek sources claim that more than 2,500 Uzbeks were killed. According to international organizations, more than 400,000 people were displaced, with 110,000 fleeing across the border to Uzbekistan.

The interim government had granted shoot-to-kill powers to its security forces, most of whom were ethnic Kyrgyz. Witnesses reported that security forces handed out weapons, uniforms, and vehicles to Kyrgyz mobs. Armored personnel carriers moved into the Uzbek *mahallas* (neighborhoods) to remove makeshift barricades, clearing the way for attacks by armed men and looters. Some observers believed the fighting was instigated by Bakiyev and his family to show that without a southerner in the White House, the south was ungovernable. The Central Asia scholar Madeleine Reeves argues that the conflict was deliberately "ethnicized." Uzbeks, who held most of the visible wealth in the south, became the scapegoats for a deteriorating economic situation in which much of the rural Kyrgyz population "felt unable to make a viable livelihood in their own state." It's estimated that one-fifth of Kyrgyzstan's working-age population is in Russia, mostly in low-paid jobs. Rather than blame a corrupt southern president for the mess, it was easier to target Uzbek shopkeepers and traders. Reeves says there were many instances when Kyrgyz and Uzbeks sheltered each other from marauding bands, or when neighbors defended their street or mosque from attack "not because they are of the same ethnicity, but because they live in the same neighborhood and want to have the chance of continuing to do so."[6] The freelance journalist Nic Tanner says the violence in Osh was systematically facilitated, an attempt to reclaim land and property that included the occupation of apartments and destruction of legal title records. "If you don't have a document that states your house is your house, then it's not your house anymore," he said. Most of the violence was perpetrated by people brought into the city. "Most Kyrgyz and Uzbek people who were living next to each other weren't fighting. They were neighbors."

More than three-quarters of those who stood trial were Uzbeks, reinforcing the official narrative that Uzbeks were primarily to blame. Dozens of prominent Uzbek community and religious leaders were arrested and charged with inciting violence and ethnic hatred. Security forces conducted sweeps of Uzbek neighborhoods and villages, ostensibly searching for weapons and criminals. Human rights organizations reported that security forces planted evidence, destroyed documents, and looted houses. Officials harassed lawyers representing Uzbeks and prevented them from meeting with their clients. A report by a seven-member international commission of inquiry, issued in May 2011, criticized the "ineptitude and irresolution" of the government, and supported claims that security forces had handed over weapons and vehicles to Kyrgyz mobs who attacked Uzbek communities. The government angrily rejected the findings and declared the commission's Finnish chair persona non grata.

Although many homes and businesses damaged or destroyed have been rebuilt, tensions in the south remain high. A radical Kyrgyz nationalist party, Ata-Zhurt, has gained support. Uzbek schools have been pressured to switch to Kyrgyz-language instruction. Uzbek-language signs have been removed from public places; a "peace bell" unveiled in summer 2012 to commemorate the more than four hundred lives lost in 2010 was engraved with "Peace all over the world" in Kyrgyz, Russian, and English, but not in Uzbek.[7] Uzbek media have been closed or forced to sell out to Kyrgyz interests. For almost twenty years, Osh TV, the first private station established in Kyrgyzstan (in 1991), had resisted legal and extralegal attempts by the local authorities to shut it down. Broadcasting in Uzbek, Kyrgyz, and Russian, it was the most popular station in southern Kyrgyzstan. Its owner, Khalijan Khudaiberdiev, says that the mayor of Osh, Melisbek Myrzakmetov, ordered him to sell 51 percent of the company's shares in return for security for his family. The company was valued at $1.5 million, but Myrzakmatov said that because of the difficult political situation, he assessed the company's value at $400,000. Khudaiberdiev said the deal was made in the mayor's office. "There were men armed with machine guns, and I had no choice but to agree." Khudaiberdiev claims he was paid only $20,000 and fled the country with his family. Osh TV now broadcasts only Kyrgyz-language programming. Asked in March 2011 if he owned Osh TV, Myrzakmatov responded, "I don't remember who owns what."

Nationalist politicians, notes Reeves, "speak of the Kyrgyz as the 'landlords' in Kyrgyzstan and other ethnic groups as 'tenants.'"[8] A referendum in June 2010 overwhelmingly approved a new constitution, with parliament choosing the prime minister and setting a six-year, nonrenewable presidential term. In October, multiple parties competed in parliamentary elections, generally considered to be fair and free by international observers.

It took two revolutions to do it, but Kyrgyzstan has moved from a presidential to a parliamentary system of government. It will take more than two relatively free elections and the emergence of political parties, civil society organizations, and independent media to restore the "island of democracy" reputation, but progress has been made. The question is: at what price? Many still live in poverty, the gap between the rich and poor has widened, and prices, especially for fuel, gas, and electricity, are rising. The government has failed to improve education, medical, and social services. Ethnic tensions remain high in the south where Kyrgyz nationalists dominate the local and regional governments, and many Uzbeks feel they are unwelcome in a country where they have lived for generations. They look north to Kazakhstan, a more ethnically diverse country. Its economy has been growing steadily and it has not suffered interethnic violence. Since independence, it has been ruled by a savvy strongman, President Nazarbayev, who is widely credited with maintaining stability and growth.

One of the legacies of the Soviet era is the belief that a strong leader—Lenin, Stalin, Khrushchev, maybe even Brezhnev—can change a country's destiny. There's a lingering sentiment in Kyrgyzstan that if it had had a president like Nazarbayev, rather than Akayev or Bakiyev, things would have turned out better.

five

On and Off the Silk Road

Warm Lake

From Bishkek, most long-distance trips begin at the bus station, the *avto-vokzal*. The busiest bus and marshrutka traffic is between Bishkek and Almaty, a four-hour journey, assuming that the weather is decent and the frontier guards are not in a foul mood. Buses and marshrutkas run east-west along the Chuy Valley to towns such as Kant and Kara Balta, south over the mountains to Toktogul, on the Bishkek-Osh road, and to Balykchy, Chol-pon Ata, and Karakol on Issyk Kul, Kyrgyzstan's premier tourist attraction.

The Kyrgyz are justifiably proud of the lake. At 106 miles long and 44 miles across, it's the tenth largest in the world, the second-largest alpine lake (more than 5,250 feet above sea level) after Lake Titicaca in South America, and the second-largest saline inland body of water, after the Caspian Sea. More than a hundred rivers and streams, their volume swelled by springs and snowmelt, flow into the lake, yet Issyk Kul has no visible outlet. It's surrounded by two mountain ranges—the Kungey Ala Too to the north and the Central Tien Shan to the south—and it is almost 2,300 feet deep at its deepest point. The combination of depth, thermal activity, and salinity means that it never freezes; in Kyrgyz, Issyk Kul means "warm lake."

In medieval times, the lake level was about 26 feet lower than today, and divers have found the remains of submerged settlements in shallow areas. In 2007, the Kyrgyz Academy of Sciences reported that archaeologists had discovered the site of a 2,500-year-old walled city, stretching over an area of several square kilometers. Excavations have also uncovered Scythian burial mounds, bronze battle-axes, arrowheads, knives, coins, and other artifacts. For centuries, the roads along the lakeshore were part of the Silk Road network. Historians retracing the route of a medieval map used by Venetian merchants discovered a fourteenth- century Armenian monastery on the northeastern shore. More ominously, archaeologists found evidence of a Nestorian Christian trading community ravaged by the bubonic plague in 1338–39. Some historians claim that this is where the Black Death, which swept through Europe and Asia in the fourteenth century, originated, with merchants carrying infested vermin in their cargoes. The region is prime habitat for marmots, known to carry a virulent form of the plague. It seems more likely, however, that traders from China brought diseased fleas with them to Issyk Kul. Whatever the case, the tiny settlement's death rate shot up from a 150-year average of about four people per year, to more than one hundred dead in 1338–39.

In the late 1860s, as the Kyrgyz tribes retreated ahead of the advancing tsar's armies, Russian, Ukrainian, and Belarusian farmers settled at the east end of the lake. A Russian military garrison was established in 1864. Karakol was founded five years later, with streets laid out in a checkerboard pattern, and the garrison relocated to the town. Its early population included military officers, merchants, and explorers. Dungans and Uighurs began arriving in the 1870s and 1880s following the suppression of Muslim uprisings in China's Shaanxi, Gansu, and Xinjiang provinces. The settlers farmed the fertile, well-watered soils of the northern and eastern shores, growing vegetables and fruits, including the apples and pears for which the region is famous; indeed, Karakol, which means "black hand" in Kyrgyz, may be a reference to the hands of farmers, blackened from tilling the dark soil.

The mild climate, hot mineral springs, and clear waters made the lake popular for convalescents. The Russian explorer Nikolai Mikhailovich Przhevalsky, returning from his fourth expedition (1883–85) to Mongolia,

China, Tibet, and the Tian Shan, traveled along the north shore of the lake. Three years later, he was in Bishkek (then Pishpek) outfitting for another expedition. While on a hunt along the Chuy River, he ignored the standard traveler's advice "Don't drink the water (or at least boil it first)" and came down with typhus. He was sent to a military hospital at Karakol and died on October 20 at the age of forty-nine. At his request, he was buried by the lake in his explorer's clothes, his grave crowned with a bronze eagle. The tsar ordered Karakol to be renamed Przhevalsk in his honor. Przhevalsky's grave, a memorial park, and museum are located a few miles outside Karakol on an inlet, which also bears his name. The honoring of the explorer is ironic, considering his contempt for the Asian peoples he encountered on his expeditions. As Meyer points out, he was not alone among nineteenth-century explorers, soldiers, and missionaries in believing he was on a mission to fast-track the natives toward civilized society. In an 1877 report, Przhevalsky wrote: "Our military conquests in Asia bring glory not only to Russia; they are also victories for the good of mankind. Carbine bullets and rifled cannon bear those elements of civilization which would otherwise be very long in coming to the petrified realms of the Inner Asian khans."[1]

The Mikhailovka inlet was selected by the Soviets for another type of exploration. The depth of the lake and its remoteness (away from the cameras of US spy planes) made it a good location for the Soviet navy to test high-precision torpedoes. You could fire one off into the lake, kill a few fish, and then recover it for further study. A military research complex grew up, with cranes, docks, warehouses, and naval cutters. In 1991, President Akayev turned down a Russian request to continue military research, ordering that the site be converted to civilian use, but no funds were available. In 2008, Kyrgyzstan agreed to lease the area to the Russian navy for about $4.5 million a year.

Of course, the Soviet industrial workers who spent their vacations at resorts and *sanatorii* (health spas) had no idea that secret torpedo experiments were going on just down the road. They were enjoying the clean air, beaches, hot springs, mountain walks, and sporting activities. Some sanatorii doubled as medical facilities. After independence, the influx of tourists abruptly ended, and some state-owned resorts, without visitors or maintenance budgets, closed. In the first wave of privatization, some were sold to entrepreneurs whose political or family connections enabled them to snap up prime lakeside property at fire-sale prices; nevertheless, the new owners often lacked the capital to invest or modernize, and the resorts went into a not-so-genteel decline. The tourist industry has since revived, with an increase in domestic, Kazakh, and Russian tourists and Westerners on trekking trips, and the resorts are again attracting investors.

On the southern shore, away from the beaches, resorts, and health spas, lies an economic asset more significant than tourism—Central Asia's largest gold mine and the second-largest operation in the world (after Yanacocha in Peru). The Kumtor mine, operated by Centerra Gold, a Canadian company, began production in 1997. Initial government hopes that gold would boost the flagging economy were disappointed as world prices declined in the 1990s, but as prices rose the mine's economic impact increased. Kumtor accounts for 12 percent of Kyrgyzstan's GDP, 40 percent of industrial output, more than 50 percent of exports, and more than 10 percent of the national budget. It has a workforce of 2,600, most of them from the local area, and wages starting at $1,500 a month are more than seven times the national average.

As in all mining operations, economic benefits are weighed against environmental costs. In 1998, soon after the mine opened, a truck carrying sodium cyanide used in the gold extraction process crashed into the River Barskoon, which flows into the lake. Of the 20 tons of chemical, 1.8 tons were found to have seeped into the river. Environmental groups claimed four people died and at least eight hundred were taken to hospital suffering from skin rashes and chemical burns. Fish and cattle were found dead along the lakeshore. Farmers lost income, because consumers would not buy their produce for fear of contamination. The government rejected the claims of death and sickness, saying the cyanide leakage was not substantial enough to harm the environment. In 2006, more than three thousand local residents, working round the clock, blocked the main road leading to the mine to protest the lack of compensation. Opposition politicians called on the government to nationalize the mine and impose stricter environmental, health, and safety standards. Instead, the government renegotiated the contract and took a 33 percent stake in the parent company. Most of the compensation claims have still not been settled.

Kumtor maintains an aggressive public relations effort, emphasizing its contributions to the national and local economies. It claims 95 percent of its full-time employees are Kyrgyz citizens and that it is hiring locals to replace foreign managers. On its website, a carefully selected group of employees—from mining engineers, welders, and mechanics to cooks and accountants—talk about how the mine has changed their lives, and the fortunes of their families and communities. They grumble about the politicians in Bishkek who want to overregulate the mine. In 2013, a state commission fined the company almost $500 million, accusing it of corruption, unpaid taxes, and environmental degradation. Parliament called for the current lease agreement, concluded under the Bakiyev regime, to be negotiated. Centerra says the agreement is legitimate and that it has invested $1.2 billion in the mine, extending its life to 2026. "It's a fraud," Kumtor's boss Michael Fischer told the *Economist*. "They should be spending their time trying to find another Kumtor rather than shaking down the one they've got."[2]

The Road to Karakol

From Bishkek, the road to Karakol runs east along the Chuy Valley, which forms the northern border with Kazakhstan. East of Tokmak, the road rises into the Chuy River gorge and across the mountains to Balykchy, the main town and bus terminus on the western shore of the lake. Along the riverbank in the mountains are memorials marked simply "1916," a reminder of the short-lived rebellion by Kyrgyz and Kazakhs against the requisition of supply cattle, cotton, and food and the conscription of men into labor battalions. The revolt was brutally suppressed, with Russian troops razing villages. In the middle of the harsh winter, an estimated 50,000 fled across the mountains, hoping to reach the Chinese border. Some were killed, but many more starved or froze to death and were buried along the roadside.

Like most journeys outside the main cities in Kyrgyzstan, the trip to Karakol is best made between May and November; in winter and spring, the road is often closed because of snowdrifts, flooding, and avalanches. We made the elementary error of taking the first bus leaving the avtovokzal, thinking it would arrive ahead of later departures. It pays to visually inspect the vehicle before boarding. Bus drivers were responsible for maintaining their vehicles, and it was common to see a bus stopped with the hood up while the driver fixed some problem. We got on board a dented blue PAZ-672 of uncertain vintage. The 672 model from the Pavlovskiy Avtobusniy Zavod (Pavlovo Bus Factory) was one of the workhorse Soviet-era buses, used for both city and long-haul transport. The PAZ "no worries, no hassles" service contract (if there ever was one)

definitely expired with the fall of the Soviet Union, leaving city governments and bus operators scrambling for spare parts. Many bus stations in
Central Asia in the 1990s had unofficial scrap yards, where old buses were
broken up for spare parts. Fortunately, there were lots of old 672s growing
weeds, and, at a pinch, a part from its precursor, the PAZ-652, might work.

Our bus would probably have made it on a city run, but it was
not up to the 250 miles to Karakol. It gasped and wheezed its way out
of Bishkek, but on the first ascent out of the Chuy Valley, it pulled
over with the radiator steaming. The driver's assistant jumped out
carrying a large gas can, scrambled down the slope to the river, and
came back half an hour later to refill the radiator. From that point on,
we stopped every thirty or forty minutes for radiator maintenance,
with the assistant filling up at roadside pumps, large puddles, and—
when we eventually reached it—the lake. The scheduled six-hour trip
turned into a nine-hour trip, but everyone on board was remarkably
good-natured about the whole affair.

Although it's the administrative and commercial center of northeastern Kyrgyzstan with a population of 80,000, Karakol in the mid-1990s
still had the atmosphere of a country town. Even on market days, the
traffic was light and some people got around by horse and cart. Children

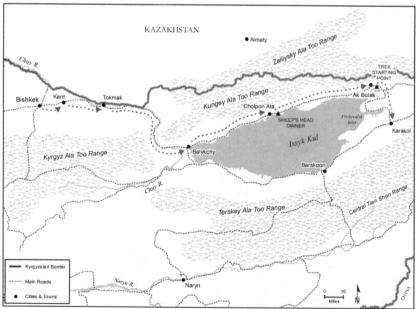

MAP 5.1 From Bishkek to Issyk Kul and Karakol (map by Brian Edward Balsley, GISP)

slid down the smooth stone step railing and played on the small square outside the oblast administration building; locals drank tea and played cards at the Santa Barbara restaurant, a long low building with a shocking-pink paint job that was supposed to make you imagine you were in Southern California. The town's sleepy charm owed much to the fact that it's on the way to nowhere in particular. Here, the lake road loops west again to run along the southern shore toward Barksoon, eventually linking back to the Bishkek road at Balykchy. A road runs east and then south, dead-ending at the thirty-seven-mile-long Inylcheck glacier in the Central Tian Shan; you can't go much further east without getting serious about jeeps and mountain guides. This makes Karakol an excellent base for trekkers, mountaineers, and skiers, but it's also well worth exploring for its own treasures.

In the older part of town, along streets lined with poplar and birch, are simple houses built in the Russian colonial era—some plain, some with attractive gingerbread trim. Most are single story, but there are a few larger, two-story homes built by merchants and professionals. The wooden Russian Orthodox cathedral was completed in 1895 but was closed by the Soviets in the 1930s; the five onion domes were destroyed, and the building was used as an officers' club. It was later restored, and services are held regularly. Eight mosques were also destroyed in the 1930s as Stalin's government sought to suppress Islam in the region. Only the Dungan (Chinese Muslim) mosque, a remarkable building constructed without nails by Chinese workers in 1910, remains. Maybe it escaped the Soviet bureaucrats' ire because it looks more like a Buddhist temple than a mosque.

FIGURE 5.1
Traditional Russian house, Karakol

FIGURE 5.2
Russian Orthodox
cathedral, Karakol

FIGURE 5.3
Chinese Dungan
mosque, Karakol

FIGURE 5.4
Bus shelter
near Karakol

As was the case with other towns and cities, the name changed with the prevailing political winds. The name Przhevalsk survived the 1917 revolution. The Bolsheviks figured that an intrepid explorer (even one with imperialist tendencies) was a suitable addition to the historical gallery of heroes of the USSR. The locals never liked it much—after all, Przhevalsky's only civic contribution had been to die there—so they protested, and in 1921 the name was restored to Karakol. Stalin changed it back to Przhevalsk in 1939 to celebrate the centenary of the explorer's birth. At independence in 1991, it became Karakol again.

Its heart is not the central square with its modest Lenin statue but the bazaar. In summer it is a blaze of colors, a feast of aromas. Although Kyrgyzstan's northern neighbor pitches the "apples are from Kazakhstan" line, the orchards around Issyk Kul, with a similar climate and soil, produce excellent apples and pears. As in other bazaars, the most tawdry section is the fashion aisle—cheap, imported clothes from Pakistan, Bangladesh, and Thailand with misspelled, sewn-in "designer labels." The Chinese rip-offs of consumer electronics even reproduced fonts. Look closely: it's not a Panasonic; it's a *Panascanic*. We found more to see at the Sunday morning animal market, where people came in from the country to trade sheep, cattle, and horses. It was a wonderful seething mass of humanity, animals, and carts.

The Hotel Karakol, one of only two in town, had definitely seen better days. There was no hot water, and the rooms, though clean, were dark and drab. However, the staff was friendly and, at $6 a night, we could hardly complain. The main challenge was getting something to eat. Snacks were sold on the street and at the bazaar, but most restaurants opened only for lunch. Twice we ended up at a bar near the hotel, eating whatever they had available. In the mid-1990s, foreign visitors were still a curiosity, so people wanted to talk with us. The second night Stephanie drove the crowd wild by attempting to teach the Electric Slide to a Turkish disco number. We were immediately invited to dance and had to pass the can-the-Americans-hold-the-vodka test.

The Rocky Road to Osh

A month later, Stephanie and I were back at the avtovokzal to plan for a longer trip. After the stop-and-start nine-hour bus journey to Karakol, we figured we would make better time in a marshrutka, even a crowded one. Unfortunately, no marshrutkas were going as far as we needed to go—to Osh, a trip of 375 miles. They went only as far as Toktogul, the main town on the country's largest reservoir. We would have to stay overnight, probably in a down-market version of the Hotel Karakol, then try to pick up another marshrutka heading south in the morning.

The trip was part business, part pleasure. After months of delays, mostly caused by lost paperwork and poor communication in Washington, the Osh Media Resource Center was finally up and running; furniture and computers had been installed, audio and video equipment was on the way, and classes had begun. I needed to spend a few days working with the manager Renat, who for over nine months had had not much more to manage than an empty room. I needed to set up the schedule for training programs, renew local media contacts, and work on equipment and technical issues. Then Stephanie and I planned to get a taste of the culture of Kyrgyzstan by attending the Osh Harvest Festival, which for now I'll describe as a cross between an old-style state fair, a Western rodeo, Wrestlemania, and a Highland games with a no-holes-barred polo game.

We had decided to travel overland rather than fly, not only to save money but to see rural Kyrgyzstan and its mountain ranges before winter arrived. Most people we talked to thought it was a bad idea. It was a long, hazardous journey and there were bandits on the road. In spring, the road was often blocked by rockslides, in winter, by snowdrifts. There are three mountain passes, the highest rising to almost 11,000 feet. In 1996, it was still a two-lane road all the way, but for long stretches deteriorated into what in the United States would be classified as a county (maybe even a township) road, full of ruts and potholes. The government was always talking about improving the road, but nothing was done. With a clear run, the trip took at least twelve hours; we ended up needing fourteen, and we'd heard of nightmare twenty-two-hour trips. Yet this was the main north-south artery in the country, connecting the two major population centers in the Chuy and Fergana valleys.

The Bishkek travel agencies were willing to take us but at an exorbitant price—$450 one way for a jeep or four-wheel drive vehicle. We figured we could find a cheaper ride with someone who had driven to Bishkek and needed to get home. That's how I found myself at the avtovokzal, along with Salavan, an Osh native, looking for cars with Osh and Djalalabad license plates. I'd asked Salavan to interpret and do the bargaining, knowing he would get a better price than I could. On a side street, we found the unofficial collecting point for passengers and goods heading south—a small group of cars, their drivers squatting on the dirt sidewalk. The cars were all about the same size (Soviet-era compact), so I picked the largest and strongest-looking driver; I figured that if there really were bandits out there, our odds would be better traveling with him. Jorobev was a Kyrgyz in his early forties with the build of a football linebacker; I imagined he had been a wrestler in his youth. Salavan told me he would take us for 1,200 som ($75). That was more than a local would pay, he said, but it was half the "foreigner's price" I'd have paid if I'd tried bargaining myself. It was also one sixth of the travel agency price. I paid Jorobev 200 som ($12) up front, and he promised to pick us up at the apartment at 6 a.m. the next morning. I had no way of knowing whether he would show up, although I reckoned the balance of 1,000 som might be incentive enough. He was right on time, and we sped off in his battered but mechanically well maintained Lada 300, the trunk stacked with our luggage and his commercial cargo—two cases of vodka he was taking to sell in Osh. It turned out we needed the extra ballast.

From Bishkek, the main road runs west along the Chuy Valley for about sixty miles to the town of Kara Balta before turning south and ascending into the Kyrgyz Ala Too range through a narrow gorge. The mountains are rough slopes of loose rocks, with little vegetation and few trees. Apart from the lack of a guardrail, the main hazards were rocks that had fallen onto the road. For Jorobev this was just normal driving. Still, it's tiring work dodging boulders, and by 8 a.m. he was feeling hungry. We stopped at a group of weather-beaten wooden shacks, parking behind a line of trucks on a narrow strip of ground overlooking a ravine. There was no sign, but Jorobev said this was the last place to find food before we ascended to the first pass. We shared a bowl of *grechka* (buckwheat) topped with boiled mutton. Two truck drivers joined us; we couldn't figure out whether they knew Jorobev, but on the road to Osh there are no strangers. They washed down their meal with a bottle of vodka. We were relieved that Jorobev was happy with tea. After the obligatory driver-posing-by-Lada-at-truckstop-with-the-Americans photos, we took off again, heading for the first pass, the Tor-Ashuu (11,765 ft.), where the Kyrgyz Ala Too and Talas Ala Too ranges meet. The views of the mountains and deep valleys were

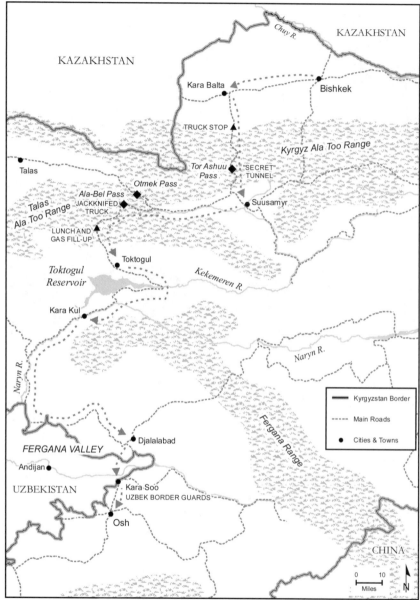

MAP 5.2 From Bishkek to Osh (map by Brian Edward Balsley, GISP)

jaw-dropping, but it was too much to ask to ask Jorobev to stop so we could take pictures because we were already in the snow. He handled the small car expertly, controlling the skids on the bends and staying in high gear to maintain traction.

FIGURE 5.5 On the road to Osh—with Jorobev outside truck stop

At the top of the Tor-Ashuu pass is a 1.8-mile-long tunnel, with bare rock walls and icicles hanging from the roof. We had heard about it from Jonathan Barth, a Peace Corps volunteer, who told us that on one trip north, he and his companions were held up for over an hour behind a line of cars waiting to enter. A driver told him that hundreds of sheep were being herded through the tunnel. For Jonathan, a photojournalist, the opportunity was too good to miss, and he started setting up his tripod. The tunnel guards spotted him and became agitated. "No pictures!" they insisted. "Why not?" asked Jonathan, "I'm only going to film the sheep." "It's a secret tunnel," the guards replied in an uneasy whisper, as if revealing its "secret" status somehow compromised its security. Jonathan was left to wonder how a tunnel on the main north-south highway, through which hundreds of vehicles passed every day, could be a secret to anyone. But the guards were simply following orders. In the Soviet era, all bridges, tunnels, railroad stations, and airports were strategic military assets to be protected. They were not shown on maps, and photographing them was prohibited. Even at the height of the Cold War, or in the most extreme Red Army war game scenario, it seemed unlikely that the United States would launch an attack by dropping paratroopers into the Kyrgyz Ala Too. But just in case they did, they should not know that the best route to the capital Bishkek was through the tunnel. And so, even though everyone knew about the tunnel, it remained an official secret because the authorities said so.

On the south side of the tunnel, the snow was deeper, and the visibility poorer. Trucks with chains on their wheels struggled up the road. A few were stranded in the snow, and we wondered if they could be pulled out before spring. The road headed west along the wide, barren Suusamyr valley where in summer the Kyrgyz come to graze herds of sheep and horses. The snow became deeper as we climbed up to the 10,446-foot Ala-Bel pass over the Suusamyr-Too range. Near the summit, traffic in both directions was stalled. A truck had jackknifed; the cab was in the ditch, the trailer blocked the road. Another truck hitched on a chain and tried to pull it out, but its tires started spinning, and the driver, fearing he would also end up in the ditch, gave up. It was time for collective action, or rather a collective heave-ho. Drivers and passengers got out of their vehicles, formed two human lines behind the truck and started pushing. More than thirty of us slithered in the snow as the truck spun its wheels, creating a minor blizzard. It took twenty minutes, but eventually we pushed the truck back onto the road.

On the other side of the pass, the snow cleared and the scenery changed as we entered a valley of evergreens and mountain streams. We stopped for a late lunch at a café, sharing our bread, cheese, and sausage with Jorobev, who ordered more meat dishes. By now we were short of gas, and hadn't seen a roadside pump for more than sixty miles. Fortunately the café owners had a supply round the back, and a bucketful was enough to take us to Toktogul, the largest town on the Bishkek-Osh road. It sits on the north shore of a vast reservoir where the Naryn River has been dammed to provide hydroelectric power. The road skirts the reservoir and continues southwest to the town of Kara-Kul, site of a Soviet-built hydroelectric plant and the massive Toktogul dam—210 meters high, and 150 meters wide—the first of a series of dams along the gorge of the Lower Naryn. The Naryn is the headstream of the Syr-Darya, one of Central Asia's two great rivers. Downstream, most of the water from the Syr-Darya and the Amu-Darya, flowing out of the Pamir Alay, was diverted by the Soviets to irrigate the cotton fields of Uzbekistan. By the time the two rivers reach the Aral Sea, they have been reduced to sluggish streams. Not surprisingly, the Uzbeks complain that their neighbors hoard too much water behind the Toktogul dam.

By now, it was getting dark. Jorobev, who had dodged rocks and driven through snow, was weaving to avoid oncoming cars and trucks, their headlights blazing. The narrow road twisted and turned, steep cliffs to the left and, on our side of the road, a dizzying drop to the dammed lakes below. We descended into the Fergana Valley, and for the last sixty miles or so traveled on flat land through cotton fields. After leaving Djalalabad, the road to Osh passes through the far eastern corner of Uzbekistan. We sped through the first border crossing where there appeared to be no controls, but as we crossed back into Kyrgyzstan near Kara Soo, the Uzbek guards pulled us over. They were looking for drugs, and two Westerners traveling in a small car late at night aroused suspicion. One guard spoke some English and seemed less interested in Jorobev's vodka than in promoting tourism. "Why are you passing through and not visiting Uzbekistan?" he asked good-naturedly. "It is a wonderful country, and the people are so friendly." We said we'd heard that too, and would love to see Samarkand and Bukhara. We finally arrived in Osh around 9 p.m., tired but exhilarated after a wonderful trip. We gave Jorobev the baklava we had brought with us (just in case we were stranded in the mountains) and a well-deserved tip.

In late 1996, there were two buildings in Osh with hotel signs outside. The Intourist, where I had stayed briefly in December 1995, had not changed—cold, spartan rooms, noisy, leaky plumbing, frequent power outages, a reception area that looked like an inner-city bus terminal, and a dimly lit restaurant that was usually closed at mealtimes. We were informed that the other hotel, the Alaii, was a couple of stars below the Intourist, so we did not bother to check it out. Instead, we rented a khrushchevka on the west side of Osh, about a fifteen-minute ride into the center by bus or marshrutka.

In most Soviet cities, a central thermal heating plant provides hot water and steam heating for apartments and public buildings. As temperatures start to drop in October, many conversations begin with the question: "When will the heating come on?" Rumors abound. The heating is already on in government buildings and high-rent districts where officials and business people have apartments, but the administration is delaying turning on the heat to the microraions. Someone who knows someone who works at the heating plant says there's a schedule, but it's an official secret. One thing is sure. The date when the heating comes on has absolutely no relationship to the temperature outside.

By mid-October, it was already chilly, and the bazaar vendors were doing a brisk business in small, electrically hazardous Chinese space heaters. There had been no hot water for months, except for apartments with bottled gas. Southern Kyrgyzstan depends on Uzbekistan for gas supplies, but the local government had not paid its bills. The Uzbeks had reduced supplies several months earlier, so gas was now available only for cooking, and the pressure was low. The government said it could not pay Uzbekistan until more people paid their utility bills, but to unemployed industrial workers, teachers who had not been paid for months, and retirees who had seen the value of their pensions decline, food came before utility payments. And so the rumors continued. Will Uzbekistan cut off the gas? Will Kyrgyzstan reduce the flow of water to irrigate Uzbekistan's cotton fields?

It hadn't always been this way. In the Soviet Union, central planning had regulated water and gas supplies. Every year, Moscow ordered the Kyrgyz to empty their reservoirs into the Syr-Darya to irrigate the cotton fields and told the Uzbeks to keep the gas flowing. Some of the cotton revenue came back in annual subsidies to the two republics. After independence, the countries struck a barter deal—summer water from Kyrgyzstan in exchange for winter gas and electricity from Uzbekistan's coal-fired power plants. Kyrgyzstan wanted to increase domestic energy production by boosting hydroelectric capacity, but had to wait until the dams filled up after summer to start producing power. Both countries started selling resources on a cash-only basis, and both complained that the other was not paying its bills on time. The victims in the energy wars were the people of southern Kyrgyzstan who endured frequent, unscheduled power outages and (even when the supply was on) low gas pressure. You have to adapt. In the morning, we put two large pans of water on the stove or hot plate, went back to bed for half an hour, and then took a standing bath.

The major attraction in Osh that weekend had the official-sounding title of the Osh Union Private Farmers Association Harvest Festival. Like other harvest festivals, it marked the end of the season when herding families packed up their yurts and came down from the summer pastures in the mountains to their villages for the winter. The passing of the season was celebrated with traditional sports—wrestling, falconry, horse races, and horseback games. Even though Soviet bureaucrats preferred structured, mainstream sports in showpiece public arenas, they allowed the traditional games to go on, perhaps reckoning that they were a safer outlet for cultural expression than Islam. The herders dutifully claimed to be competing for the honor of their collective farm, but everyone knew that it was all about individual strength and horsemanship.

In the mid-1990s, Kyrgyzstan was going through the long and acrimonious process of privatizing farmland by breaking up the *kolkhozes* (the contracted form of *kollektivnoye khozyaystvo,* meaning collective farm or economy). Foreign agricultural consultants descended with their marketing plans, technical advice, and microfinance schemes. The major challenge was to divide land and resources equitably, and then enforce legal title. Herding families claimed hereditary grazing rights from the pre-Soviet era, although claims were often challenged by other families; because these rights were part of local oral tradition and never written down, it was often impossible to know who was right. Russians and Volga Germans who had settled in the region from the late nineteenth century tried to reclaim their family farms. In the Fergana Valley, Kyrgyz and Uzbeks fought for control of the cotton fields—first in the riots of 1990, and then in the courts and local administration. The process was fraught with corruption and influence-buying, with officials and business people taking over large tracts, despite having no clear legal claim. In any case, it was never simply a matter of dividing up the land of a collective farm between families. How were the herds of sheep, horses, and cattle to be shared? Who got the farm buildings, the dairy equipment, the tractors, and other farm machinery? Whatever decision was made, someone felt aggrieved.

The privatization was part of what foreign donors liked to call the transition to a market-driven economy. The Osh festival celebrated the achievements of a new and growing class of private farmers, who were presumably applying scientific breeding and crop-rotation techniques and MBA-caliber business planning to their traditional practices. In fact, it was difficult to know how well private farmers were doing because, as in other sectors of the economy, statistics were notoriously unreliable. Most transactions took place informally; farmers tended to underreport livestock and crop sales to avoid taxes, and the local tax agency did not have the resources to count sheep. Nonetheless, the consultants reported statistics on the growth of the private sector in agriculture, and the usual cast of donors—the United Nations Development Programme (UNDP), USAID, the European Union—sponsored the festival to celebrate the progress of privatization.

The festival was held at the hippodrome, the horse racing track, about nine miles south of Osh. The field inside the track was lined with decorated yurts, their floors covered with *shirdaks.* Most competitors had arrived on horseback. In the fold of the lower Ak Burra valley, with sweeping views of the mountains, it was a fine spectacle. Behind the yurts was a line of steaming *kazans*—steel kettles, about three feet in diameter, heated over wood fires: the *plov* cook-off contest was under way.

FIGURE 5.6 *(above)* Kyrgyz man on horseback at Osh Harvest Festival

FIGURE 5.7 *(right)* Kyrgyz herders, Osh Harvest Festival

FIGURE 5.8
Competitors
in *Ulak
Tartyshy*,
Osh Harvest
Festival

FIGURE 5.9
Competitors
in *Ulak
Tartyshy*,
Osh Harvest
Festival

FIGURE 5.10
Competitors
in *Ulak
Tartyshy*,
Osh Harvest
Festival

Although you could see everything from the bleachers, it was more fun to be down on the field. We watched the wrestling competition, in which burly Kyrgyz (with the build of our driver Jorobev) grappled and whirled each other around in the air. In another game called Oodarysh, the wrestlers were on horseback, competing to be the first to throw the other from his horse; there was a referee, who periodically separated human and horseflesh for infractions, but the rules were never entirely clear. In Kyz Kuumai, male and female riders chase each other around the track; if the man catches the woman, she has to kiss him; if the woman catches the man, she horse-whips him. There was no scoreboard but, as far as we could tell, there was more horse-whipping than kissing going on. The highlight was Ulak Tartyshy, a cross between polo and rugby, popular throughout Central Asia. Two teams of riders struggle for possession of an animal carcass, try to pick it up, and race with it toward the opposition's line for a touchdown. In the minor-league version, a headless, legless sheep or goat is the ball, but this was the big league, so they used a 250-pound calf. Picking up 250 pounds is tough at the best of times, but when you're on horseback with other riders jostling, punching, and whipping you, it's a real challenge. For most of the game, all we could see was a tight knot of riders; they would reach down to try to pick up the calf and get pushed or kicked out of the way. One team, sporting what looked like Soviet World War II aviator headgear, clearly had the edge (with the help of some sideline coaching), and made two touchdowns. This dangerous game was played with true passion, with the crowd cheering each block, tackle, and fumble. We were happy we had made the long road trip to Osh. The Kyrgyz are justly famous for their horsemanship, and this was our best chance to see the traditional games.

Too High in the Tian Shan

The guides looked doubtful. "You really want to go on a trek?" asked Pavel. "In the *mountains?*" Harvey and I nodded. "How about a nice trip to the beach at Issyk Kul instead? The weather will be lovely." No, we insisted. Some of us were leaving Kyrgyzstan soon, and we wanted to do a trek in the Tian Shan. Pavel shrugged, went over to a desk and started pulling out maps.

There were seven of us in the group, ranging in age from my son Richard (eleven) to my fellow Fulbrighter, Harvey Flad. Harvey was in his mid-fifties, but like many geographers was an avid hiker and in excellent shape. Jeania, an English teaching fellow, was in her late twenties and fit. Our friends Bob and Jane had traveled up from Osh, where Bob ran a USAID-funded agricultural development project; both were in their early thirties and in good shape, though Jane had a dodgy hip.

Stephanie and I were in our mid-forties and in better physical condition than we had been in years. That's because we walked almost everywhere in Bishkek—to the universities, to the local market, to dinner and the theater. Still, ambling along the level tree-lined streets, and stopping to rest and have an ice cream in one of the many parks, did not exactly prepare us for a trek in the mountains.

The guides did a quick assessment, surmising, as Harvey put it later, that "we were not all twenty-five-year-old mountain climbers." They spread out the maps of the Zailiskiy Ala-Too, north of Issyk Kul, and the Central Tian Shan range to the south. "The trails south are longer and more difficult," said Pavel. "Let's go north toward the border with Kazakhstan. Easy to moderate."

"Easy to moderate" sounded fine to us, although in retrospect it depends what scale you're using. What was "easy" to an experienced guide or trekker might fall into the "really difficult" category for the novice; "moderate" into "mission impossible." We assumed they had assessed our physical capacity and decided what we could manage.

Today, trekking and adventure travel in the Tian Shan is a profitable niche of the tourism industry in Kyrgyzstan and southern Kazakhstan, with companies in Bishkek and Almaty offering packages to visitors, most of them from Europe and North America. They have modern equipment, medical supplies, GPS, and satellite phones; if there's an emergency, they call in the helicopter mountain rescue unit. However, in the mid-1990s, few tourists had discovered Kyrgyzstan. The tourist agencies in Bishkek did most of their business selling air tickets and package vacations to Thailand and Turkey. They could put you in contact with guides, but it was quite informal. "Here's Vladimir's number. He did two treks for foreigners last year, speaks English, and can arrange for porters. However, I haven't seen him for a few months. My brother-in-law said he heard he has been working in Germany, shipping secondhand cars through Karaganda. Or perhaps he is back in Russia. Maybe he is available—maybe not. Posmotrim [We'll see]."

That's pretty much how we ended up with Pavel (Paul) and Sasha (Aleksandr). In Soviet times, both had had well-paying industrial jobs but lost them at independence when the factories closed. Like other ethnic Russians, they considered moving to Russia, but relatives had said that economic conditions there were not much better, so they decided to stay in Bishkek, learn English, and benefit from the tourism boom that, according to the government and the more optimistic newspaper reports, was going to happen any day now. In July 1997, they were still waiting for the influx of well-heeled foreigners. They were happier in Soviet times, they said, before Gorbachev and his cursed perestroika ruined it all. But business was business, so they agreed to take us on the trek.

We set out from Bishkek early on the morning of July 12—our group of seven, the two guides, and two Kyrgyz porters to carry the tents and cooking equipment. Collectively, we would not have made good models for an outfitter's catalog. We brought layers of clothing and hiking boots, but the guides and porters wore sweat pants and sneakers or flip-flops. A few miles from Tyup (see map 5.1), where the lakeshore road turns south, we pulled over and put on our packs. It was a warm, sunny afternoon, and we were in high spirits. "That will be our campsite tonight," said Pavel, vaguely waving his arm northward. I could not figure out where he was pointing, and could not see a trail, so it was reassuring to know that he knew where we were going. We hiked up a steady incline through the mountain pastures. The views back toward the lake were spectacular, and the mountainside was ablaze with color—wild irises, edelweiss, and other wildflowers. Stephanie wanted to stop to pick flowers, but the guides urged us to keep going: we had to make the campsite before darkness. We stopped for brief breaks, but the guides told us not to drink too much water because it would sap our strength. We weren't sure of the medical basis for the advice. We didn't want to become dehydrated, but we resisted temptation, passing cool mountain streams without pausing.

We camped the first night in a narrow valley. We realized why the guides had pushed on so they could set up the tents and gather wood before darkness fell. In these deep valleys, shaded by the high mountains from the sun, darkness comes early, even in midsummer. We gathered around the campfire for dinner, and went to bed early. When we woke up, the sun had not yet reached down into the valley, but brilliantly illuminated the top third of the peaks, a dramatic visual contrast. After kasha and tea for breakfast, we set out, climbing over two passes. As the day went on, the party became strung out. Harvey and Jeania kept up with the guides, but the rest of us straggled along with one of the porters. Then the clouds moved in and the rain began. With visibility dropping, we lost sight of the forward party. The porter wasn't sure of the way, and we ended up wandering along a ridge, looking for the lake that marked our campsite. The rain turned to hail. We plodded on, wondering whether we would find the rest of the party that night. Eventually, we spotted the lake below and scrambled down a hillside through rocks and across a stream. By the time we reached the campsite, we were soaked, and our mood didn't improve when we found Pavel and Sasha sitting in their tent drinking cognac. There was a brief argument, which ended with a new protocol for the trek: one guide would lead the party, while the other would stay at the rear, keeping pace with the slowest-moving member.

As we gathered around the campfire to drink tea and dry out our socks and boots, the mood was more subdued than on the first night. There was a minor alarm when Harvey's socks caught fire and the soles of Stephanie's boots partly melted. The next day dawned bright and sunny, and it was an easy three-hour walk to our lunch spot at another mountain lake. From there, the trail rose abruptly through forests and across streams. With one of the guides at the rear, the party did not become separated, but it was a steep and tough climb. Jane's hip was hurting, and she was having trouble keeping up, so we took turns walking with her. As we emerged from the timberline to the high mountain pastures, she said she couldn't go any further and collapsed. Sasha, Harvey, Jeania, Bob, and I were ahead of the rest of the party, resting on a small ridge, when we saw Pavel run toward us shouting. We hurried back. It was clear that Jane was in a bad way; she was feverish, and a porter was massaging her feet to restore circulation.

I had heard of altitude sickness, but I thought it was the kind of thing that happened only to people who fly into nose-bleed cities such as La Paz in Bolivia or Lhasa in Tibet and then go jogging, or to serious mountaineers attacking Himalayan peaks on *National Geographic* specials. I didn't expect it on an "easy to moderate" trek in the Tian Shan. But the guides immediately diagnosed it. Because air is thinner at high altitudes, when you make a rapid ascent—as we had done from the lake to about 9,000 feet—the body cannot take in as much oxygen as it needs. In mild cases, the symptoms are like a hangover—headache, dizziness, weakness, sickness in the stomach, and loss of appetite. In severe cases, the lungs and brain can be affected. You become confused, unable to walk straight, and feel faint; your toes and fingers may start to turn blue.

This case was severe. We put up a tent, and Jane was laid down. Bob, Stephanie, and the guides massaged her feet, which were beginning to turn blue. The only solution was to get her down in altitude as quickly as possible. Today, trekking parties use satellite phones to call in rescue units, and provide GPS coordinates. In July 1997, for all we knew we were the only people on that mountain slope near the Kazakhstan border, and we had to face the challenge ourselves. One of the porters ran off to see if he could find a shepherd. He returned an hour later, saying he had been to the next ridge, but there was no one in sight.

And then, as if in a scene from a Western movie, two Kyrgyz herders appeared on the skyline. We waved and shouted, and they rode toward us. There was a brief negotiation, and dollars changed hands. Jane, who was looking and feeling worse than ever, was helped onto a horse with Sasha walking behind to hold her. Bob, one of the porters, and the herders followed with the other horse. The plan was to head north toward the nearest road, and on to Almaty where Jane could receive medical treatment. We divided the remainder of the food between the parties. There were hugs all around, and Jane's party started its descent. The rest of us turned south again.

We had hoped to get over the final pass, which rose to almost 11,000 feet, that day, but it was now late in the afternoon and everyone felt drained, physically and emotionally, by the events of the past few hours. After two hours, we stopped to camp in a wonderful, lonely, treeless place by a stream. At almost 10,000 feet, it was cold, and we were glad we had brought our long johns. In the morning, we awoke to find the tents surrounded by horses. We pushed on to the pass, and moved from the pastures to a barren landscape of glacial scree, the loose rocks left by the ice when it retreats in summer. The scenery was, if anything, even more wild and spectacular than any we had seen so far on the trip, with beautiful alpine meadows and sweeping views of the mountains.

The descent to Issyk Kul was long and strenuous. I stopped worrying about the blisters on my heels, because my big toes were hurting so much from the downward pressure (both of my big toenails turned blue from the bruising, and one detached a few weeks later). By late afternoon, we caught sight of the bus waiting for us on the road. It felt good to soak our feet in a cold stream and, an hour later, to stop by the roadside and pick up beer.

We learned later that Jane's group had made it down to the lake, hired new horses, headed north and picked up a ride to Almaty. The doctor who examined Jane confirmed altitude sickness, and prescribed a few days rest. That's what the rest of us took, without prescription. Opinions on the trek were divided. We all agreed the scenery was fantastic, but that "easy to moderate" was more challenging than we expected. And, as someone said after the second day, "Are we really paying money to be cold, tired, and eat lousy food?" Harvey, Jeania, Bob, and I all said we would do it again; Richard, who did wonderfully well for an eleven-year-old, wasn't so sure. Stephanie and Jane said they would have preferred a gentler outing that involved picking wildflowers and mushrooms.

The Eye of the Sheep

A month later, Richard and I took Pavel and Sasha's original advice with a trip to the beach at Issyk Kul. We traveled with my university interpreter, Gulkhan, and rented a small apartment in Cholpon Ata. In Kyrgyz, Cholpon Ata literally means "Venus father," the name of a mythological protecting spirit, and the town was renowned for its healthy climate and clean beaches. Most visitors stayed at a *dom otdykha* (rest house) or *turbaza* (tourist center), a rambling holiday camp with chalets or apartments, landscaped grounds and gardens, a common dining hall, and a beach. By the 1990s, the camps, and Cholpon Ata itself, had fallen on hard times because it was too expensive for people from other former Soviet republics to travel there. Still, it remained a favorite for vacationers from Central Asian countries. President Akayev had a summer home there with a yacht for entertaining foreign visitors.

We spent three days lazing around on the beach and walking around the town. This is one of the major fruit-growing areas of the country, and in August the trees were laden with apples, apricots, and cherries. On our last night, we drove out to a village for a traditional Kyrgyz feast with colleagues from the KSNU journalism faculty and their relatives. Stephanie came out from Bishkek to join us. I had completed my second semester of teaching in June, so the feast was in my honor. This was an offer you definitely can't refuse, but I'd heard enough about such occasions from Western colleagues that I approached it with trepidation.

The family put out a huge spread, and we started eating at about 7 p.m. In the backyard, they had slaughtered a sheep and were boiling it over an open fire. The patriarch sat next to me, filling my glass, and talking to me in a rural Kyrgyz dialect that even Gulkhan could not understand. On schedule at 10 p.m. they brought in the *besh barmak* (five fingers)—boiled mutton served with noodles, so called because it is traditionally eaten with the fingers. I was presented with the sheep's head. As the honored guest, I was supposed to carve it up and distribute slices to the company at the table. It's not a random process because tradition determines who gets which part. Richard, as the youngest at the table, was expected to eat an ear, on the assumption that by doing so he would be more likely to listen to adult advice (he refused, of course). I don't think they seriously expected me to do the carving, but I gamely chopped at the thing for a few minutes before passing it off to another guest who knew what to do.

Regular power outages were common, particularly in rural areas, so I was not surprised when the lights went out a couple of minutes later. I breathed a short sigh of relief, thinking I had been rescued from eating the part destined for the honored guest. However, soon after they brought in oil lamps, the lights came back on, and I smiled through clenched teeth as I was presented with one of the eyes. It was a bit late to claim an allergy to mutton, so I tried to swallow it without thinking about what I was eating. It nearly came right back up but a quick swig of cognac did the trick. Richard sat looking at me in amazement. "Dad, how did it taste?" he asked. I just gulped.

Heads and eyes apart, it was an enjoyable evening, enlivened by one guest, who was drunk when we arrived and who kept on drinking (presumably also in my honor) and trying to speak French. At that time, my French was better than my Russian, but his Russian was easier to understand. About fifteen of us stayed in the house that night. When they served the innards and boiled mutton again for breakfast, I felt I could now politely refuse. "Just some bread and tea, please," I said.

Visaless in Uzbekistan

Although the borders of the Central Asian republics are artificial, crossing them can be a serious business, involving visas, vehicle searches, minor interrogations, and bribes. In the mid-1990s, the most open border was between Kyrgyzstan and Kazakhstan. Guards would routinely wave through buses and marshrutkas on the Bishkek-Almaty road without examining documents or checking the luggage. I made two trips to Almaty by marshrutka in 1997 but have no way of proving it because my passport was neither examined nor stamped. In principle, I should have been traveling with a Kazakhstan visa, but other expats said they didn't bother. "Just say you're on the way to the airport," one advised me. "You may have to pay a few tenge to the Kazakhs, but it's cheaper than a visa and less hassle." Cars with foreigners—especially those "from countries with convertible currencies," as my source put it—merited more attention (and more tenge), but I'd never heard of anyone being turned back.

Uzbekistan was a different proposition. More than any other Central Asian republic apart from Turkmenistan, it had retained the Soviet police-state mentality. Official censors in the capital, Tashkent, still wielded their blue pens, removing any hint of criticism of the regime of President Islam Karimov from the newspapers. The government had some reason to fear the growth of Islamic fundamentalism but used it as a pretext to imprison political opponents, social activists, and journalists. It was difficult for NGOs, even those working in health, education, and poverty alleviation, to operate. It could take up to two years for an NGO to obtain official registration, and even after that it was subject to harassment by the tax police and other agencies. The government exercised strict controls over the economy. Starting a business required forms and fees, plus bribes to make sure the paperwork was processed; for foreign firms, it could take months (and more bribes) for a piece of equipment to make it through customs.

The regime seemed paranoid about all foreigners, including tourists. This was a pity because of all the Central Asian republics Uzbekistan has the most to offer—from the great Silk Road cities of Samarkand, Bukhara, and Khiva and the museums of Tashkent to the environmental disaster of the Aral Sea. The food is wonderful, and the people hospitable. Most tourists were required to book vacations through the state travel agency Uzbektourism, which offered overpriced guided tours with accommodation at official hotels. Tourists saw what the guides wanted them to see, and contacts with ordinary Uzbeks—apart from museum and hotel staff and official souvenir vendors—were not encouraged. It was possible to travel independently, but it could be, as *Lonely Planet* put it, "an endless series of petty bureaucratic irritations and not-so-petty official hassles."[3]

I decided to try anyway, and flew with Richard from Bishkek to Osh (Stephanie was getting ready to leave Kyrgyzstan and stayed home to start packing). We joined Jane, now fully recovered from her altitude sickness, and her friend Diane who was visiting from the United States. We found a driver, Ilya, who agreed to do the five-day trip for $300. Obtaining a visa was difficult because Uzbekistan—perhaps in reprisal for the ongoing spats over water supplies and unpaid gas bills—did not have a consulate in Bishkek. The nearest was in Almaty, and we would have to wait for a few days while the visa paperwork was processed. The only other place offering visas was Tashkent airport, so we settled on the story to use with border guards and police: we were on our way to the airport. We supported it with a large passport stamp from the Kyrgyz Otdel Viz i Registratsii (OVIR—the Department of Visas and Registration) in Osh.

OVIR was a classic example of how little independence had done to remove the layers of government bureaucracy. In the Soviet era, its main purpose had been to keep records of citizens who moved to a new city or district. Foreigners were required to register (and pay a fee) within three days of arriving in the country. Hotels took care of registration for guests, but long-term residents and independent travelers had to join the line at the OVIR office to obtain what was, for all intents and purposes, a second (if cheaper) visa. Nevertheless, we were happy to pay OVIR about $12 for a passport stamp that stated that we could travel in Uzbekistan for a week. What gave the Kyrgyz authorities the right to let people travel in another country is a diplomatic technicality that eluded me, but we hoped that the stamp would look official enough to confuse, if not convince, the border guards and police.

No one checked us at the Uzbek border two miles outside Osh, but from midmorning on we were stopped by the police and asked for our papers every hour or so. As the only one in the group (apart from Ilya) who spoke any Russian, I was the designated negotiator. For the first 150 miles or so, I stuck to our story: we were going to Tashkent airport to obtain visas. Jane, Diane, and Richard, sitting in the backseat, nodded on cue. After passing the city of Khokand, it was clear that we were not heading north to Tashkent after all, so we dropped the story and replaced it with a narrative that went something like this, "Your colleagues back in Andijan and along the highway checked our papers, and welcomed us to your wonderful country. Why is there a problem now?" Then Ilya shook hands, slapped backs, and chatted with the police. As far as I could tell, we were fined for having tinted windows, having Kyrgyzstan plates, or simply for being there. Most of the fines were small—$2 or $2.50—and even when Ilya picked up a speeding ticket, it was under $5. But we still had two borders to cross.

The road to Samarkand runs west through the northern panhandle of Tajikistan, a region of the Fergana Valley lopped off from the Uzbek SSR in 1929 when the Tajik SSR was created. I now had to deal with officials who wanted to see Tajik visas. Sometimes they just wanted to chat and were sincerely curious about these four foreigners passing through, but they were also ready to impose a service charge. Fortunately, we had stocked up with small gifts. Entry to Tajikistan cost us two blank audio cassettes. At the other side of the panhandle, I was forced to play the sex card. In the office, the middle-aged, sullen-looking border guard absentmindedly thumbed through the passport pages, but paused when he got to Diane's passport picture. She was an airline steward, tall, shapely, and blonde. I sensed an opportunity. "Ochen' krasivaya devushka [a very beautiful young woman]," I observed, in as offhanded a fashion as I could. He grunted in agreement and kept looking at the photo. I asked if he would like to meet her, and his face broke into a smile. Diane did a runway-style walk into the office and flashed a smile. The passports were returned. Back in the car, I apologized to Diane and Jane for my tactic. They said they didn't care. Whatever it took to get across the border.

Our plan was to do the five hundred miles from Osh to Bukhara on the first day, and then return via Samarkand, but the car kept stalling because of bad gas, so we were happy to make it to Samarkand. We stayed with Ilya's uncle's family in a traditional Uzbek house with a courtyard, about a ten-minute drive from the center. We still had time to go into the city and visit Registan square, the heart of medieval Samarkand's religious, intellectual, and commercial life, its three great madrassas with their minarets, arches, and courtyards sparkling in the evening light. Many of the city's architectural wonders date from the reign of Tamerlane (Timur) who chose Samarkand as his capital in 1370 and over the next thirty-five years made it a center of commerce and religion. Samarkand's architecture and art were financed by Timur's conquests; by 1395, his empire included most of Central Asia, modern-day Iran, Iraq, eastern Turkey, and the Caucasus. His grandson, the educated and cultured Ullughbek who ruled until 1449, made the city a center of learning in the Islamic world. Ullughbek was more inter-ested in astronomy than governing. He built an observatory where he spent many nights using a marble astrolabe to chart the positions of stars and make calculations of time. Maybe he should have spent more time on earthly affairs. The Islamic clerics of Samarkand resented his preference for science over the Koran; one his sons hatched a plot in which Ullughbek was dethroned and decapitated and the observatory (but not its astrolabe and records) destroyed.

The drive to Bukhara was uneventful, except for the regular police checkpoints. We found a bed and breakfast, again in a traditional Uzbek home. The emirs of Bukhara were a nasty bunch, running a huge slave trade and beheading foreigners, including the unfortunate British offi-cers Connolly and Stoddart. We visited the Ark, the emir's fortress, and other scenes of dastardly deeds. Although the madrassas and mosques of Bukhara are not as visually dramatic as those of Samarkand, there are many more of them. The artisans' covered markets have been restored, but much of the old city with its dirt streets remained pretty much as it used to be. We had more of a sense of being in an ancient city than in Sa-markand, where the Registan is bordered by wide, wooded boulevards.

It was a long day's drive back to Osh, with the usual hassles from police and border guards. In Tajikistan, one guard asked me to swap a $100 bill, which he claimed had been burned by a cigarette, for a new one; surely, I could exchange it at a bank in the United States. I wasn't buying, and we gave up a can of car shampoo to cross. In midafternoon, a cop pulled us over and began examining our passports. He said he was learning English, and started reciting the names of the US states printed on the visa pages. I went along with this performance for about twenty minutes, good-naturedly correcting his pronunciation. "No, not Ar-kan-sas, it's Ar-kan-saw, and please don't ask me why." I gave up when he could not wrap his tongue around Mississippi, and said we had to move on. The Uzbeks were searching cars (for drugs, they said) and asked us to pull out all of our bags. We were worried they would confiscate our purchases, so we all got out and started scattering dirty clothes and toilet articles all over the road. This was too much for them on a hot afternoon, so they waved us through. We got back to Osh late in the evening, slightly amazed that a mixture of charm, bluff, deceit, and the occasionally choreographed show of indignation had got us all the way through Uzbekistan and northern Tajikistan, and back again.

The Rapids of the Chuy

Stephanie, Richard, and I made one more trip that summer—whitewater rafting in the gorge of the Chuy River, east of Bishkek. In September, the water level was fairly low, and the trip was deemed easy-to-moderate. I'd heard that phrase before (in reference to our trek in the Tian Shan), so I wasn't sure what to expect. For those of us rafting for the first time, it was wild enough. There were seventeen in the party (mostly expats living in Bishkek) on three rafts, ably handled by what we were told was Kyrgyzstan's international kayak team. They kitted us out in what looked like Soviet World War II aviator gear. Some of us tried to paddle, although it probably didn't help much because we didn't know what we were doing and the directions—except for the occasional "rock 'n' roll"—were shouted out in coarse Russian. We were on the river about four hours, including brief stops. It was all great fun, and everyone got happily soaked.

In later years, when Richard and I went on rafting trips on the New and Gauley rivers in West Virginia, we would pretend to compare the rapids with those of the Chuy. Someone else in the raft would invariably say, "The Chew-ee? Never heard of that one. Is it in Georgia?" "No, Kyrgyzstan in Central Asia," we replied casually, gaining instant river cred.

Customer Disservice

When the Soviet Union broke up, its national airline Aeroflot suffered the same fate. From Baku to Bishkek, the governments of cash-strapped new republics seized the aircraft sitting on the tarmac, repainted them in the new national colors, and hoped they could round up enough spare parts to keep them flying. National airlines have since modernized their fleets, adding Boeings and Airbuses for long-haul flights, but Soviet-era planes are still the standard on most domestic and regional flights, and travelers still struggle with bureaucracy at ticket offices and airports.

In the early years after independence, foreigners had to pay the "foreigner's price" for tickets. It was usually at least 50 percent higher than the regular fare and often had to be paid in Western hard currency. The only advantage, as far as I could tell, was that you entered the terminal through a separate "foreigners' entrance," waited (usually alone) in an area with an overpriced souvenir shop, had your passport inspected multiple times, and then were escorted to the plane by a uniformed official. Special treatment had nothing to do with being nice to foreigners. It was a holdover from Soviet times, when foreigners were segregated for undisclosed security reasons.

In July 1998, I needed to fly from Osh to Bishkek. The Kyrgyzstan Airlines ticket office was inconveniently located in a suburb, a twenty-minute cab ride from downtown. The agent told me she could not sell me a ticket. "Only Gulmira is authorized to sell tickets to foreigners," she announced, "and she is at the airport today. You will have to come back tomorrow." I asked if I could buy a ticket at the airport. "That is impossible," said the agent. "Tickets are only sold here." I went to the airport anyway and found Gulmira, who sold me a ticket at the foreigner's price with, um, a small commission. It was cheaper than another trip to the ticket office.

Foreigners' prices have largely disappeared, but there's still the foreign passports line at most airports. And sometimes the line can turn ugly.

Until the late 1990s, Dushanbe, the capital of Tajikistan, was not on the business (and certainly not on the tourist) itinerary. A five-year civil war meant that the airport was periodically "closed for fighting" (about as routine in Tajikistan as "closed for construction" anywhere else). With the return of peace, if not prosperity, the airport is open, if not exactly ready, for business.

The arrivals hall, a ramshackle building separated by a few city blocks from the main airport terminal, has limited staff and a single baggage carousel. When three flights (including mine) arrived within a half-hour period, the fragile infrastructure was quickly overwhelmed. Only one passport booth for foreigners was open, and it took the officer at least five minutes to review and stamp each passport. And there were many foreigners—most of the passengers on my flight from Almaty were Kazakhstan citizens. Occasionally, a policeman climbed over the barrier, waded into the crowd and pushed some people around, but it seemed to make no difference. Apparently the only way to get ahead was to slip a few bills to a policeman who would go into the booth and have the officer process the passport (while the person at the booth waited).

The foreigners' "line" became more unruly when a group of Tajiks, tired of waiting in their equally slow-moving nationals' line, decided to join us (but at the front, not the back of the line). People clambered over barriers and passed papers back and forth. Meanwhile, baggage from all three flights was arriving on the single carousel. All bags had to pass through a scanner; however, it was not connected to a computer, so no one actually inspected what was inside. Two airport staff collected baggage tags, but did not match them to the bags you were carrying. The trip had taken four hours—a two-hour flight and a two-hour ordeal in the arrivals hall.

Preflight Shakedown

Customs and security officials at Central Asian airports have gained a reputation for trying to shake down weary travelers by inventing airport taxes, selling transit visas you don't need, and charging for excess baggage both on departure and arrival. Some travelers have had luggage impounded for weeks by officials demanding thousands of dollars in import duties or fines. Other scams involve currency controls. Because of capital flight, Central Asian countries imposed strict limits on the export of currency. However, the official inquiry, "How much money are you carrying?" can be the prelude to a search and an on-the-spot and undocumented fine.

Fortunately, most attempted shakedowns are minor and often played like a game. Arriving at Almaty for a flight to Europe, I was stopped by two policemen who inspected my passport. One noticed that my OVIR registration stamp had expired two days earlier. "That's a $100 fine," he declared with triumph. I figured that fines in the Kazakhstan Civil Code were denominated in tenge, not dollars, so I asked him to show me the regulation. As he skimmed through papers, failing to find the one that described my offense, I became impatient. "Even if you're right, I don't have $100," I said, not entirely truthfully. The policemen looked crestfallen. "How much money do you have?" the other asked. "One thousand tenge [at that time, about $8]," I replied. "That will do," the first policeman said. "Have a nice flight, and if anyone else in the airport asks, please don't say this happened." I handed over the money, shook hands, accepted a shot of vodka and went on my way. In a country where police do not earn a living wage and routinely stop drivers to extract small fines, it was an additional, and not unexpected, travel expense.

The secret to shakedowns is to apply (or invent) obscure regulations. On another departure from Almaty, customs officials emptied the contents of my two suitcases, pulling out the three large Soviet-era school maps I had bought at a bookstore in Bishkek. "It is forbidden to export rare cultural artifacts, including historical maps," declared the customs official. I pointed out that maps like this hung on the walls of schoolrooms all over the Soviet Union. They were neither rare, nor valuable. "Show me the regulation on historic maps," I insisted. I unfolded the map pinpointing the sites of labor unrest in the United States in the late nineteenth and early twentieth centuries. "So what am I going to do with it? Invade the United States?" I asked rhetorically. That settled the issue.

Camping Indoors, Soviet Style

I don't deliberately stay in rundown Soviet-era hotels so I can write about them later. Sometimes, there's just no alternative.

From the mid-1990s, my work in Central Asia has taken me to places where the accommodation choices are pretty limited. I usually try to rent an apartment, if only for a couple of days. But sometimes I have to take my chances at whatever establishment displays a *gostinitsa* (hotel) sign. The Hotel Intourist in Osh. The Hotel Karakol. And the Hotel Molmol in Djalalabad in southern Kyrgyzstan in July 1997.

The municipally owned hotel had probably been a decent enough place in Soviet times when party bosses came to town to roll out the latest five-year plan, cook up inflated statistics on the cotton harvest, relax in the hot springs at the local spa, and dine in the hotel ballroom. There also used to be tourists—factory workers and their families who came to the spa and walked in the walnut groves. But few officials (and fewer tourists) had been there for almost a decade, and the place was in sorry shape.

I paid the foreigner's price of $10 for a "luxury room" that consisted of a dormitory-style bed, a chest with broken drawers, and a few cockroaches. There was no running water. The staff—cheekily described by *Lonely Planet* as "breathtakingly rude"—told me the electricity would go off at 10 p.m. By 8:30, I was sitting in the dark, feeling hungry. The hotel restaurant was closed—for renovations, so they said. At breakfast the next morning, Buffet No. 37—the sign was a throwback to communist times, when all eating establishments were state-owned and numbered—offered cold piroshki and tea.

Most Soviet-era hotels reflect the ostentatious public architecture of the Stalin, Khrushchev, and Brezhnev eras with colonnades and cavernous lobbies. The impressive facades often conceal dark and drab interiors with poor heating and ventilation, dangerous wiring, and leaky pipes. The Soviets built their hotels large, and even small cities boasted establishments with several hundred rooms. Of course, the number bore no relation to the expected number of guests. In an economy based on artificial production quotas, not on demand for products and services, there was no place for market research.

So there they stand today—large, and largely empty. Hotel occupancy rates may still be a state secret in some former Soviet republics, but my guess is that most government hotels in provincial centers don't fill more than 20 percent of rooms most of the time. And without guests, they don't have the money to modernize.

These hotels have one saving grace—the dezhurnayas, the floor ladies. The dezhurnaya sits at a table opposite the stairs or elevator and discreetly monitors the comings and goings of guests. You hand in your room key to the dezhurnaya, not at the front desk. Even in Soviet times, the dezhurnayas were not very busy, except when the hotel was full. Today, they while away the hours reading magazines and watching TV. But in hotels where room service is not an option, they keep things running, rustling up late-night cups of tea and retrieving linens, blankets, and toilet supplies from secret stashes.

On a later trip to Mongolia, I learned that conditions in former Soviet satellite states were similar. I asked a friend who had traveled to the provinces to rate the hotels. "Pretty grim," she said. "Rather like camping indoors."

I've learned three valuable lessons about camping indoors. If you're six feet tall (as I am) or taller, sleep at an angle because the beds are short. Carry a few tools so you can fix the furniture and, if you're handy, the plumbing, too. And tip the dezhurnaya on the first day of your stay.

A Seven-Star Hotel and a Seven-Dollar Breakfast

My traveling companion Sergey nudged me as the aircraft began its slow descent from the Pamir Mountains to Dushanbe, the capital of Tajikistan.[4] "We'll be staying at the only seven-star hotel in Central Asia," he said, with almost a straight face.

I was doubtful. If there's a seven-star hotel anywhere in the world, I was pretty sure it wasn't in Tajikistan. In any case, our travel budget didn't cover such extravagances. I forgot Sergey's remark and returned to my struggle with Tajik Air in-flight catering. The tray contained an array of small and hard-to-open items including meat paste, a slice of brown bread, impregnably shrink-wrapped Russian cheese, a cookie, and at least six condiments.

If I'd known about the seven-dollar breakfast at the seven-star hotel, I'd have eaten it all.

The Poytaht (Tajik for capital) Hotel, a massive, concrete, Soviet-era extravagance in Dushanbe's central square, does indeed have seven stars in the crown atop its roof. So do many other establishments in this pleasant city with tree-lined boulevards, parks, and public buildings painted in shades of pink and blue. In Tajik culture, seven is a magic number. According to legend, paradise consists of seven beautiful orchards separated by seven mountains, each with a bright star at its summit. Tajikistan adopted a new national flag in 1992, ditching the proletarian hammer and sickle for the more ethereal crown with seven stars. The country didn't need a Western-style branding campaign to adopt the emblem. In short order, the seven stars popped up on public buildings, restaurants, stores, and karaoke bars. Dushanbe has no shortage of seven-star establishments.

The Poytaht once had star quality. In Communist times, party bigwigs from Moscow stayed there while they checked on the affairs of the Tajik SSR. They threw banquets in the ballroom and lavishly entertained local officials. The Poytaht has at least two hundred rooms (though no one seemed to know exactly how many), but we saw only a handful of other guests. The staff seemed to spend their time dozing in the dimly lit lobby or hanging out in the karaoke bar waiting for customers. For $50 a night, I got a suite, with a lock that had been jimmied a few times. No stars for the furnishings or plumbing, but enough room to easily sleep seven people, which is apparently what the locals do to stretch their budgets.

Sergey and I had turned down the Poytaht's offer of full board with dinner, opting only for the rooms and a $7 breakfast. The only moving bodies in the breakfast room the first morning were a few hungry flies. Sergey woke up the waiter, who was fast asleep despite the pounding sound of Tajik techno-pop from the DVD player.

He came over to our table. Could he buy us SIM cards for our cell phones? The latest Harry Potter movie with Chinese subtitles? Cheap plane tickets to Novosibirsk?

"How about some food?" Sergey asked. He looked disappointed, but ambled off to the kitchen. After some shouting, he reappeared with cold, slightly stale lipioshki, green tea, jam, and four small slices of cheese.

Sergey complained and the waiter returned to the kitchen. After more shouting, he showed up with two omelets. "Bon appétit," said Sergey. "Remember that if this was really a seven-star hotel, we'd be paying a lot more than seven dollars for breakfast." I was already nostalgic for Tajik Air in-flight catering.

SIX

To Be a Kazakh Is to Be "Brave and Free"

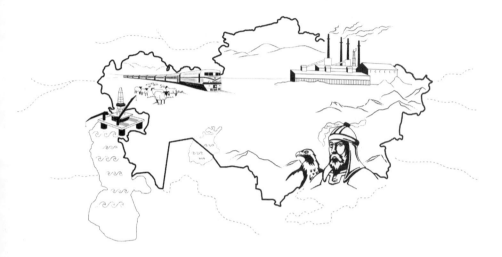

It's a Really Big Country

On October 14, 2013, Alex Trebek, host of the long-running TV quiz show *Jeopardy*, announced the category for Final Jeopardy: Big Countries. The clue: "Outside of Russia, it's the largest country in the former Soviet Union, and the largest country not bordered by oceans."

One contestant responded, "What is Ukraine?" Another wrote, "What is Kazakhstan?" adding $4,701 to her total. The reigning champion, Greg Buzzard, asked, "What is "Kazakhistan?" That extra syllable cost him dearly. "We don't normally penalize misspelling," said Trebek, but in this case it changed the pronunciation of the country's name. It cost Greg his $6,600 bet, and he landed in second place.

The decision ignited a minor controversy on *Jeopardy* fan sites, with viewers citing precedents for rulings on misspelling issues. "I am going to stop watching *Jeopardy*," wrote one. "This Kazakhistan should have been acceptable. This was a rip-off." A European viewer lamented American ignorance of "anything foreign: geography, history, language."

The viewer had a point. I've asked colleagues and friends to show me where Kazakhstan is situated on a topographical map. Their fingers move confidently east from Europe, but then hesitate over the Himalayas or Siberia. They know that if they reach the Pacific or Indian Oceans, they've gone too far. They're not sure.

The confusion is surprising because, at over one million square miles, Kazakhstan is the ninth-largest country in land area in the world, larger than Saudi Arabia, Mexico, or Indonesia. Its northern border with Russia is 4,350 miles long. You could fit all of Western Europe (and a couple of Balkan republics for good measure) into it. It's more than twice as large as the other four Central Asian republics put together, and more than ten times the size of the United Kingdom.

It may be even larger, according to government boosters. It's all a question of how you present it on the map. Like other countries, Kazakhstan uses cartography to emphasize its size and geopolitical importance, placing itself squarely in the middle of maps of Asia.

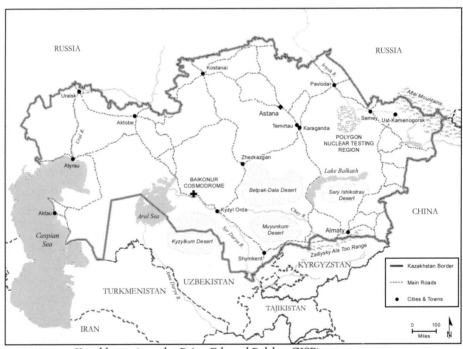

MAP 6.1 Kazakhstan (map by Brian Edward Balsley, GISP)

In January 2011, I was in the concert hall at Eurasian National University (ENU) in Astana to hear Dr. Kerri-Ann Jones, US Assistant Secretary of State for Oceans and International Environmental and Scientific Affairs, speak about the role of women in science. Dr. Jones was on a visit to promote bilateral relationships in biotechnology, renewable energy, health, environment, and science education.

I tried to listen, but my eyes kept wandering to the backdrop on the stage—a graphic map of Kazakhstan. The country looked roughly the right shape, but appeared to have been rotated on its axis to occupy most of the horizontal frame, pushing China and Russia to the geographic fringes. From where I was sitting, it looked larger than China (which is more than three times the size of Kazakhstan). To the north, it stretched almost to the Arctic Sea; to the west, European Kazakhstan reached across Ukraine and Russia, stopping only a few map inches short of the Baltic Sea. I wondered if I'd missed the international news. Was Kazakhstan about to exploit Arctic oil reserves? Were Kazakh troops on the Polish border?

Being a big country has disadvantages. In Kazakhstan's case, the main one is the low population density (an average of fifteen people per square mile). Of course, in remote and barren areas there may actually be no people per square mile, or just the occasional herder passing through. Just over half the population now lives in cities, and more are moving from rural areas. The size of the country makes transportation and communication difficult and costly. Because air travel is expensive, most people use the train for long-distance travel. On the map, Almaty looks pretty close to Taraz (Zhambyl), an ancient city in the southeast, but it's twelve hours by train. It's eighteen hours from Shymkent, the main city in southern Kazakhstan, and twenty-three hours from Kyzlorda in the Aral Sea region. From Uralsk in the far northwest, it's fifty-four hours by train to Almaty, almost twice the time for a trip from Uralsk to Moscow (thirty hours).

Another disadvantage of looming large on the world map is that it's difficult to escape notice when international organizations, think tanks, and Western journalists provide rankings. When data are presented in a table or list, all countries are equal in size, but on a map the perceptual proportions change. Depending on what is being measured,

Kazakhstan appears as a large blob with some level of color saturation in the explanatory chart. Kazakhstan has roughly the same population as Burkina Faso, one of the smaller states in the geographical melee that is Francophone West Africa, or Malawi, a sliver of a country wedged between Zambia, Tanzania, and Mozambique. Burkina Faso and Malawi may rank high or low on various indices, but you don't notice them unless you're really looking. It's difficult to avoid Kazakhstan because it takes up so much space.

With a growing economy and booming natural resources sector, Kazakhstan ranks high on macroeconomic indices and usually earns good marks for the business and investment climate, although corruption knocks it down a few pegs. That's the kind of map the government likes to reprint in brochures and advertising supplements in Western newspapers. On human rights and press freedom, Kazakhstan languishes in a lower-tier, mildly saturated category on the maps of Amnesty International, Human Rights Watch, Reporters Without Borders, and Freedom House. The government dismisses such rankings as Western bias and a misunderstanding of "Asian values" where peace, stability, and central authority are valued more highly than personal freedoms.

Government budgets have increased, but so has the gap between the rich and the poor, between the upwardly mobile middle class of Astana and Almaty, living in modern apartments, shopping at upscale malls and ordering takeout sushi, and residents of provincial cities and villages, living in draughty khrushchevkas or single-story houses, and scraping out a living. Although the government has invested heavily in elite higher education institutions such as Astana's Nazarbayev University, underpaid teachers in village schools struggle to give their students the basics. Medical and social services in many provincial areas are inadequate.

On a positive note, Kazakhstan excelled in a September 2011 *Newsweek/Daily Beast* survey of data from 165 countries to determine which offer women the most rights and best quality of life. The index weighed factors including justice, health, education, economics, and politics. Kazakhstan ended up in the second tier, along with the United Kingdom and Germany. It's difficult to reconcile the ranking with a 2012 Economist Intelligence Unit (EIU) survey of 80 countries to determine which "provide the best opportunities for a healthy, safe, and prosperous life in the years ahead." In other words, which are the best and worst countries to be born into today? The EIU linked the results of subjective life-satisfaction surveys—how happy people say they are—to more objective determinants including income, health, crime, education, and trust in public institutions. Kazakhstan finished in the bottom tier, just ahead of Pakistan, Angola, Bangladesh, and Ukraine. Kazakhstan's government and business community point to economic and social data that tell a different story on quality of life.[1] There's plenty of data to go around and support any argument, positive or negative, so Kazakhstan boosters and detractors can continue to feed their agendas and color their maps appropriately.

Kazakhstan likes to position itself as the heart of Eurasia, a bridge between continents and civilizations. Geographically, it's much more Asia than Europe, but the region west of the Ural River in the northwest is in Europe. This allows Kazakhstan to play on several political stages, as a member of the Shanghai Cooperation Organisation (along with China, Russia, Kyrgyzstan, Tajikistan, and Uzbekistan) and, more importantly, as a member of the Organization for Security and Cooperation in Europe (OSCE), a body of 57 states that works on a range of security-related concerns, including arms control, human rights, national minorities, democratization, policing, counterterrorism, and the environment. To the chagrin of human rights and press freedom advocates, Kazakhstan chaired the OSCE in 2010, despite not passing promised reforms and enacting a repressive Internet law.

Being part of Europe means Kazakhstan can compete in European sports competitions. Football matches are usually lopsided affairs, although in 2013 Shaktyor Karaganda beat Scottish champions Celtic 2–0 at home before losing 3–0 in Glasgow. In the 2014 World Cup qualifying group, Kazakhstan won only once—a come-from-behind home victory over that other football powerhouse, the Faroe Islands—although it managed a 0–0 home draw with Austria. The team would do better in an Asian group. Kazakhstan walloped Pakistan 7–0 in Lahore in 1998, and Nepal 6–0 in 2002. But, as in politics, Kazakhstan wants to play in the big leagues. It does better in boxing, wrestling, weight-lifting, cycling, skiing, and horseback riding. And in the winter sport of bandy, Kazakhstan is the team to beat.

Every country needs to establish its place in the world, and President Nazarbayev has used soft diplomacy, public relations, and foreign direct investment, rather than military force, to try to make Kazakhstan a world leader. However, the digitally enhanced map was one more example of the harder-we-try-the-less-convincing-we-look strategy.

Kazakhstan spends lavishly on hosting international sporting events, conferences, and concerts, most of them in Astana. It eagerly welcomes foreign visitors—politicians, diplomats, educators, and entertainers. It has contracts with lobbyists in Western capitals and international public relations companies, produces glossy English-language magazines, and regularly buys advertising supplements in Western newspapers to promote investment and signature annual events such as the Astana Economic Forum. At the foreign ministry, young multilingual press assistants scour the foreign media, monitoring and summarizing all reports on Kazakhstan. In 2014, it launched a competition, sponsored by the Ministry of Foreign Affairs, a luxury hotel, and Air Astana, to reward what it called "high-quality and objective international journalism" about the country. It attracted forty entries from twenty-three countries. Predictably, the winners were all puff pieces about the energy sector, national traditions, and interethnic harmony with titles such as "The Fairy Tale of the Steppes."[2] There was no mention of official corruption, rigged elections, or social unrest, but then the media that report on such issues did not bother to enter the competition.

The country's "sultan of spin" is former British Labour Prime Minister Tony Blair. Nazarbayev and Blair, who first met in 2006, renewed their relationship in January 2011, a few months before Kazakhstan's presidential election, when Blair visited Astana. Blair was followed by Alastair Campbell, the former Downing Street media consultant, and Jonathan Powell, Blair's former chief of staff. Another close associate, Sir Richard Evans, former chair of the UK defense firm BAE Systems, chairs the Kazakh state holding company Samruk, which owns the national rail and postal services, KazMunayGaz (KMG), the state oil and gas company, the state uranium company, Air Astana, and financial groups.

In October 2011, Blair, through his PR firm Tony Blair Associates, reportedly signed a contract worth $13 million a year to advise Nazarbayev on social and political issues, although his press team says he makes no money from the deal. In an interview for a promotional video produced by state television in April 2012, Blair called Kazakhstan's progress remarkable and said that Nazarbayev had "the toughness necessary to take the decisions to put the country on the right path" and "a certain degree of subtlety and ingenuity that allowed him to maneuver in a region which is fraught with difficulties." Blair called Kazakhstan "a country almost unique . . . in its cultural diversity and the way it brings different faiths and cultures together."[3]

Human rights activists criticized Blair's involvement. Blair, who "prevented the genocide of Kosovan Muslims and defended the rights of Sierra Leoneans, is now the counsel of oil-rich dictators," lamented Mike Harris of the London-based Index on Censorship. Steve Swerdlow of Human Rights Watch told the *Daily Telegraph*: "Tony Blair is in a better position than most to know that a country that violates fundamental human rights is not a good environment for economic investment."[4]

Blair is the celebrity in a concerted strategy to burnish Kazakhstan's image. A report by Deidre Tynan for EurasiaNet.org lists three other major PR firms—BGR Gabara, Portland Communications, and Berlin-based Media Consulta—with contracts to promote Kazakhstan through outreach to government officials, the business community, and media. Some activities, such as infomercials on global satellite TV channels, are routine, what many governments do to promote investment and tourism. Other activities are more subtle. EurasiaNet.org reports that Web records show that Media Consulta inserted two new sections on Nazarbayev's Wikipedia page, titled "Dialogue between Religions" and "Preventing Global Nuclear Threats," and made changes in other sections and in the entry for Kazakhstan. The goal, wrote Tynan, is "to counter any negative perceptions" and to "shape an image as a modern, open and investment-friendly nation."[5]

As Ken Silverstein revealed in an investigative report for *Salon.com*, Central Asia's strongmen—particularly Uzbekistan's Islam Karimov and Nazarbayev—employ a range of tactics. "These include making contributions to think tanks, universities and nonprofit groups, and setting up business associations that advocate for better ties with the U.S. but aren't legally defined as lobbying organizations," wrote Silverstein. In 2008, the Central Asia-Caucasus Institute at Johns Hopkins University, headed by leading Central Asia scholar Professor S. Frederick Starr, "published three upbeat reports on economic and political developments in the country without mentioning that the Kazakh government had paid for them through one of its Washington lobbying firms, APCO Worldwide," reported Silverstein. The US-based Institute for New Democracies and the Center for Strategic and International Studies held a Washington conference "stacked with pro-Nazarbayev viewpoints" and were paid $290,000 to write reports about democratic reforms.[6]

And then there was the election that wasn't.

What's it like to run against an incumbent president with a 90 percent approval rating? In March 2011, I spent a couple of hours with Melis Yeleusizov, one of Nazarbayev's three challengers in the April election.[7]

Yeleusizov was head of the Tabigat (Nature) Ecological Union, an NGO he founded after independence. I had no problem arranging the interview. After a couple of calls to his campaign HQ in Almaty, he called me back himself. We met in Astana after a sparsely attended press conference at a shopping mall. He looked exhausted after a road trip north to give a speech at a college, and was already on his third cup of black coffee. After the interview, we walked outside, and I took a photo of him in front of Bayterek, the national monument. There was no security. As far as I could tell, his Astana campaign organization consisted of two people and an SUV.

FIGURE 6.1 Mels Yeleusizov, the "can't win candidate" in Kazakhstan's 2011 presidential election

By Kazakhstan standards, Yeleusizov was a political veteran, having run for president in 2005 when he got just 0.28 percent of the vote and in parliamentary elections. "I don't miss any elections—it's my credo," he said. His main asset was his name recognition, bolstered by media coverage of his environmental advocacy. "People know me because they have seen me on TV. People know the Communist party, but I'm better known than its candidate," he said. For the campaign, he said he was relying on a loose coalition of environmental groups, and volunteers who "appear from time to time." He talked about his plan to visit all regions, but admitted that the one-month campaign period would limit his appearances.

As an independent, Yeleusizov lacked a party organization. He was also short of money and time. Kazakhstan's size and scattered population centers make television the most effective medium for a national campaign, but Yeleusizov did not have the money to buy commercials. The government allocated each candidate about $42,500—enough, according to Yeleusizov, to buy six thirty-second spots on TV in Almaty. He wasn't planning to buy any. His advertising plan consisted of roadside billboards—two each in Almaty and Astana, and one in each region. He didn't even have a campaign poster. By contrast, on the first official day of campaigning, members of Nazarbayev's Nur Otan (Ray of Light of the Fatherland) party plastered posters listing the president's achievements and priorities—with the slogan "Forward, Together with the Leader—Let's Build the Future Together"—on apartment blocks, shops, and bus stops across the country.

Nazarbayev called the election after a bizarre series of events. Kazakhstan's parliament had already made him exempt from term limits. A group of supporters led by university rector Yerlan Sydykov took the president-for-life argument more seriously: why bother with elections when everyone knows what the result will be? In short order, they gathered over five million signatures (about 55 percent of the electorate) on a petition to hold a referendum to abolish presidential elections and extend Nazarbayev's term to 2020. The proposal was endorsed by the parliament. Nazarbayev bashfully vetoed the measure, but the parliament, dominated by Nur Otan, overrode the veto. Western governments were horrified, and Nazarbayev knew that he stood to lose more in international standing than he would gain in job security. On January 31, the Constitutional Court ruled against the proposal. Nazarbayev needed to send a positive signal to referendum supporters and reassure the international community about the country's democratic credentials so he called a snap election almost two years ahead of schedule.

"Nazarbayev is a clever man," said Yeleusizov. "He didn't want to lose his voters, and he needed to calm down the opposition. All the European and OSCE leaders supported the election decision." While Yeleusizov and the candidates from the Communist People's Party and the right-wing Patriots' Party were scrambling, Nazarbayev said he would not personally campaign and asked Nur Otan's regional offices not to hold public events. Instead, he said he would focus on the country's business. His Ak Orda (White House) strategy provided plenty of positive media coverage.

So why was Yeleusizov running when he had no chance? "It is not to become president because I am 100 percent sure Nazarbayev will win," he said. Yeleusizov said he wanted to boost his name recognition and test the waters to see if voters were ready to accept an environmental political party. He described his campaign as "a kind of training—to give me experience."

"It's all just a play—and the opposition candidates are puppets," said Dr. Zhas Sabitov, a senior lecturer in political science at Eurasian National University in Astana. "They have no chance of winning, and they don't want to win." The main audience, according to Sabitov, was the international community. It was not even a new play. The 1999 presidential election had featured a similar cast, with a Communist, a right-wing military leader, and an ecologist running against Nazarbayev. "It's just a remake, and the 2011 candidates are all playing their roles," said Sabitov.

I wondered if Yeleusizov would be offended by being called an actor. He wasn't. "Life is itself a play," he said, "and an election is a great play with characters. I will take my part."

The plot had a final surreal twist. Emerging from the polling station in Almaty, Yeleusizov informed journalists that he and his family had all voted for Nazarbayev.

Election Shenanigans

The day after the election, my friend Hal Foster called me. "Want to go for dinner at the Uighur place?" he asked. "OK, let's meet at the Ramada. I'm covering one of the press conferences by election observers."

I wandered into the room where a small group of local and Western journalists had gathered. The Independent International Observer Mission—a panel of academics and former diplomats—gave a positive accounting of their monitoring. The Western journalists asked a few softball questions; the local journalists were silent. I wondered how this group could come to such a different conclusion from the OSCE observers who had reported "serious irregularities." No one asked that question.

As the press conference was ending, I raised my hand. "Who paid for your trip to Kazakhstan?" I asked. The mission's leader, Daniel Witt, answered: "The International Tax and Investment Center." I'd never heard of it, but it didn't take more than a few minutes to find its website. What I learned and reported in an article for *Transitions Online* (later cited in Silverstein's piece on *Salon.com*) provides a glimpse of Kazakhstan's image-making machine.[8]

Facing weak opposition, Nazarbayev won the election by a landslide. The turnout of registered voters was almost 90 percent, with Nazarbayev receiving more than 95 percent of votes. The OSCE, with more than four hundred election observers on the ground, noted "serious irregularities, including numerous instances of seemingly identical signatures on voter lists and several cases of ballot box stuffing." Witt's mission, which deployed only eight observers for four days, visited sixty-five polling stations in four regions and said it witnessed no irregularities. While the OSCE reported that "many local authorities intervened in the election process in order to increase turnout," the mission saw "no visible signs of centrally directed administrative mobilization of voters to show up at the polls." Instead, it reported, "voters seemed motivated by a sense of civic consciousness and patriotism." The mission's goal, said Witt, was to communicate "the success story of democratic, social, and economic reforms to our colleagues in the U.S. and Europe." The theme was summarized in the title of its press release, "Kazakhstan's Democratic Roots Deepen."

How can two election observer groups come to such different conclusions? It didn't take long to figure out that the International Tax and Investment Center (ITIC) had a horse in the race.

ITIC is a Washington, DC–based group that provides tax and investment policy advice for governments and commercial clients in the former Soviet Union and has worked with the government of Kazakhstan since 1993. Its main Kazakhstan office is in Astana's government complex, and its Almaty office in the Ministry of Finance. Its funding comes mainly from commercial sponsors, including multinational corporations doing business in Kazakhstan. They include oil companies (BP, Chevron, Exxon-Mobil, Lukoil, and Shell), mining and tobacco companies, banks, and business consulting and accounting firms (Ernst & Young, KPMG, and PricewaterhouseCoopers). Kazakhstan sponsors include Air Astana, PetroKazakhstan, and the Kazakhstan Petroleum Association. The American Chamber of Commerce in Kazakhstan is also a sponsor. ITIC's work is even endorsed by Nazarbayev. Its website quotes him as saying that ITIC has helped the government "to define problems and lay out ways of further perfecting tax legislation and establishing a favorable investment climate in our country."

At the press conference, Witt did not mention ITIC's ties to the government or the business sector but repeatedly referred to his team as independent observers. He acknowledged that they were not "technical experts on elections" and said the OSCE was "second to none" at examining the "nuts and bolts." Yet team members went on to comment on their observations at polling stations. There is no evidence that the observer mission or ITIC has monitored elections in other countries.

"I think that the vast majority of the world knows who the definitive voice is when it comes to election observation—and that's the OSCE," said OSCE Parliamentary Assembly spokesperson Neil Simon. While declining to comment on the group's report, Simon said that the OSCE findings were "clearly the true picture of what happened in Kazakhstan over the past few weeks. Everything from the ballot box stuffing we observed on election day to the lack of a genuine competitive election due to blocked freedom of media and assembly shows that the country still needs to make improvements to live up to its democratic commitments."

History on the Streets of Almaty

In winter 2009, on one of my longer trips to Almaty, I rented an apartment on Vinogradov. I didn't spot any grapevines (in Russian, vinograd means vine or grapes) but it seemed a fitting name for a quiet, leafy, street with wide sidewalks and park benches. Like most city streets, Vinogradov was officially renamed after independence in an effort to erase the Soviet legacy. The new government reached into its gallery of eighteenth-century Kazakh warrior chiefs, and Vinogradov became Karasai Batyr. It's taken some time for the new name to stick.

The Kazakh word *batyr* is derived from an old Turkic word for a hero, knight, or brave warrior, a title bestowed upon individuals for military service among the Turkic and Mongol peoples. Many batyrs are celebrated in Kazakh history, because there was a lot of fighting.

With the death of Genghis Khan in 1227, his empire was divided between his sons. Most of present-day western and northern Kazakhstan became part of the Golden Horde, whose domain extended to European Russia and Ukraine. Central and southern Kazakhstan, as well as present-day Uzbekistan and western Xinjiang, became the Chaghatai khanate. In the fourteenth century, the khanate split, with the region south of the Syr-Darya river adopting settled agriculture and Islam, and the north retaining its nomadic, animal-herding culture. The northern tribes became the Kazakhs and by the end of the fifteenth century they had established one of the world's last great nomadic empires, stretching from the Caspian Sea to the Altay Mountains, from southern Siberia to the Tian Shan. The Kazakh khan was reportedly able to bring 200,000 horsemen into the field, and the empire was feared by all its neighbors.

Kazakh unity and central authority began to weaken in the first half of the sixteenth century as the khanate broke up into three separate "hordes," or *zhuz*—the Great Horde in the south, the Middle Horde in the center and northeast, and the Little Horde in the west. In each horde the authority of the khan was curtailed by tribal chieftains, and even more by the *bis* (the sages or judges) and batyrs who headed the clans or extended families that made up each tribe.

From the 1680s, the Kazakhs were involved in wars with the Oyrats, a federation of four western Mongol tribes, including the aggressive Dzungars. In 1723, the Dzungars invaded the eastern Kazakh lands, slaughtering entire clans, taking captives and seizing pastures, an era known in Kazakh history as the "Great Disaster." In 1726, the leaders of the three hordes—Tole Bi, Kazybek Bi, and Ayteke Bi—met at Ordabasy near Shymkent to form a confederacy against the Dzungars, and the Kazakhs won major victories in 1726 and 1729. Meanwhile, Russia's westward expansion into Siberia brought it into conflict with the Oyrats. Between 1731 and 1742, the khans of the three hordes, considering the Russians the lesser of two evils, swore allegiance to the tsar and asked for Russian protection. Although the Russians established a line of forts across northern Kazakhstan, the Dzungar threat was ended by the Manchu Chinese. In two campaigns in 1757–58, imperial troops virtually wiped out the Dzungars and incorporated their lands into China. Stuck between two great powers, Ablai Khan of the Middle Horde did the smart diplomatic thing; he offered his submission to the Qianlong emperor. In 1771, Ablai was confirmed as ruler by both the Chinese and the Russians. After almost a century of warfare, the Kazakhs had survived as a people but had been forced to surrender their independence.

The street names of central Almaty evoke this turbulent period. Walking west from my apartment on Karasai Batyr (Vinogradov) brought me to the junction with one of the main north-south streets, Nauryzbai

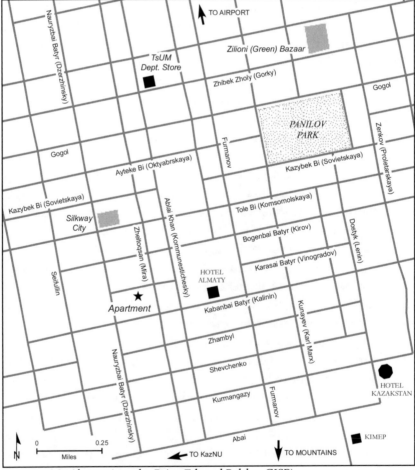

MAP 6.2 My Almaty (map by Brian Edward Balsley, GISP)

Batyr, named for another chieftain who fought against the Dzungars. Although many residents still used the Soviet-era name, Dzerzhinskiy, I preferred walking along a street named for a Kazakh warrior than one named for the founder of Cheka, the precursor of the KGB, which became notorious for torture and mass summary executions during the Russian Civil War and the 1920s. One block north, at the junction with Bogenbai Batyr (formerly Kirov), my friend Sergey Karpov lived in an apartment in a solid three-story block built by Japanese POWs in World War II. One more block took me to the junction with Tole Bi (formerly Komsomoloskaya) and Silkway City, the downtown mall where I often shopped. From there, Kazakh history continued north—Kazybek Bi (Sovietskaya), then Ayteke Bi (Oktyarbr'skaya). South of my apartment, it was one block to Kabanbai Batyr (Kalinin). To reach the university, I took a bus on Ablai Khan (Kommunisticheskiy), which runs one-way north-south. Coming back, I got off at the stop on Zheltoqsan (Mira), a street whose name, which means December, commemorates a more recent conflict—the 1986 riots to protest the appointment of a Russian as head of the Kazakh SSR Communist Party.

Clan and Language Politics

It's difficult to blame Ablai Khan and the other eighteenth-century Kazakh chieftains for doing deals with the Russians to save their people from the Dzungar raids, but that's when the demographics started changing. The troops that established a line of forts across northern Kazakhstan—Omsk in 1716, Semipalatinsk in 1718, and Ust Kamenogorsk in 1719—were followed by Russian, Tatar, and Cossack settlers who plowed up the steppe and planted crops. A century before the range wars of the American West, when ranchers and farmers fought it out over grazing and water rights and bands of cowboys cut fences across Texas, Kazakh herders were battling to preserve their traditional grazing grounds.

Although they had forged a confederacy to fight the Dzungars, the Kazakhs failed to unite against Russian expansion. Internal disputes weakened the hordes, with some tribes overthrowing their leaders. Exploiting the divisions, the Russians formally abolished the hordes as political entities—the Middle Horde in 1822, the Little Horde in 1824, and the Great Horde in 1848. In the 1840s, Ablai Khan's grandson, Kenisary Qasimov, was able to rally enough horsemen from the supposedly defunct Middle Horde to launch one more brave but futile campaign against the Russians. Militarily, it was the last gasp of a fading power. The Russians steadily extended their grip over the region, moving south to conquer parts of the Khokand khanate and founding a fort at Verniy (later Almaty) in 1854.

With the abolition of serfdom in Russia in 1861, the pace of agricultural settlement increased as freed peasants headed east to claim lands. The settlement pattern closely paralleled that of the American West. The military led the way, establishing a line of frontier forts with supply lines. Farmers followed, fencing lands for arable crops. Railroads, such as the Trans-Aral line from Orenburg in the Urals to Tashkent, transported agricultural produce and supplied the farmers with manufactured goods. The farmers were followed by administrators, lawyers, tax collectors, customs agents, traders, teachers, fortune seekers, and criminals. The more upstanding migrants established villages and towns with shops, banks, hotels, bars, and theaters. Depicted in late nineteenth-century photographs, the main streets of towns in northern Kazakhstan look much like frontier settlements in Kansas, Nebraska, Colorado, and the Dakotas— frame and clapboard storefronts with boardwalks, horse-drawn wagons, and the occasional carriage. For the tsarist government, the frontier was a convenient dumping ground for high-profile dissidents and political opponents such as the writer Fyodor Dostoyevsky, exiled to Semipalatinsk. In this frontier drama, the Kazakhs played the part of the tribes of the northern Great Plains, driven from their ancestral grazing and hunting grounds. No one knows how many Kazakhs died from revolts or famines.

The 1917 revolution gave brief hope to Kazakh nationalists when moderate upper-class intellectuals formed a political party called Alash Orda, named for the mythical ancestor of their people. "Alash Orda!" (Horde of Alash) had long served as their traditional battle cry. Despite later Soviet charges, the party was progressive on social issues while calling for the creation of an autonomous Kazakh region. After vacillating between the White and Red Armies, most leaders accepted Mikhail Frunze's promise of amnesty and in December 1919 recognized Soviet authority. Acquiescence did not save them. The provisional government was abolished, and Alash Orda members were expelled from the Communist Party, executed or sent to labor camps. Thousands of Kazakhs and Russian settlers died in the civil war. And the economy was devastated. From the mid-1920s, Kazakhs became an ethnic minority in the country.

After establishing military and political control, the Soviets embarked on the next stage of social reform—the elimination of private property and the collectivization of industry and agriculture. Technically, it wasn't much of a challenge to nationalize the steppe because the boundaries between the grazing lands of families and clans were a matter of oral tradition, not of legal title. If the Kazakhs had been left free to travel in family groups with their herds, they might not have cared much that their animals were grazing on state property. However, the Soviets viewed the traditional economy and the social organization of clans and tribes as primitive and potentially subversive. They forced the Kazakhs to move onto kolkhozes and surrender their herds. Collectivization threatened not only their livelihoods but a centuries-old nomadic culture. Many killed their livestock rather than hand them over to the state. Unaccustomed to settled agriculture, more than 1.5 million people died between 1926 and 1939, mostly from famine and disease. Those who openly opposed collectivization were executed or sent to labor camps. Thousands fled to China, although many died on the journey; others fled to Uzbekistan and Turkmenistan. Kazakhstan's population fell by more than two million between 1926 and 1933.

From the late 1920s, the Soviets embarked on a systematic program of deporting ethnic groups from their ancestral or adopted homelands to remote areas of Siberia and Kazakhstan. The program, which reached its zenith under Stalin in the 1930s and World War II, was motivated by two factors: the need to supply cheap labor to the mines and industrial plants exploiting the region's natural resources, and fears that ethnic groups would support a foreign invasion. In the mid-1930s, the two Polish Autonomous Districts created in Belarus and Ukraine in the 1920s were abolished, and their leaders executed. The rest of the population was deported in 1936, 75,000 of them to northern Kazakhstan, with many dying on the journey. In 1937, almost the entire population of ethnic Koreans, about 170,000 in number, was deported from the Russian Far East to Kazakhstan. In public pronouncements, the Soviets denounced Koreans as potential collaborators with the Japanese. Maybe the Soviets had not forgiven the Japanese for Russia's defeat in the war of 1904–5 when Japan gained control of the Korean peninsula, formally annexing it in 1910. However, claims of collaboration were ludicrous; if any ethnic group hated the Japanese more than the Russians, it was the Koreans. In June 1941, days before Germany invaded the USSR, almost 30,000 ethnic Romanians from Moldova and western Ukraine were deported to Kazakhstan and Siberia. In August, the Supreme Soviet issued a decree to deport the largest ethnic group—some 480,000 Volga Germans. Deportation of other non-Slavic nationalities from the Black Sea region followed—Crimean Tatars and Greeks, Chechens, Ingush, Balkars, Kalmyks, Karachays, Meskhetian Turks, and Armenians. Many were sent to the Kazakh SSR or were moved to its labor camps from Siberia.

The camps were closed after Stalin's death in 1953, but many members of the so-called Trudarmiya (Labor Army) remained in Kazakhstan. A new wave of Russian and Ukrainian migrants arrived in the 1950s under Khrushchev's Virgin Lands scheme, which aimed to convert the steppe into arable land, growing wheat and other grains for the rest of the Soviet Union. Others came to work in the coal and iron mines, the power plants and factories. In 1959, the SSR's population stood at 9.3 million, but only 2.7 million (29 percent) were ethnically Kazakh, and Kazakhs were in a majority in only seven of the 20 oblasts. From the 1960s, primarily because of a relatively high birthrate, the proportion of Kazakhs in the population increased, so that by the 1989 census they made up 40 percent of a population of 16.4 million, with Russians at 38 percent. History determined that when Kazakhstan became independent, it was the only Central Asian republic where the ethnic group that gave its name to the country constituted less than 50 percent of the population.

Although all Central Asian republics experienced population decline after independence, Kazakhstan's was dramatic. In the first post-Soviet census in 1999, its population was just 15.6 million—the result of economic hardship which contributed to out-migration and a declining birthrate. More than a million Russians and 800,000 Germans, almost 11 percent of the 1989 population, left the country in the 1990s. In 1999, TV commercials by a charity backed by businesses and the president's wife, Sara Nazarbayeva, lamented the sharp drop in the birthrate and went on to offer "real money for real children"—100,000 tenge ($1,150), almost the annual average wage—to the parents of the first 2,000 babies born in 2000.

From 2000 onward, Kazakhstan's economy grew by close to 10 percent a year, creating a modest baby boom and population rebound. Although ethnic Russians and Germans continued to leave, the country attracted migrants from its impoverished Central Asian neighbors to work on building sites, especially in Astana and Almaty, and in the cotton and tobacco fields of the south. The proportion of Kazakhs increased dramatically, not only because of the birthrate and out-migration by other groups, but because of immigration by Kazakhs from China, Mongolia, Russia, and western Uzbekistan—the so-called oralmans. Today, Kazakhs account for almost two-thirds of the population of over 17 million.

One of Our Cows Is Missing

In the Soviet era, many Kazakhs simply chose to ignore their troubled history and learned to live and work in a multiethnic society. Indeed, for the generations born after World War II, the past was literally a foreign country, absent from school textbooks, museums, monuments, media, and official histories. Although the Soviets recognized ethnicities and subsidized minority-language publications and cultural events, it was always within the safe and sanitized framework of official party activities and ideology. You could learn to play the dombyra, weave traditional rugs, and study the Kazakh language, but you might not learn about the batyrs and certainly not about Alash Orda or the Stalin-era writers, artists, and activists executed or sent to labor camps.

Islam was a sensitive topic. Although Arab armies had introduced Islam to Central Asia in the seventh and eighth centuries, it was Sufi missionaries with their moderate, nondogmatic teachings who were most successful in spreading religion. Among the nomadic tribes of Kazakhstan and Kyrgyzstan, Sufi mysticism and tolerance of other beliefs allowed their followers to easily mix Islam with animism and shamanism. The Bolsheviks feared religion as a force that could unite ethnic groups, as the spectacular but short-lived rebellion led by Enver Pasha in the early 1920s had shown. In the 1930s, Stalin systematically suppressed Islam, closing mosques and madrassas, dismantling Shari'a courts and arresting mullahs. In 1943, the Soviets established formal Muslim religious boards, each headed by a state-appointed mufti, to control and supervise religious activities. Nonofficial Islam went underground, preserved largely by the clandestine Sufi brotherhoods. Openly practicing religion outside the official state structures was dangerous. The journalist, blogger, and media educator Asqat Yerkimbay learned how his grandfather, Isaghazy, led secret prayers in a village near the copper-mining town of Karsakpay in central Kazakhstan in the 1930s:

All the mosques had been ruined, destroyed. What they would do was tell others, "One of our cows is missing and we're going to go out and find it." And they would go far away from the village to pray so that no one could see them. During Ramadan, they prayed every day. They closed all the windows in the house, and they had all the women go out. My grandfather usually led the prayers.[9]

Asqat, born in 1983, did not hear the story from his parents, who never discussed religion and said little about their ancestors. It was not until he was in his early twenties, after graduating from university, that a great aunt told him about Isaghazy. By that time, he had become a practicing Muslim:

> When I started praying one day, she gave me this prayer rug and told me it had belonged to my grandfather. Holding this prayer rug—it was a very emotional moment for me. It was just a piece of material without decoration. In one corner there was a red triangle to symbolically indicate the Qibla [the direction to Mecca]. She also showed me his prayer book. I started wondering why my parents were not talking to us [their children] about our grandfather, and she said they didn't want people to know they prayed because it was a small village.

Isaghazy's name derives from Ishaq, the Arabic version of Isaac, the son of Abraham and father of the Israelites, revered in the Jewish and Christian traditions, and in Islam as a prophet. He is mentioned fifteen times by name in the Qur'an. Many Kazakhs in Isaghazy's generation were given religious names, but most in the next generation had secular names; Asqat's father and his brother were named for the day of the week when they were born.

Asqat grew up in Zhezdy, a mining town hastily built by the Soviets in 1942 to extract manganese deposits for the manufacture of tanks and other military vehicles. In Kazakh, *zhez* means the "place of the miner." The regional center, the copper-mining city of Zhezqazgan, means the "place where minerals are dug." Asqat's father was a miner, and his mother worked as an accountant for the mine. By the 1980s, after waves of migration and deportations, Zhezdy was a multiethnic community. At the Russian kindergarten, Asqat realized that other children "were different because they had blonde hair and names like Konin. There were German girls but they had Russian names like Sveta and Lena. That's probably why we didn't know there were different ethnicities." The family lived in a three-story khrushchevka. At home, as at school, ethnic identities were blurred.

> In the central part of Kazakhstan, Kazakhs were in a minority because the Soviets had deported other ethnicities to the region. Our neighbors were Russian, Belarusian, Ukrainian, German, but we couldn't distinguish them—we thought they were all Russian. Russian culture was very strong. We celebrated all the Russian holidays. Most of my mother's friends were Russian speakers—I think there were only two or three Kazakh speakers. When she had her birthday or celebrated an achievement at work, they sang Russian songs. There was candy, vodka, and cognac on the table, and it felt like a Russian celebration.

Asqat's family was from the Naiman tribe of the Middle Horde, Kazakhs who had moved to central Kazakhstan from the eastern Altay region after a famine in the 1930s. At home they spoke Kazakh. Until he went to school, he "learned Russian from TV, from the street." As a young child, he did not have a strong sense of ethnic identity. "All my friends were Russian speakers, all the neighbors were Russian speakers. At that time the word Kazakh did not mean ethnicity or nationality."

His views started changing during the Gorbachev period, as the local mining economy declined and neighbors started leaving. "I asked my mother, 'Why are they moving out?' and she said it was because they were going back to their motherland. At that time, I started to realize who they were. That this neighbor was Dungan, and another was Armenian, and the family on the first floor were Germans."

From the age of five, Asqat had listened to Kazakh fairy tales from his grandmother. After independence, the school curriculum was changed to include textbooks on Kazakh history and literature. Asqat started reading about the Alash Orda movement and the works of Saken Seyfullin, the poet, writer, and national activist from central Kazakhstan who called for greater Kazakh autonomy and was executed in 1939. At school, the students staged plays and concerts to mark Kazakhstan's independence day, December 16.

All this built a sense of Kazakhness in my mind. However, I realized that I could not use my Kazakh language in my everyday life, and I wondered why. I started subscribing to a youth newspaper called *Ulan* [in the Soviet era, it was *Kazakhstan Pioneer*] to read what kids from other regions were saying. I sent them my first poem. They rejected it but sent me a letter encouraging me to continue writing. I was really good in Kazakh language and literature classes. I started to participate in high school competitions, and was motivated to be a journalist.

Zheltoqsan

For a quarter of a century, the dominant figure in Kazakh politics was Dinmukhamed Kunayev. In the 1950s, he became a protégé of Leonid Brezhnev, who served as first secretary of the Communist Party of the Kazakh SSR. In 1960, Kunayev was appointed first secretary, the first native Kazakh to hold the top post; all his predecessors had been Russian. During his long tenure, Kazakhs occupied prominent positions in the government, economy, and educational institutions. In December 1986, the Politburo, under pressure from Gorbachev, fired him on charges of corruption. His replacement, the Russian Gennadiy Kolbin, had never lived in the Kazakh SSR. On December 17, thousands of demonstrators—mostly young, ethnic Kazakhs—took to the streets of Alma-Ata (now Almaty) to demand a stake in the political process. Nazarbayev, who was serving as prime minister but had been passed over for the post of first secretary, urged the demonstrators to disperse, warning that the authorities would use force. His pleas were ignored. Moscow brought in security forces, and the riot was brutally suppressed. Many doubt the official death toll of three (one Kazakh student, two Russians), claiming that more than 100 were killed. Some demonstrators received long prison sentences while others saw their careers ruined. The so-called Zheltoqsan (Kazakh for December) protests were the first major riots of the perestroika period. They showed that the grip of the central government was weakening and revived latent Kazakh nationalism.

Word of Zheltoqsan reached Zhezdy, as Asqat recalls. "There was a neighbor who was Dungan—I knew she was Dungan because she made Dungan *lapsha* [noodles]—her husband was Kazakh, and their son studied in Almaty. She came to my mom crying that her son was involved. My mom tried to calm her." To Asqat, it was an early sign that the old Soviet order was beginning to break apart.

In the 1990s, with Kazakhstan facing an economic slump, Russian and German out-migration and potential social unrest, Nazarbayev's government pursued a dual strategy—providing more opportunities for ethnic Kazakhs in higher education and government service and promoting Kazakh language and culture, while telling non-Kazakhs that the country was a multiethnic society where all were welcome. At school, Asqat struggled with the notion of identity.

> There was a strong message "Be a Kazakh" in all school activities, but they didn't tell us what it means to be a Kazakh. At that time, being a Kazakh to me meant to follow the culture—to wear the national costume, play the dombyra, and speak Kazakh. When I went to university to study Kazakh language and literature, my view started to change. The Kazakh language was not widely spoken in Zhezkazgan. For me, being Kazakh then meant to fight for the status of the Kazakh language.

After two years at the state university in Zhezkazgan, Asqat moved to Almaty to complete his studies and started working as a journalist for an opposition weekly newspaper. Asqat and his Kazakh colleagues were responsible for the three or four Kazakh-language pages in a mostly Russian publication, and he worked closely with Russian journalists.

> At first, I did not want to work with Russian speakers because I believed they never wanted to learn the Kazakh language. They were in Kazakhstan, but their mentality was still Russian. But when I started working with them, we didn't talk much about language. We talked more about social issues and that started to change my mind about what it means to be a Kazakh. I thought, "Why should I be happy to say that I am a Kazakh?" It's like saying I was born on a Monday or a Tuesday or I have black hair. It's not an identity I chose. What does it mean to be Kazakh? Does it mean to play the dombyra? Anyone can learn to play a dombyra. Does it mean the Kazakh language? Well, anyone can learn the language, and that does not make them Kazakh. For many, their tribal identity is more important than being a Kazakh.

Asqat, like most Kazakhs, can trace his family and tribal lineage back for at least seven generations. It's not a matter of genealogical interest or family pride, but a biologically based tradition with socioreligious support to avoid overlap in bloodlines. You need to be able to identify the lineage so that you don't marry a close (or even distant) relative from the same tribe. That's why, when Kazakhs meet for the first time, the conversation often begins with two questions: Where were you born? And what is your *zhuz* (horde) and *ru* (tribe)?

If zhuz and ru are more important, then what does it mean to be Kazakh? For Asqat, national identity—or Kazakhness—should derive from a sense of common purpose, what he calls [in Russian] a *grazhdantskaya pozitsia* (a citizenship position) in a multiethnic society.

> There should be one visible and understandable goal for everyone—that's more important than language. The word Kazakh, translated from the old Turkic, means "brave and free." Being Kazakh is not so much about politics or ethnicity as about citizenship, a grazhdanskaya pozitsia. Some people in government are sending the message that being a Kazakh does not mean simply to speak Kazakh. Being a Kazakh means we should all have the same goal and respect others.

The concept is admirable for its inclusiveness, but Asqat's views may not be shared by those who suffered from economic and cultural discrimination in the Soviet era. For some, independence offered an opportunity for payback for almost three centuries of Russian (and then Soviet) political, economic, and cultural oppression. They did not embrace Nazarbayev's vision of a multiethnic state, and they didn't mind if the Russians (and other minorities) left, even if it meant the loss of talent.

The Politics of Language

The Soviets did not outlaw the study of Kazakh language and literature, but they did little to promote it. Despite the recognition of nineteenth-century literary greats such as Abai Qunanbayev, Shakarim Qudayberdiev, and Mukhtar Auezov, whose writing (unlike Seifullin) was considered politically safe, Kazakh (like Kyrgyz) was regarded by many as a village language. Knowledge of Russian was key to a successful career and advancement in the Communist Party. The best and brightest studied in

Moscow or Leningrad. At independence in 1991, it was estimated that about half the ethnic Kazakh population were either unfamiliar with their own language or could manage only conversational Kazakh.

Language has become a powerful weapon in the struggle to establish the new nation states of Central Asia. To create a national culture separate and distinct from the Soviet past, each republic has actively promoted its native language and attempted to restrict the use of Russian. Kazakhstan is officially a bilingual country. In 1999, Kazakh was declared the state language; Russian was given a constitutional status allowing its use in state bodies, and it remains the lingua franca in interethnic communication, especially in business. According to the 2009 census, only two-thirds of citizens claimed a decent command of Kazakh, whereas 94 percent understood Russian. The government has set a goal of 95 percent of citizens speaking Kazakh by 2025, while preserving fluency in Russian at about 90 percent. More children are learning the language in school, studying Kazakh history and literature and other subjects in Kazakh. University-level education is offered in Russian, Kazakh, and (at some institutions) English. National and local government agencies and public facilities such as hospitals are switching to Kazakh. Many forms and documents are still issued in Kazakh and Russian, but increasingly official business is conducted in Kazakh. Any applicant for government service is now expected to show proficiency in Kazakh.

That includes the presidency. Potential candidates have to pass a three-part test—writing an essay, reading a text aloud, and delivering a fifteen-minute speech. That's no problem for Nazarbayev, who is fluent in Kazakh and Russian, but in 2011 the test eliminated two opposition candidates. The tests are conducted behind closed doors by a panel of five university professors who vote on whether a candidate can run. One candidate was disqualified for making too many spelling errors; he claimed the decision was politically motivated, that the panel had asked him about issues rather than checking his language. Vladimir Kozlov, of the unregistered Alga party (later jailed for his alleged support of the oil workers' protests in western Kazakhstan), simply pulled out, saying he didn't have enough time to get his Kazakh up to snuff.

The slow adoption of the Kazakh language has frustrated academics, writers, and artists who deplore what they regard as continuing Russian cultural influence, especially in the media. Russian-language newspapers are more successful in selling advertising because they attract urban readers with higher income and education than the largely rural readership of Kazakh-language newspapers. Faced with declining circulation and scarce advertising revenue, most Kazakh-language newspapers depend on state subsidies for survival.

In 1997, Kazakhstan introduced a broadcast language law, requiring all TV and radio stations to devote half their air time to Kazakh-language material. Little licensed programming or music was available in Kazakh, and few stations had the resources to dub or subtitle programs. Even if stations could have complied, it would have been financially disastrous to do so because they would have lost Russian-speaking viewers and their advertisers; stations in Russian-dominated northern Kazakhstan would quickly have gone out of business. Commercial TV stations made a token effort to meet the quota without breaking the budget, airing a few Kazakh-language talk shows and shooting cheap music videos with Kazakh pop stars. This was not the high-brow cultural programming that the Kazakh culture-boosters had expected, but it was all that the stations, struggling for advertising revenue in a stagnant economy, could manage. In 1999, a group of seventy academics, writers, and artists wrote an open letter to Nazarbayev, deploring the "spiritual and cultural anarchy" of radio and TV and demanding that 70–80 percent of broadcasts be in Kazakh. They also called for the creation of a state artistic council to select programs for both state-owned and privately owned radio and TV stations—essentially a return to Soviet-style censorship. To his credit, Nazarbayev ignored the petition.

As with other legislation, the problem with the broadcast language law was not so much its intent, but how it was used. The government attempted unsuccessfully to close two stations in the predominantly Kazakh southern city of Shymkent—Otirar TV and Umax Radio—for alleged violations of the law. The maneuver was clearly politically motivated; both stations aired more programming in Kazakh than stations in other cities but had been critical of government policies. Meanwhile in northern Kazakhstan, TV stations were filling over 75 percent of their schedules with Russian-language programs, and the authorities refused to intervene as long as news coverage broadly supported government policy.

Over the years, the quantity of Kazakh-language TV and radio programming has increased, not because of the law but because the Kazakh-language entertainment industry, especially movies and music, has grown, and quality has improved. Social and cultural change achieved what legislation could not. The broadcast language law achieved little beyond giving authorities another tool—in addition to licensing fees, fire and building codes, and the tax police—to stifle critical coverage, and to jump-start the careers of a few starlets and boy bands.

While the Kazakh language is gaining ground, another thorny debate is under way: Which alphabet to use? In the nineteenth and early twentieth centuries, the Kazakh language was written in Arabic script. It was replaced by the Latin alphabet in 1929, but it was in use for only a decade. In 1940, Cyrillic was introduced as a common alphabet for all the Soviet republics; Kazakh is written in a forty-two-letter version of the Cyrillic alphabet (with nine extra letters). After independence, Uzbekistan switched to the Latin alphabet in an effort to distance itself from Russian cultural influence. In the 1990s, some Kazakh academics and nationalists proposed following suit, but the idea lacked support because Russian was still the dominant language, and political and economic ties with Russia remained strong. The debate has rumbled on in the media but gained new impetus in late 2012 when Nazarbayev announced that the switch would take place—but not until 2025. The change, he said, would provide "an impulse for the modernization of the Kazakh language" and promote "our global integration."[10]

The proposal was criticized by Kazakh-language supporters who argued that it would widen the linguistic divide. In a letter to the president, a group of sixty-six writers, academics, and journalists said the change would discourage Russian speakers from learning Kazakh. Some linguists argued that the change would free Kazakh, a Turkic language, of syntactic and semantic influences from Russian. In writing, Kazakh sentences often follow the rules of Russian syntax. And then there's the issue of spelling. Let's take the example from the preface: the country and its people. When the Russians decided in the 1920s that the Kazakhs were not Kyrgyz after all, they needed to distinguish them from the similar-sounding Cossacks. They did so by using the Cyrillic letter "х" (transliterated as "kh"); in English, the country becomes Kazakhstan and its people Kazakh. In the Kazakh [sic] language, both "k" sounds are hard ("қ"—a "k" with a diacritic, transliterated as "q"), so the correct transliterations are Qazaqstan and Qazaq. To fervent nationalists and some scholars, the continued use of the "x" and "kh" is another sign that the country has not escaped from Russian cultural imperialism; to many others, it's just normal spelling.

In July 2009, in the midst of the global economic crisis, I asked friends and colleagues how the region was weathering the storm. The most perceptive comment was shared by Tarja Virtanen, director of UNESCO's Central Asia office, who had asked her driver, Yuri, the same question. He replied laconically: "Crisis? You don't understand. I've been dealing with crises most of my life, so I don't see any difference now." Yuri remembered the early 1990s when the factories closed, thousands lost their jobs, and the currency suffered a massive devaluation, making savings and pensions virtually worthless. Today, he spends most of what he earns because he does not believe that savings can be protected. People in Central Asia were not particularly shocked by the global crisis because they had seen it all before.

The sense of resignation was expressed in proverbs, jokes, songs, and media. It was epitomized by an Almaty-based opposition weekly newspaper in the late 1990s. Its name, probably a take-off on the 1968 Soviet romantic film, *Dozhivyom do Ponedel'nika* (Let's survive until Monday) was *Nachniom c Ponedel'nika*. It means simply "Let's Start from Monday." In uncertain times, you try to get through the day, hope that next week will be better, and never think too far ahead.

Walking around downtown Astana or Almaty today, with their highrise office buildings, luxury goods stores, and expensive restaurants, it's difficult to imagine just how bad conditions were in the 1990s. You begin to grasp the economic and social reality better as you move to the outskirts of a city and see an industrial wasteland—shuttered factories and warehouses, weeds growing in cracks through the concrete foundations and walls, abandoned vehicles and equipment rusting on muddy, trashstrewn land and railroad sidings.

Small, single-industry towns such as Asqat's Zhezdy were hit hardest; when the factory or mine closed, there were no other jobs. By the mid-1990s, conditions were desperate. "In winter, it was freezing," Asqat recalls. "There was no heating, electricity, or water. We did not have money for bread. We just boiled macaroni every day." The story of Zhezdy was repeated in cities, towns, and villages throughout Central Asia. Factories and farms closed, and no other jobs available. Families surviving on what they had saved or could sell, shivering through subzero temperatures with no heating, light, or water. Teachers and government officials showing up for work, even though they hadn't been paid for months. Street crime, drug and alcohol use rising. What Asqat saw as a child, coupled with his religious beliefs, turned him firmly against alcohol. "My generation was not raised well because many of the parents drank. It's still a problem in towns in central Kazakhstan where they consume a lot of alcohol." But he understands how deeply the loss of jobs and dignity affected his father's generation:

> People didn't have anything except their miners' jobs, and they lost all confidence in themselves. My father's friends just sat around drinking and cursing the future. They did not believe in anything anymore. They became addicted to alcohol, and so many families were ruined. There were a lot of suicides. The father of one of my friends got drunk and collapsed in the street. When they found him, he had frozen to death.

seven

Father of Apples

Welcome to Almaty?

For travelers in the mid-1990s, Almaty airport was not a welcoming port of entry. Flights from Europe arrived in the wee hours of the morning, and passengers trudged bleary-eyed through a seemingly endless series of document inspections. At one counter, my customs declaration was scrutinized and stamped; at the second, the stamp was inspected and initialed; at the third, an official tore off part of the form; finally, another reattached it. The process was observed by uniformed police and unsavory looking characters in leather jackets, whose scowling faces made you think you were doing something illegal, even if you weren't. Kazakhstan wasn't thinking about customer service rankings on global tourism surveys.

On my first visit in 1995, the US embassy in Bishkek sent a driver to pick me up. We drove into Almaty on an almost deserted highway, the darkness broken only by an occasional light from a house. Even in the downtown area, few lights were on. At 2:30 a.m., I checked into the

Hotel Almaty and quickly fell asleep, my six-foot frame wedged sideways on the five-and-a-half-foot bed.

I was awakened around 8 a.m. as morning sun filled the room. In my late-night stupor, I had forgotten to close the drapes. I stepped out onto the balcony and literally gasped. Before me was a mountain panorama unlike any I had ever seen before. The winter sun illuminated the rugged snow-covered peaks of the Zailiysky Ala Too. I almost forgot about the grim airport and undersized bed and pinched myself to make sure I wasn't dreaming. No, I was not. I was in Central Asia.

I didn't see much of Almaty on that trip. It was not until 1999, when I was doing media research for USAID, that I spent more than a couple of days in the city. Although Astana had become the capital two years earlier, there was no sense that Almaty faced an uncertain future. It was the largest city in the country and its commercial hub, with headquarters for domestic and foreign companies, universities, hospitals, and a lively music and arts scene. New hotels, restaurants, shops, and supermarkets were opening, and a growing middle class was flaunting its wealth, building houses in the new suburbs toward the mountains and driving imported cars. Since 1999, I've been to Almaty half a dozen times, for periods from a week to a month, and have seen the city grow, its population increasing to close to two million.

Although some Soviet histories suggested that Almaty was not much more than a wide place in the road to Tashkent until the Russian army arrived in 1854, there's evidence of prehistoric settlements in burial mounds from the Saka period (from 700 BCE). By the eleventh century, the settlements were part of the Silk Road network, trading agricultural produce and crafts. An area called Almatu was first mentioned in thirteenth-century books. Although academics don't agree on the origins of the name, the most likely explanation (and the one accepted by many Almaty residents) is that it comes from *alma,* the Turkic (and later Kazakh) word for apple. The wild varieties found throughout southeastern Kazakhstan and across the mountains around Issyk Kul are said to be ancestors of the modern domestic apple. In Soviet times, the city was called Alma-Ata, a combination of two Kazakh words meaning Father of Apples.

The region witnessed fierce fighting in the early eighteenth century, as the Kazakhs tried to repel the Dzungar invaders. In 1730, the batyrs won a major victory in the mountains northwest of Almaty. Although the three hordes accepted Russian protection, southeastern Kazakhstan fell under the control of the Khokand khanate until 1854 when Russian troops built a fort and named it, in homage to the tsar, Verniy (faithful). The population grew, with Russian and Cossack farmers arriving, particularly after the 1861 emancipation of the serfs, and Tatar merchants and craftsmen established a settlement. In 1867, the fort was incorporated as a town and divided into residential districts according to a city plan. Although it was devastated in an earthquake in 1887, it was quickly rebuilt.

After the 1917 revolution, southern Kazakhstan became part of the Turkestan Autonomous Soviet Socialist Republic (ASSR), which included most of Central Asia. Northern Kazakhstan and southern Siberia were in a separate Kazakh ASSR. In 1924–25, the Kazakh ASSR was enlarged to include the rest of present-day Kazakhstan, with its capital at Kyzylorda in the barren southwest. After two blisteringly hot summers, the ASSR administrators moved the capital to the more moderate climes of Alma-Ata.

The town grew rapidly over the next two decades, especially after the completion of the Turkestan-Siberia Railway, the Turksib. The line, first proposed in 1886, was built to carry cotton north from the Fergana Valley to the Trans-Siberian Railway and cheap grain south, and to reinforce Russia's economic and military presence along the Chinese border. The northern section from Novosibirsk on the Trans-Siberian to Semipalatinsk was opened in 1915, but World War I delayed construction of the rest of the line to Tashkent. During the civil war, the White Army extended the northern line by almost ninety miles. The Red Army tore it up, an action it was to later regret because it had to be rebuilt. Construction resumed in 1926, and the Turksib, over one thousand miles long, finally opened in 1930, a construction feat celebrated in Soviet newsreels and the classic 1929 documentary *Turksib*. Alma-Ata became an important railway and industrial center, with the Turksib giving its name to a mixed industrial and residential district. The city grew rapidly, with construction of government buildings and apartment blocks.

During World War II, Alma-Ata's location, far from the front line, spurred its growth. The Soviets packed up more than thirty factories— equipment, supplies, and workforce—and moved them to the city. Fifteen universities, institutes, and technical schools, eight hospitals, theaters, museums, and motion picture companies from Leningrad, Moscow, and Kiev were relocated. The influx of industry and scientific and artistic talent turned a provincial capital into a manufacturing and cultural center. Its major economic sectors were agricultural processing (meat, flour, cereals, milk, fruit, tobacco, and alcohol), light industry (textiles, footwear, printing) and heavy industry (iron and steel, building materials). The building boom resumed in the mid-1960s as apartment blocks—khrushchevkas and later *brezhnevkas*—sprang up in the micro-raions. New hospitals, theaters, and sports stadiums were opened, and a dam was constructed across the Malaya (Lesser) Alamatinka River above the Medeo winter sports complex to prevent mudslides and avalanches.

Renamed Almaty in 1991, the city became the ready-made capital of independent Kazakhstan. It was a pragmatic choice. The new government simply took over the buildings that had housed the SSR government, Communist Party, and other institutions, hoisted the turquoise and yellow flag of the new republic and changed the signs on the doors. Many officials made a similarly effortless transition to government service; some did not even have to move out of their offices. Chief among them was Nazarbayev, who had risen in the party ranks in the 1980s to become prime minister of the Kazakh SSR. In 1989, he succeeded the unpopular Gennadiy Kolbin, whose appointment had precipitated the Zheltoqsan riots, in the top job—First Secretary of the Communist Party. In December 1991, he became president of independent Kazakhstan. In the difficult years after independence, when the country faced economic dislocation, out-migration by Russians and Germans, and social unrest, governing from Almaty provided a sense of continuity between the certainties of the Soviet past and an unpredictable future.

Almaty was laid out on a grid pattern, with broad north-south and east-west avenues. As in Bishkek, the mountains are always south (see map 6.2). In places, high-rises obscure the view, but if the road or sidewalk is rising gently, you can be confident you are heading south. It's a pleasant walking city, especially in spring and fall, with tree-lined streets, shady parks and squares, and outdoor cafés and restaurants. In some cities, Soviet-era public architecture seems ludicrously out of scale, dwarfing apartment and commercial blocks; in Almaty, except in the ostentatious Republic Square, it's more modest, in harmony with other structures. With the economic recovery, the real estate market has picked up, and new commercial and residential buildings have gone up. Most older buildings are at or below the khrushchevka maximum of five stories. For Almaty, the issue was not so much one of construction cost, but safety. The city is in a region of seismic activity; earthquakes in 1887, 1889, and 1911 destroyed many buildings.

The Pollution Bowl

Moroz y solntse, dyen' chudesnyi

[Cold frost and sunshine, a wonderful day]

—Opening line of Aleksandr Pushkin's 1829 poem,
Zimneye Utro (Winter Morning)

This is the kind of line you write in the middle of a long, cold, dark Russian winter to keep up your spirits (and those of your readers). Pushkin describes a cold morning when the sun shines brilliantly on the snow, lifting your mood (if not the temperature). That's the feeling I experienced on my first morning in Almaty in December 1995. I've had a few more Pushkin-like mornings in Almaty, but not many. Kazakhstan has a continental climate with hot summers and cold winters. Sheltered by the mountains, Almaty never gets as hot or cold as cities in the north where temperatures can rise to 40 Celsius (104 Fahrenheit) in July, and drop to minus 40 (both Celsius and Fahrenheit) in January, but it's chilly from November through March, with snow on the ground for an average of 111 days a year. On milder days, the snow turns to rain and freezes, leaving a thin layer of ice on the sidewalks. Many days, it's simply overcast, the clouds mixing with the smog.

In the basin below the mountains, rain and fog combine with industrial and power plant emissions and smoke from household fires to raise the pollution level. There's no wind to move the air, so it just hangs over the city like an unhealthy blanket. At street level, it's difficult to see the air quality, although residents complain of throat and eye irritation. For perspective, you need a bird's-eye view from the Shymbulak ski resort or another mountain perch; on a sunny day, the views across the mountains are clear, but the city is shrouded by a blanket of haze or smog. And pollution is just one of the environmental problems the city faces. Higher in the mountains above Shymbulak, the glaciers are retreating.

Climate Change? What Climate Change?

In 2009, a long, cold spring delayed the snowmelt in the Zailiysky Ala Too. Driving in from the airport, Feodor, a travel agency owner who was taking me to my rented apartment, told me there was still snow at lower altitudes. Feodor knew this was a blip in long-term weather patterns, and that the glaciers were retreating. Other Almaty residents looked at the mountains and wondered why the scientists and environmental groups were making a fuss. Although the more serious newspapers reported on long-term scientific predictions, there were plenty of naysayers on the Internet and in the *zholti* (yellow or tabloid) press.

I wasn't sure that people would buy the "climate change is a hoax" story line until I heard other rumors spread in the media. One driver asked if it was true that Barack Obama would be the last president of the United States. Why did he think so? Because the United States was destined to break up into separate states, just as the Soviet Union had done, he said. He was likely referring to the apocalyptic vision of the Russian academic Igor Panarin, a former KGB analyst and dean of the foreign ministry's academy for future diplomats, that mass immigration, economic decline, and moral degradation would trigger a civil war and collapse of the dollar in 2010. The United States would break into six regions. The Atlantic states might join the European Union; the new Texas Republic (southern states) would become part of Mexico or under Mexican influence; the Californian Republic (from Arizona to Washington) would become part of China or under Chinese influence; the Central North American Republic would become part of Canada or under Canadian influence; Hawai'i would go to either China or Japan, and Russia would reclaim Alaska.[1] Panarin's prediction, eagerly embraced by the Kremlin and Russian state media, was reported in Central Asian media, usually without his caveat that the risk of disintegration was 45–55 percent. Anyway, if you believed that the end was nigh for the United States, it wasn't difficult to accept that climate change was a Western invention, the latest fiendish plot to enslave the developing world by reducing its industrial growth through caps on carbon emissions.

I was in Almaty to try to counter bad science and rumors about the environment. The UNESCO Central Asia office had hired me to lead a workshop for scientists on communicating climate change issues to public (nonscientific) audiences. The challenge was not only to persuade the scientists to abandon jargon and explain complex processes in language ordinary people could understand. That's a problem for scientists everywhere. I was also up against the venerable Russian literary tradition of long sentences packed with dependent clauses, parenthetical phrases, and passive constructions. We discussed the use of short declarative sentences, active verbs, strong leads, and the inverted pyramid, but the scientists' models were still the Russian literary greats of the nineteenth century, whose elegant sentences are painstakingly dissected for their literary merits.

I tried to suggest a three-sentence structure. Number one: What's the problem/impact? "The glaciers of the Tian Shan are retreating, depleting Kazakhstan's water resources and increasing the danger of floods and mudslides." Two: Why is it happening? "Global climate changes and local carbon emissions are causing earlier and more rapid snowmelts." Three: What is your organization doing about it? I've found that this formula works for almost every climate change story. The scientists' tendency, however, was to back into the issue. Example: "Within the framework of the Kyoto Protocol and in accordance with pertinent national legislation relating to the protection of the future of the environment on the territory of Kazakhstan, the Information section of the Ministry of Environment, acting under the authority of the legislature of the Republic of Kazakhstan and His Excellency President Nursultan Nazarbayev, is engaged in the distribution of information—in newspapers, magazines, broadcasting, and other media—that will educate the population. . . ." And so on. On the second day, I asked one participant to read the first two paragraphs of his draft press release and asked my interpreter to translate them one at a time. I had enough time to walk over to the snack table, pour myself a cup of coffee, and come back before he had finished the first one.

Although progress was slow, by the end of the workshop the scientists had grasped the importance of tailoring messages to different audiences—for popular or specialized media, funding agencies, politicians, university administrators—even if they still struggled to write them. I encouraged them to communicate by telling stories rather than presenting data. And they had good stories to tell. One scientist spent every summer in the mountains, monitoring the glaciers. He had survived five avalanches (with broken bones) and been chased by bears. The region is popular with trekkers, and he often encountered groups decked out with the latest outfitters' gear. He says the trekkers were amazed when they were overtaken by his unfashionably dressed but physically fit scientific party, striding up the slopes carrying heavy monitoring equipment.

The problem goes both ways. Media in Central Asia do not have a good record for reporting on pollution, the depletion of water resources, deforestation, soil erosion, and other environmental issues. Compared with politics, celebrity sex scandals, crime, and other contact sports, the environment seems dull. It's a challenge to have journalists conduct research on complex topics that involve statistics, scientific data, and sometimes conflicting evidence. They are overly reverent toward scientists and experts. I ask them: You don't trust politicians, right? Their heads nod. Well, why should you trust scientists and environmental experts any more than politicians? They agree, at least in principle, but faced with bulky reports and tables of data, it's easier to package than to probe.

The challenge is to take large, difficult-to-grasp issues—greenhouse gas emissions, ecosystems, biodiversity—and turn them into stories readers and viewers understand, stories that may lead to individual and collective action. Public opinion polls in Central Asia reveal a widely held attitude that goes something like this: there's nothing I can personally do about these problems, so I'll just leave them to the government and international organizations to fix. And why should the media report on them if people can't do anything? To improve media coverage, you have to start with an issue that directly concerns many people. Almost everyone in Central Asia eats meat. That's why, on a bright November morning in 2010, I headed west out of Almaty with a group of journalists to grazing lands in the foothills of the Zailiysky Ala Too.

In the Hills

If you travel across the steppe of Kazakhstan, it's easy to think that the whole country is one large pasture. That's an exaggeration. Although the country has the largest steppe area in the world, grasslands occupy just over one-third of the total land area; another third, mostly in the west and southwest, is either desert or too barren to support any vegetation. In the north, where Khrushchev's Virgin Lands program was launched, large tracts were plowed up to grow wheat and other grains, although the arid climate makes yields unpredictable, and some are now being turned back into pasture. The chief livestock products are meat, dairy products, wool, and leather. Despite the fact that more than two-thirds of the land area is devoted to crops and livestock, agriculture accounts for less than 10 percent of the country's GDP. There's more money to be made mining and drilling under the land than using it to produce food.

Since the 1970s, overgrazing has reduced the amount of pasture land. Overgrazing causes native perennial grasses to be consumed and trampled and destroys native lichen and algae, which are important for fixing nitrogen and holding water. Their loss further depletes the land, reducing its ability to replenish itself and remain stable. Soil erosion, caused by the harsh winds that blow across the steppe in all seasons, follows.

With the breakup of the kolkhozes, most pasture areas were turned over to individual farmers, leading to a decline in livestock numbers. In contrast to Kyrgyzstan, where many herders maintained the nomadic system, moving livestock from villages to mountain pastures in the summer, herders on the Kazakh steppe started to keep their herds close to villages, leaving more distant pastures unused. The government and development agencies realized that herders needed to rotate pastures, or more land would be lost or become barely sustainable. Pilot projects were launched to allocate and regulate grazing areas. In a reversal of the usual top-down administrative system, herders came together in pasture committees to make decisions about who could graze where, and for how many seasons. Farmers whose work had once simply consisted of moving their herds, protecting them from wolves and other predators, birthing lambs and calves, and slaughtering and selling livestock, now found themselves collecting data on herds, breeds, and forage resources, and working on pasture and management plans. On that November morning, we were on our way to a herding community that was participating in a United Nations Development Programme (UNDP) project to restore lands for livestock through pasture rotation and the planting of new, hardy grasses.

As we drove into the countryside, the Russian-language signs became rarer. Outside Almaty, the rural population is largely Kazakh-speaking. We eventually turned off the main road onto a dirt track to a village. It was a treeless landscape, with small hills and dried-up streams, which reminded me of the Sand Hills of Western Nebraska or other areas east of the Rockies. Our inquiries began at the home of the chairman of the pastures committee, who was responsible for working with his neighbors to implement the grazing plan. We were welcomed with traditional hospitality—a table laden with breads, cakes, and the sweetest homemade butter I've ever tasted. Then we left to meet one of the herders.

It was a roller-coaster ride up and down the hillocks and across streams to the farmstead, which sat in a small gully. In winter, the only way to reach this place is on horseback, so such farms need to be self-sufficient. There was a stack of dried animal manure for heating (wood is scarce and expensive), farm animals, supplies, and a kitchen full of canned fruits and vegetables. The only power source was a single solar panel—enough, we were told, for a couple of lights and to recharge the mobile phone. We were told that almost every herding family had a mobile. It was not a technological luxury but a necessity in a region where the roads are poor and the nearest doctor or vet may be miles away. We talked to the herder's wife, then set out to look for the herder. Every half mile or so, we stopped the van and our guide would run up a small hill, scan the horizon, shake his head and run back. Eventually, we spotted small white dots in the distance. Sheep! If they were there, the herder would not be far away. We heard him before we saw him, shouting to the sheep. Then he galloped up, leaped off the horse and welcomed us. It was a desolate yet magical place. A cloudless sky, a light breeze, the sheep moving slowly across the grassland, the snow-covered mountains to the south. After the smog of Almaty, we almost drank the fresh, clean air.

Who Locked the Room Yesterday?

Visits to rural Kazakhstan provided a welcome respite from the city, where smog was not just in the air, but often seemed to pervade my daily work. Bureaucratic smog can also be dangerous to your health.

According to my colleague (and sometime interpreter) Irina Velska, any foreign teacher should learn three Russian phrases before entering a university classroom in Kazakhstan. The first is *"Gde kliuch?"* ("Where's the key?"). The response is usually another question: *"U kovo kliuch?"* ("Who has the key?"). Which is generally followed by a third question: *"Kto zakril auditoriyu vchera?"* ("Who locked the room yesterday?"). Only after the keeper of the keys is found can class begin.

Teaching in Central Asia requires patience, flexibility, and knowledge of a labyrinthine university bureaucracy where responsibilities—for keys, copying, repairs, and other services—are ill-defined. Transactions such as checking out the key require at least a signature, if not a picture ID. Higher-level tasks, such as memos, schedule changes, and expense reimbursements, require multiple forms and signatures and often an official and difficult-to-obtain departmental stamp. That's assuming you can find the person authorized to use the stamp. The same mind-set permeates government and the commercial and NGO sectors. A business manager told me how she received a letter from the European Union (EU) authorizing the transfer of funds for a media legal reform project. She took the letter to the bank, but it was not accepted because the signature did not contain a stamp. The EU project officer explained that the EU does not use stamps. The bank was not satisfied. It demanded a letter from the EU stating that it does not use official stamps, and said the letter should be signed by a responsible official and contain (I am not joking) an official stamp. Despite all the billboards and promotional campaigns proclaiming that Kazakhstan is open for business, Soviet-era traditions die hard.

I was at Kazakh National University (KazNU) to conduct a curriculum development workshop for teachers and working journalists. The seminar room was set up in conference style with chairs and tables that could be moved. Its main limitation was the single electrical outlet. We ran several extension cords to laptops but eventually our power demands overwhelmed the fragile system and the outlet failed. After several phone calls, a maintenance crew arrived. They said they could fix the outlet, but were reluctant to start work. "What's the problem?" Irina asked. They said they were assigned to another building on campus. They could do the repair, but we would have to pay them for their work. We refused and threatened to report them to the dean. By the next morning, they had repaired the outlet, although they did not clean up the plaster dust on the floor. That's must be someone else's responsibility.

The sign on the door stating that a workshop was in session did not deter casual visitors. Every ten minutes or so, the door would open, and a teacher or student would look around the room, nod in my direction and then close the door. Occasionally, people would walk in, sit in the outside circle of chairs and leave after twenty to thirty minutes without explanation. By midweek, I noticed a pattern—the traffic was heavier just before coffee breaks with the visitors grabbing tea, coffee, and snacks on their way out. A couple even signed the daily attendance sheet.

Such distractions did not seem to bother the participants. And the journalism faculty dean, Galiya Ibrayeva, smiled when I quietly remonstrated about keys, power outlets, and interruptions. She's a veteran academic administrator, with progressive ideas, but she knows that change comes slowly. We talked on a Sunday lunchtime outing to a resort in the mountains south of Almaty. It was an upscale development, with a hotel, spa, and (sadly) a few mountain animals (a fox, some deer, and falcons) in cages to divert the visitors on their after-lunch strolls. We ate shashlyk and *khachiapury* (cheese bread) at what I thought was a Georgian restaurant, although Galiya said it was actually Abkhazian. The resort was a kind of gastronomic theme park, with national/ethnic restaurants—Russian, Kazakh, Turkish, Chinese, and Japanese—set in gardens and walkways. Each had an appropriate statue of a national hero, although the Kazakh batyrs were the dominant species. It also boasts a historical anomaly—a *new* statue of Lenin in his most famous pose, right arm raised, gazing upward toward some Communist utopia. However, in this setting, Lenin was pointing the way to the Russian restaurant. It's really the same as the Che Guevara T-shirts. Revolutionary icons recycled to raise profit margins.

FIGURE 7.1 Lenin's commercial arm: "This way to the Russian restaurant." With KazNU journalism dean Galiya Ibrayeva and her daughter at a mountain resort near Almaty.

Over the years, I've grown to know what to expect from state universities in Central Asia. They have good people, but in a top-down bureaucratic system where curriculum is mandated by the government and rectors control resources, they are not free to make many changes. These universities, despite their glitzy brochures and websites and lists of centers, institutes, and international partners, are still trying to claw their way out of a Soviet-era time warp. Most teaching is lecture-based, with students required to attend many hours of classes; they have little opportunity to critically examine content through research or assignments. At most universities, teachers are paid according to the number of hours they spend in the classroom, not by the credit hour or course level. Asked to describe higher education in Tajikistan, my colleague Jovid Mukhim had a succinct, if discouraging, reply: "Long hours in cold classrooms." He was talking about both students and teachers.

Overall, the higher education picture in Kazakhstan is better than in the other Central Asian republics, where universities face serious budget pressures. In 2001, Kazakhstan launched a multiyear program (now extended to 2020) to improve education. Many universities are stronger and healthier than in the 1990s, with higher salaries and state funding for research and development. Standards have been improved with the introduction of the Unified National Test, roughly equivalent to the SAT, the standardized test used for most college admissions in the United States. After signing on to the European Commission's Bologna Process in 2010, Kazakhstan introduced degrees at the bachelor's, master's, and doctoral levels and adopted the European Credit Transfer System (ECTS) to improve student mobility. Between 2004 and 2008, the Ministry of Education and Science closed about forty underperforming universities and branch campuses. Nationwide, about 620,000 students are enrolled, most at state institutions; about 285,000 (46 percent) are part-time or distance education students, completing their requirements by examination. About one-fifth of students are supported by merit-based state scholarships (which do not cover living expenses); the rest pay tuition.

In the 1990s, entrepreneurs started opening private universities to attract upper- and middle-class students dissatisfied with state institutions. Some were little more than diploma mills, storefront colleges with letterhead, a website, and a handful of teachers whose own diplomas probably would not pass muster. In 1999 Shymkent, the leading city in the south with a population of over 400,000, reportedly boasted over twenty faculties of law. Law, like business and diplomacy, was a fashionable undergraduate major, both for students and their parents. Even in an increasingly litigious society, there was a limit to the number of lawyers Kazakhstan needed. It was the same with diplomacy. Kazakhstan has expanded its diplomatic corps, but again the supply of freshly minted diplomacy graduates expecting to be posted to London, Paris, or Washington far exceeds demand. At least business degrees were more marketable. By 2010, about a quarter of the hundred-plus private institutions had either failed because of financial problems or been closed because they did not meet minimal standards.

One higher education entrepreneur was Dr. Chan Young Bang, a Korean-born economist from the University of San Francisco who came to Kazakhstan in 1990 to serve as Nazarbayev's principal economic adviser. In 1992, he founded the Kazakhstan Institute of Management, Entrepreneurship and Strategic Research (KIMEP). Nazarbayev and Bang believed the country needed an elite institution, following Western standards, to train a new generation of business and political leaders for the global economy. Nazarbayev backed the scheme with money and prime real estate in Almaty's business district. KIMEP adopted a Western education model, with most teaching in English, and high admission standards. In the boom years, KIMEP prospered, attracting excellent students and faculty, many from overseas. It broadened its academic offerings to public administration, journalism, and other areas. It was the most expensive institution in the country, but some students were funded by scholarships from the government, foundations, and international agencies.

Like the banks and financial companies, KIMEP probably expanded too fast. For at least a year after the global financial crisis of 2008, high oil prices cushioned the impact on the economy. When the price dropped to below $50 per barrel, the downturn hit every sector—construction, housing prices, government tax revenues, and education. In just one week in 2009, the tenge lost 20 percent of its value against the dollar. Middle-class families found it difficult to pay for private education. KIMEP's enrollment of about 4,000 declined precipitously.

The administration's response makes for a good case study of how *not* to handle a crisis, because it succeeded in alienating almost everyone—faculty, staff, students, and parents. Bang's advisers, meeting behind closed doors, arbitrarily slashed faculty and staff. By late 2010, it was apparent that KIMEP's problems were not all attributable to risky mortgages in the West. Most of the finance department staff was fired for fraud or incompetency. The university came under criminal investigation for the embezzlement of about $1 million. The administration instituted checks and balances that improved accountability but increased frustration. Simple transactions took months to complete and required extensive documentation. One proposal (happily shelved) would have required department chairs to produce pencil stubs before they could requisition new pencils. There were sex scandals, and an attempt to withdraw KIMEP's license to issue degrees, later overturned by a court order.

At other universities, widespread malfeasance would have resulted in student sit-ins and critical editorials in the student newspaper. Not at KIMEP. Indeed, student leaders were also damaging the institution's reputation. First, the victorious party in student government elections was found to have hired a hacker to change the electronic vote count. Then the elected student officers appropriated $4,000 to finance a trip to Washington, ostensibly to attend a conference. Finally, the student president hired two other students to take summer session final exams for him. The administration suspended him for a year—a penalty most faculty considered too light. What's more worrying than the offenses themselves is that these students are supposed to be the best and brightest, destined for leading positions in government and business. If they can rig elections, steal money, and cheat on exams, what will they do when they're in the parliament or running major corporations?

None of the issues rated mention in the so-called independent student newspaper, the *KIMEP Times*. In 2010, the *Times* was moved from the journalism department to the Bang (named after the university president) College of Business. The paper and printing quality improved, but the content left much to be desired. Whereas local media reported on the scandals, the *Times*'s definition of news (according to its student editor) included "new friends, interesting trips, absorbing movies." The lead story? "Dr. Bang introduces new course [on leadership]." What's inside? "Minor in tourism introduced," "Different organizations at our institute," "Chess tournament," and "Dormitory—my home." Then there was the must-read "I'm a KIMEP student" column. This edition featured the first runner-up in the Miss Popularity category of the Miss KIMEP competition. I can't wait to read the story on "KIMEP Core Values."

As a young Soviet ham radio champion in the 1960s, Gennadiy Khonin, now a Lutheran pastor, remembers radio enthusiasts from the German Democratic Republic visiting his home in Almaty. "They would ask my mother if she was German. She would answer: No—never! Even our dog is not a German shepherd! My father was in a labor camp, but my mother never talked about it."

In the half century after World War II, anti-German discrimination ran deep in the Kazakh SSR. Ethnic Germans were afraid to speak their language outside the family. They were prohibited from traveling more than thirty kilometers from their homes and from gathering in groups of three or more. As late as the mid-1990s, youths spray-painted swastikas on German houses.

Official policy and public opinion began to change in the perestroika period, according to Aleksandr Dederer, president of Kazakhstan's Wiedergeburt (Rebirth) national association. "Today, people have memories of clean and tidy German villages. Companies hire Germans because they have a reputation for accuracy, punctuality, and hard work. On the real estate market, 'German-built' houses fetch higher prices because they were built to last. Attitudes have changed—from total hatred to something like respect."

The shift came too late to stem massive out-migration to Germany in the 1990s. At independence, about 960,000 ethnic Germans lived in Kazakhstan. Over the next decade more than 700,000 left. Although the tide has slowed to a trickle, and a few have returned, the country lost skilled professionals, including teachers, engineers, scientists, and doctors. Coupled with out-migration by Russians, Kazakhstan suffered a huge brain drain, precisely at the time when it needed an educated workforce to rebuild a shattered economy.

Although German peasant farmers began arriving in Central Asia in the middle of the nineteenth century, most ethnic Germans in Kazakhstan are members or descendants of the Trudarmiya (Labor Army), deported from the Volga region of Russia. Their ancestors had lived there since the mid-eighteenth century when Catherine the Great invited German farmers to settle the sparsely populated region. With the promise of religious freedom, exemption from military service and thirty years of tax exemption, they founded more than one hundred settlements along the banks of the Volga by the 1770s. For 150 years, the communities prospered, growing wheat, winter rye, sunflowers, potatoes, and other vegetables and fruits. Volga Germans suffered heavily in the civil war as the Red and White Armies fought for control of the region, destroying crops and villages; it is estimated that one-third of the population died from famine. In 1918, the Soviets established the Volga German Autonomous SSR and restored limited autonomy; the German language was promoted in education, media, and the arts, and Germans moved into government jobs.

Germany's invasion of the Soviet Union on June 22, 1941, changed official attitudes to the Volga Germans. On August 28, 1941, the Supreme Soviet, fearing that they would side with Hitler's advancing army, abolished the autonomous republic, stripped Volga Germans of their citizenship and ordered their deportation to Siberia and the Kazakh SSR. About 480,000 were rounded up by troops. Each was given as little as five minutes to pack one suitcase with belongings and food. Those who resisted or tried to hide were summarily shot.

"They were packed into cattle cars for a journey that could last up to two months," said Dederer. "They had little food or winter clothing, and some died on the journey. When they arrived, those selected for work were sent to the labor camps. Others were driven out onto the steppe and abandoned. They tried to dig holes in the ground, but most of them died."

"The labor camps and prohibitions against German language and culture were bad enough, but what was worse was the hate cultivated by Soviet movies and propaganda," he said. Dederer recalls the 1942 poem "Kill Him" by the Russian writer Konstantin Simonov that urged patriotic Soviet citizens to protect their homes and families by killing Germans.

Dederer, a factory engineer, began secretly organizing Germans in the city of Kostanai in northern Kazakhstan in the 1980s. In the perestroika period, Germans were allowed to hold meetings organized by the Communist Party. "The authorities were talking about peace and friendship, but the people wanted to discuss injustices and the preservation of their language and culture," he said. History was rewritten at a national congress in Moscow in 1989 when the Soviet authorities formally stated that the deportation and injustices suffered by Germans were wrong. The question of reestablishing the Autonomous Republic of Germans in the Volga region was discussed. Yeltsin dashed those hopes on a visit to the Volga region, stating that the region would never be returned to the Germans. According to Dederer, he said: "If the Germans want to come back, let them live in Kapustin Yar [a region near Volgograd used for nuclear and chemical missile tests]."

Yeltsin's statement provoked anger, and Germans in Kazakhstan who had considered returning to Russia decided to migrate to Germany. The German government supported migration, offering free flights and assistance with housing, jobs, and social services. Dederer credits Germany with "taking responsibility," but notes that only those who could prove they had been deported were accepted with their families. Since the late 1990s, stricter language tests, legal requirements and annual caps on visas have significantly reduced migration.

With financial assistance from the German government, the twenty Wiedergeburt centers provide social support for elderly Germans living on pensions and families in need. There are free lunches, care packages, and medical assistance—free eyeglasses and hearing aids and discounts on doctors' visits and prescriptions.

For Viktor Kist, president of the Karaganda oblast branch of Wiedergeburt, the rising Phoenix in the society's emblem represents cultural rebirth after two centuries of official repression of language, religion, and tradition. The Karaganda region, where most of the labor camps were located, has the largest concentration of ethnic Germans, estimated at 48,000. Because fewer than 10 percent speak fluent German, the Karaganda center offers language classes, now funded by the German government. In the 1990s, according to Kist, people studied German to prepare for emigration, but now they "feel they should know their language to preserve their traditions."[2]

The Lutherans

The German language is still alive at the Lutheran church in the Turksib district of Almaty. Half the hymns, prayers, and readings are in German, half in Russian.

Empty pews are a vivid reminder of the mass exodus in the 1990s. After independence, the church regularly attracted more than a thousand worshippers, with the service relayed over loudspeakers to an overflow congregation in the basement and churchyard. "The German language and the Lutheran faith were always part of our national identity," said Pastor Khonin, a former nuclear physicist. "In 1992, when I became a member of this congregation, everything was in German. People talked to each other in German—they had the feeling of being at home. But today most young people don't know German."

In the 1990s, according to Khonin, the church acted as a migration way station, helping people prove their German identity. Many who attended Khonin's confirmation classes emigrated. "One man asked me for two confirmation certificates. He said he needed one for himself and one for the embassy."

Today, the church has about fifty members, most of them elderly. The oldest, ninety-four-year-old Aleksandr Riel, a Trudarmiya veteran and retired music teacher, is the only male member of the choir. He has relatives in Germany and could have emigrated, but his Russian wife and family members were denied visas. "Before she died, my wife told me—don't ever leave your children. I gave her my word."

For Germans who stayed, the psychological effects of seeing relatives and neighbors leave could be devastating. "In some villages, almost every family was German," said Dederer. "When only one or two families are left, how do you think they feel? These people are depressed. They could not leave for Germany, and they now feel that they are in the minority."

FIGURE 7.2 Pastor Gennadiy Khonin and Aleksandr Riel outside Lutheran church in Turksib district, Almaty

The government has worked to improve the status and rights of minority groups. Article 2 of the constitution protects minority languages and culture and religious freedom. The government provides operating funds and staff salaries for Wiedergeburt branches and the *Deutsche allgemeine Zeitung (DAZ)*, a weekly published in German and Russian. It has a small print circulation, but the online edition, with over 30,000 unique monthly visitors, reaches ethnic Germans and the larger diaspora in Germany.

DAZ covers "issues of integration in Germany, both successful and unsuccessful," said chief editor Olesja Klimenko. "In the 1990s, people thought Germany was a paradise. Some migrants were successful— they learned the language, used their qualifications, and continued their education. Others found that their qualifications as engineers, scientists, doctors, and teachers were not accepted. They were already middle-aged, and it was difficult to re-train. Some ended up as lab assistants or drivers. It's good to present a picture of what it's really like to live in Germany."[3]

The Brain Drain

Dederer and Kist are leaders in the Kazakhstan-German Association of Entrepreneurs, helping Germans start their own companies and find business partners in Germany. With trade between the two countries growing, there is potential in mining and natural resources, equipment supply, retailing, and the service and tourism sectors.

"There was a huge brain drain in the 1990s," said Paul Kirol, who owns a vegetable storage and food processing plant, a transportation company, an industrial equipment importer, and a hotel in Astana. Kirol was part of the brain drain. With his family, he migrated in 1995 and became a German citizen. Most of his relatives live in Germany, but Kirol decided to return to take advantage of Kazakhstan's growing consumer market. "Germany is a safer place, but I feel freer here because my business is not restricted," he said. "I know the language, I know the business culture. In Germany, I would have to learn all over again."

Dederer says that emigrants have few incentives to return. Kazakhstan companies cannot match German salaries and will not make contributions to the German social welfare fund. Migrants can earn almost as much from unemployment benefits in Germany as in a full-time job in Kazakhstan. "Why would you give up almost 900 euros a month in unemployment to come to Kazakhstan and work full-time for 1,000 to 1,500 euros?" said Dederer.

Ethnic Germans in Kazakhstan continue to face a complex push-and-pull relationship with a country where most of them have never lived. Yana Baumgartner, president of a German youth club in Astana, is an energetic advocate of German culture. Her group holds folk music and dance performances at city festivals, celebrates German holidays, and conducts a youth leadership program and a summer ecology camp. "It's so important to maintain our traditions and let other people know about them," she said.

Baumgartner credits Nazarbayev with supporting minority cultures and says she feels no discrimination against ethnic Germans. "I am lucky," she said. "I have a choice between German, Russian and Kazakh cultures." But long ago she made a choice to move to Germany for graduate study and work. "It's my dream. I have lived in Kazakhstan all my life, and I love the country. But in my heart, I'm German."[4]

eight

The President's Dream City

Planet Astana

To look at, Astana is so strange that it has one grasping for images.
It's a space station, marooned in an ungraspable expanse of level
steppe, its name (to English speakers) having the invented sound
of a science fiction writer's creation. It's a city of fable or dream,
as recounted by Marco Polo to Kublai Khan. Except it's not quite
so magical: it's also like a battery-operated plastic toy, all whirring
noises and flashing colours, of a kind sold by the city's street
vendors.

—Rowan Moore, *Observer*, August 2010[1]

For many visitors, the capital of Kazakhstan is an astonishing sight—
unlike any other city they've seen. I visited Astana for the first time in
September 2010, one month after Rowan Moore. My first impressions—
from the air and then from the airport highway—evoked otherworldly

metaphors. Strange shapes rose out of the steppe—spires, domes, globes, ovals, and pyramids in gold, silver, blue, and turquoise. The taxi passed the gleaming facade of Nazarbayev University, then sports stadiums and arenas built for the 2011 Asian Winter Games, with their massive, curved metal and concrete spans. Then triumphal arches, monumental public buildings, upscale apartment blocks, the huge Nur Astana mosque, shopping malls, and manicured parks, most of which on a chilly Saturday afternoon were almost deserted.

Whatever you think about futuristic architecture (or what it cost to build it, and whether the money could have been better invested in Kazakhstan's social needs), Astana is unlike any other capital city in Central Asia. Almaty (the former capital) and Tashkent look like other Soviet-era cities with their colonnaded public buildings and monotonous apartment blocks. Bishkek and Dushanbe have similar architecture, but are rougher around the edges. Astana looks more like Dubai or Abuja. It is growing fast, but even by the latest (2012) population estimate of 775,000, it is still less than half the size of Almaty or Tashkent (each of which has about two million inhabitants). However, the futuristic architecture makes Astana look and feel bigger. Which is exactly what its chief conceptual architect, President Nazarbayev, intended.

It's fun to depict Astana in the language of science fiction, but Moore's Marco Polo analogy may be more appropriate. Like other capital cities throughout human history, Astana is designed to impress visitors. Just as medieval travelers returned home with tales of the fabulous cities of the East, modern travelers to Astana are treated to a visual spectacle. Astana is a twenty-first-century version of Karakorum, the thirteenth-century capital city of the Mongol Empire.

Contemporary visitors to Karakorum were suitably awed, perhaps because they thought the Mongols were too busy rampaging and pillaging their way across Asia and Eastern Europe to actually build anything more than siege fortifications and campfires. In 1253, the Flemish Franciscan William of Rubruck, who had accompanied the French king Louis IX on the Seventh Crusade, set out from Constantinople for Karakorum. Louis had given the monk the medieval version of mission impossible—convert the Mongols to Christianity. Whether or not William knew the futility of his assignment, he set out to record his party's journey in detail, producing one of the great travel narratives of the age, comparable to that of Marco Polo.

After traveling for almost seven thousand miles William and his companions entered a wealthy, bustling city at the heart of a major trading network, with markets, temples, and a cosmopolitan population, including Christians. The Great Khan even staged a debate at court among adherents of Islam, Christianity, and Buddhism. William's detailed account of the journey and the six-month stay at Karakorum, and the reports of other missionaries and merchants, helped to counter popular views of the Mongols as a murderous horde.

Like Karakorum, Astana is the concrete symbol of a modern and business-friendly Kazakhstan, an emerging economic and cultural power at the crossroads between Europe and Asia. In his writings and public speeches, Nazarbayev positions Kazakhstan within Eurasia, arguing that the nation embodies the best of the West and the East in its economy, education, religion, civil society, and values. The Eurasian motif is visible in the signature architecture of Astana, where elements of Western and Eastern design are combined. Astana hosts Eurasian conferences and events; businesses claim to reach the Eurasian market; Eurasian National University is the largest institution of higher education in the capital.

For Nazarbayev, Astana was never the otherworldly, utopian fantasy that its critics have claimed. "It was a dream," he wrote in 2006. "Now it is a true city, the pride and heart of Kazakhstan."[2] Astana is a combination of Karakorum and Dubai, the center of a new Mongol empire built, not on military conquest, but on oil and gas revenues, authoritarian government, investments in technology and education, and soft diplomacy with the West, Russia, and China. In a commentary for the *Kazakhstanskaya Pravda* newspaper to mark Astana Day, the city's fifteenth anniversary, on July 6, 2013, Nazarbayev wrote: "The fate of Astana is the fate of all Kazakhstanis who have boldly crossed the threshold between two centuries. This is the fate of independent Kazakhstan, which has walked the great path from the obscure fringe of a fallen superpower known to few in the world to a dynamic modern state which the international community knows and respects."[3] Astana Day was also (not coincidentally) Nazarbayev's seventy-third birthday. For the crowds who attended the birthday celebrations and the millions who watched the spectacle on TV, the association between city, country, and president was more than metaphorical. Astana *was* Kazakhstan. Nazarbayev had created Astana. Ergo, Nazarbayev was Kazakhstan.

An expensive government PR campaign, including glossy spreads in travel magazines and advertising supplements in Western newspapers, has failed to convince most Western journalists of the legitimacy of Nazarbayev's vision. The *Economist* critique is typical: "Astana has all the weirdness of Pyongyang. . . . It is a collection of monuments and boulevards on a scale that screams 'L'état, c'est moi.'"[4] "Despite the president's efforts to highlight Astana's 'reality,'" writes Natalie Koch, a Syracuse University geographer, "the city is consistently read and interpreted by Western observers as a 'Potemkin village' or 'utopia.'"[5]

She provides a sampling of unflattering labels—"Nowheresville" (*New Yorker*), "the space station in the steppes" (*Guardian*), "the Jetsons' hometown" (*Slate Magazine*), "Tomorrowland" (*National Geographic Magazine*), and "the Disneyland of the steppe" (German magazine *Merien*). Such negative images infuriate a government that is still battling the "Borat effect." In the 2006 satirical film, *Borat: Cultural Learnings of America for Make Benefit Glorious Nation of Kazakhstan,* and in his *Da Ali G Show* on TV channels, British comedian Sacha Baron Cohen plays Borat Sagdiyev, "the number two" television reporter in Kazakhstan, where, he says, the favorite hobbies are "disco dancing, archery, rape, and table tennis." In the movie, Borat travels through the United States recording real-life interactions with Americans, who believe he is a foreigner with little or no understanding of their customs. Many viewers understood that Cohen was satirizing political and cultural intolerance. In Kazakhstan, both government officials and citizens took it literally, believing it portrayed the country as backward and intolerant; some accused Cohen of being the agent of a foreign power. *Borat* was banned, of course. The government redoubled its own PR efforts, launching the multimillion-dollar "Heart of Eurasia" campaign to rebrand Kazakhstan and its capital.

Unlike many, I did not make a flying visit to the city to report on an event or the opening of a new building. I lived in Astana for six months, traveled and walked in the city and talked with residents. In June 2011, Koch was in Astana, completing research for her dissertation, "The City and the Steppe: Territory, Technologies of Government, and Kazakhstan's New Capital." Her perspectives point to the dangers of jumping to conclusions about the city.

Koch argues that describing new city projects as utopias or Disney-style theme parks is stigmatizing. "From Dubai to Shanghai to Tokyo to Astana," she writes, "the political language of 'utopia'—fantasy and extravagance—is in full force in much Western writing about these cities. In the hegemonic interpretive frame, 'underdevelopment' is seen to propel Eastern 'others' to pursue extravagant, overwrought, desperate attempts to achieve an impossible modernity. The discursive frame, however, only allows these (urban) spectacles to be facades, covering up a lack of modernity 'underneath.'"[6]

Academics will excuse me for skipping the next step in building an argument for what Koch describes as the "political bordering" of Astana. This involves parading the usual cast of theoreticians—Foucault, Gramsci, Said, and others—to outline (sorry, I meant to say "explicate") their theories and critiques of hegemony, orientalism, poststructuralism, postmodernism, postcolonialism, and post-other-isms. They are important thinkers, but they make for heavy reading, and I'm not going to let them slow down this narrative. Let me leave them where I know they're welcome (in the theory and literature review sections of dissertations and journal articles). I'll return to Koch's analysis of the real, stigmatized Astana.

Koch reviewed about forty articles in the English-language (US and UK) and German press from 1997, the year the city became the capital. The most common themes described Astana's "inhospitable environment, bad weather, barrenness of the steppe," characterized the city as "strange, utopian, fantastic, and futuristic," or "as somehow false, a façade, a Potemkin village," and connected the city "to Nazarbayev's megalomania" or to Kazakhstan's oil wealth. Articles also mentioned the unpopularity of the decision to move the capital from Almaty, the rushed speed of development, divisions between the new (left bank) and old (right bank) cities, and other criticisms of the project.[7]

That's not the way many residents view Astana. Thousands have moved to Astana in search of jobs and business opportunities. For them, the city is not a theme park; it's where they live, work, and raise their families. Although living costs are higher than in other cities (except for Almaty), wages and city services are better. "I'm from Shymkent," one taxi driver told me. "There are no jobs there. I miss my family, but I can earn enough picking up fares from people like you at the airport to live and send money home. Why would I go back?"

For longer-term residents, seeing the city grow in size, wealth, and prominence has been a source of pride. My Russian teacher, Galiya Suleimenova, moved from Almaty in the early 1990s for her husband's health. In winter, Almaty has high levels of air pollution, and the clean air of the steppe improved his breathing. "When we arrived, this was just a small, sleepy town," Galiya told me. "There were few businesses, few cars on the street. We've seen it grow so fast. There are more jobs, more people, just more life and activity. And it's still growing. We're proud to live in Astana."

In 2010, Koch commissioned a survey research company to conduct doorstep interviews with more than 1,200 citizens over the age of eighteen in all sixteen of Kazakhstan's provinces. Eighty-one percent (996) said that Astana has improved Kazakhstan's international image. The government has worked hard to brand Kazakhstan, as represented by Astana, as modern, progressive, and open for business. The city has hosted major international conferences, festivals, and sporting events, and established special economic zones and technology parks. "The goal is to have people talk about Astana like Dubai," the city's master planner, Amanzhol Chikanayev, told Koch.[8]

But Please Don't Write about Astana

In the summer of 1997, I took the four-hour marshrutka ride from Bishkek to Almaty to work with my colleague Elizabeth Sammons. We'd been asked to write the Central Asia chapter for a book on global journalism ethics, and Elizabeth had arranged interviews with Almaty journalists.

Journalists in Kazakhstan, as in other Central Asian countries, face threats and dangers—from harassment by the police and security forces to libel actions and economic pressure from owners and advertisers with political alliances. Inevitably, such pressures result in self-censorship, with journalists either not covering topics that can get them into trouble or covering them in such a way that hackles are not raised.

Which are these touchy topics? Over the years, I've talked with journalists in many countries and developed a standard question: Which topics, not specifically prohibited by law, such as state secrets or military information, do you not cover, or cover only with extreme caution? In Almaty in 1997, there was virtual unanimity on the "prohibited" or "report-only-with-care" list. In rough priority order, the topics were:

1. The private life (including the health) of President Nazarbayev and his family

2. The transfer of state property to private ownership

3. Private companies, such as banks, in which government officials and other prominent figures have financial interests

4. The financial status of government officials

5. Interethnic and racial issues

6. Problems in Kazakhstan's new capital, Astana

Quttyqadam Seydkhamet, a politician who wrote a column for the Kazakhstan edition of the Russian-language weekly *Argumenti y Fakti,* told me that the first five topics had been on the list since independence. Number 6 was new. Government sensitivity on the topic had been growing since the move was announced in 1994. Now, in the summer of 1997, with ministries scheduled to move by October, criticism was viewed as, if not exactly treasonous, at least unpatriotic.

Opposition politicians had questioned the price tag of moving government ministries when the country faced a budget deficit and major economic and social problems. In 1997, the cost was estimated at between $500 million and $1 billion, the sheer range indicating that either the cost was a state secret or, more likely, that no one had the faintest idea of what it would be. Foreign diplomats and businesspeople did not relish the prospect of leaving comfortable, sophisticated Almaty, with its moderate climate, for a remote city on the northern steppe. Journalists were discouraged from reporting on these issues or on infrastructure problems in the new capital—gas, electricity, and water shortages, and the eviction of residents to provide apartments for government officials.

Why did Nazarbayev decide to move the capital? The government claimed Almaty was overcrowded, prone to earthquakes and too close to China. However, the main reasons were economic and political. The move put the capital, with its good rail links to Russia, closer to Kazakhstan's industrial region and mineral resources. Most important, it would be easier to govern the predominantly Russian north of the country.

There's no law of political geography that says you have to locate a capital city in the middle of the country, although some such as Brussels, Madrid, and Ankara are reasonably centrally situated. However, few capitals were further away from the geographical center of their country, or so close to the border with a politically unstable neighbor, as Almaty. The city is tucked into the fold below the Zailiskiy Ala Too in the southeast corner of the country, close to China and only 150 miles by road from Bishkek. The nearest large city in southern Kazakhstan, Shymkent, is 450 miles away.

After independence, the new government realized that trying to govern the country from its far southeastern border was too great of a geographical, logistical, and political challenge. The most immediate concern was the northern provinces where most ethnic Russians lived. The area—from the uranium processing city of Ust Kamenogorsk in the northeast, through the coalfields of the Karaganda region to the wheat-growing region of Kostanai and the Cossack town of Uralsk— had historically closer links with Southern Siberia and the Urals industrial region than with the rest of the Kazakh SSR. Most of the country's coal and iron resources and industrial plants were in the region, and oil exploration had begun in the northern section of the Caspian Sea. The north also had a more dangerous Soviet legacy—a stockpile of around a thousand nuclear warheads, more than a hundred rockets, forty bombers, and the Semipalitinsk Polygon, the site of Soviet above- and below-ground nuclear tests.

In the early 1990s, Russian nationalist politicians on both sides of the border—including the popular and anti-Muslim Vladimir Zhirinovsky, who was born in the Kazakh SSR—openly advocated that the northern provinces secede from Kazakhstan and rejoin Mother Russia. Nazarbayev and his advisers knew it was vital to the country's economic and political future to build a sense of national unity. One way to do this was to move the capital north.

Aaarghmola

First it was called Akmola. Then Tselinograd. Then Akmola again. Today it is Astana.

The place has been on history's center stage before. Until the 1950s, Akmola, about 150 miles northwest of the industrial city of Karaganda, was a small mining settlement, an undistinguished demographic dot in the steppe. In the 1950s, Khrushchev selected it as the center for his Virgin Lands campaign, a scheme to convert almost 100,000 square miles of grassland into arable land and make Kazakhstan (with Ukraine) the breadbasket of the Soviet Union. Thousands of Soviet citizens were moved to the region, and Akmola was symbolically renamed Tselino-grad, the "City of the Virgin Lands."

Soviet economic planning was never sensitive to the lessons of history. If it had been, Khrushchev's agricultural advisers would have studied what happened in the American Dust Bowl of the 1930s. The ecosystem of the steppe is similar to that of the plains of Texas, Okla-homa, Kansas, and Nebraska, where hardy prairie grasses reach down to hold the thin topsoil together. Except for some areas near rivers, the arid land is best suited for livestock grazing. That's what the Kazakhs had been doing for hundreds of years. Plowing up the steppe to plant grains exposes the topsoil to wind erosion. Although northern Kazakhstan has never experienced a catastrophic dust bowl, much of the land originally designated for wheat has now been returned to grazing. Within a de-cade, the USSR had moved onto other grand schemes. The Virgin Lands campaign was forgotten by most Soviet citizens, except for those who ended up in Tselinograd.

At independence, the name was changed back to Akmola. In Kazakh, ak means "white." There's disagreement over the precise meaning of mola. In 1997, government historians declared that it meant "abundance of white," apparently a reference to dairy products. A more plausible version, confirmed by Kazakh colleagues, is that it means "way," making Akmola the "White Way," a suitably inspiring name for a future capi-tal. More skeptical sources claim it means "death" or "tomb." In 1997, this interpretation was a convenient fit for those who did not want to leave Almaty. They could complain over cocktails in Almaty's bars that they were being sent to their "white death" on the northern steppe. The Economist summed up their angst in a July 1997 article playfully entitled "Aaarghmola." "Bureaucrats, diplomats and businessmen generally felt no desire to leave relatively sophisticated Almaty . . . for remote and inhospitable Akmola. Many people hoped that Mr. Nazarbayev would think again—after all, he has to live there too."[9] The president didn't change his mind, and the government quickly settled the semantic issue by renaming the city Astana, which in Kazakh means "capital." This gave Kazakhstan one more international distinction. It is the only country in the world where the capital is called, in the native language, capital.

Akmola, with a population of about 300,000 (70 percent of them Russians, Ukrainians, and Volga Germans), was situated on the right bank of the River Ishim. To create a futuristic new city on the site would have involved tearing down blocks of khrushchevkas and older, single- story houses, displacing thousands of residents. It was easier and cheaper to make a fresh start on the undeveloped left bank. The right bank was not neglected, however. New government buildings were constructed on Akmola's main square as temporary homes for the parliament, ministries, and presidential administration; later, they became the lavish quarters of the oblast and city administrations. The railroad and bus stations were renovated, new hotels built, roads repaired, and the main north-south drag, Virgin Workers' Prospekt, was renamed Republik Prospekt. But most of the construction was under way on the other side of the river.

For several years, Western journalists (as indicated in Koch's analysis) stressed the Potemkin-village quality of the place. "It's all a show," a construction company owner told a *New York Times* correspondent in November 1997, a month after the official move. "The buildings have three sides and no back."[10] The evocation of the final scenes of Mel Brooks's *Blazing Saddles,* where the false storefronts collapse and the fistfights spill onto other movie sound stages, seems harsh. The right bank, even with its new government and commercial buildings and improved roads and sidewalks, still looked like an ordinary Soviet-era city. The left bank was another matter—a huge construction site with a steadily rising skyline. Most of the contracts went to foreign companies, with Turkish concerns the big winners; on the sites, many workers were poor migrants from Kyrgyzstan and Tajikistan.

It was a good time to be in real estate in Astana, with land prices rising fast. Of course, all the embassies had to move. Most ended up in an embassy row, a gated compound of almost identical McMansions distinguished only by the national flags outside. The United States needed more land than embassy row could offer to build its cookie-cutter Fortress America mission with high walls, topped with menacing spikes, and independent security systems. In 2010, a foreign service officer boasted to me that the United States had entered the real estate market early and secured a prime location for the embassy. "Prime" seemed a relative term to me. In September 2010, I asked a taxi driver to take me to the US embassy. He assured me he knew where it was. After half an hour of driving around unnamed streets on the left bank, he admitted he didn't know, and stopped to ask pedestrians. None of them knew. Eventually, I called my embassy contact who, rather like an airport traffic controller, guided us in to land by the main gate. I still don't know the street name.

The multinational companies, especially those in the oil, gas, minerals, and banking sectors, moved their headquarters from Almaty and provided apartments for staff. They realized that even though Astana did not yet have a large business sector, it would grow quickly because the government was there. As the foreign service officer put it, in succinct realpolitik language: "The power has moved here, and the money will follow."

Fulbright Conspiracy Theory

Astana interested me enough to want to spend a few days in the city. I never planned to spend six months there. When I applied for a second Fulbright Fellowship in the summer of 2010, my plan was to teach in Almaty. I had visited the city regularly for workshops and university teaching, had friends there, and had a letter of invitation from Dean Galiya Ibrayeva of the Journalism Faculty at KazNU, the leading mass media department in the country. I expected to guest-lecture at other universities, do workshops for journalists and media managers, and spend spring weekends relaxing in coffee shops and hiking in the mountains.

I was caught off guard at the Fulbright orientation session in Washington, DC, when the US embassy education officer suggested I go to Astana and teach at Eurasian National University (ENU). I knew nothing about the institution, and a web search yielded little because most of the web pages were under construction. All I could glean was that there *was* a Faculty of Journalism and Politology (political science), with faculty with advanced degrees in philology (not journalism or media). I e-mailed a few colleagues. "Why would you want to go there?" one asked. "ENU has no reputation for teaching journalism." Galiya agreed when I told her of the embassy proposal. Most of the ENU faculty, she sniffed, had been fired by KazNU. She said the government was putting pressure on the embassy to bring in a Fulbrighter to boost ENU's (and Astana's) profile. At the time, I dismissed this as a crazy conspiracy theory. Subsequent events indicated that, while there may not have been a conspiracy, there was substance to Galiya's claim.

The embassy's pitch was about spreading the Fulbright wealth. Few US academics check Kazakhstan (or any Central Asian country) on the application box. Most who came to Kazakhstan had worked in Almaty, so now it was time for other cities, including the capital, to benefit. I agreed and started thinking about winter clothing.

I had a preview of Astana and ENU in September 2010 when I spent a week there conducting a curriculum workshop for journalism educators. ENU's new academic buildings, housing the science, business, and law faculties, line the banks of a canal feeding into the River Ishim. Unfortunately, journalism is not considered a prestige faculty, and is almost hidden from view down a side street in a former student dormitory surrounded by Soviet-era apartment blocks. The building was once home to the philology faculty. It looked as if the staff had left in a hurry, because several classrooms were still set up as language labs, although none of the technology worked. In smaller classrooms, the blackboards were installed on a side wall; any student behind the third row risked whiplash to read what was written.

After many years of teaching in Central Asia, I was accustomed to inadequate facilities. What mattered was what I'd be teaching and to whom. The dean, Namasaly Omashev, agreed to the courses I proposed and said that I would be advising master's and PhD students on their research. This was to be my first and last meeting with the dean. My classes never made it onto the faculty schedule. And I never met—let alone worked with—a single graduate student. But in late September 2010, I was not to know this. I had agreed to teach at ENU, and now I needed to find an apartment.

Apartment Hunting

On an afternoon break from the workshop, my interpreter Irina Velska and I took a bus tour of Astana. It was not a tour in the strict sense of the term with a route and a guide. We simply got on a public bus on the right bank, paid the 50 tenge (30 cent) flat fare, stayed on the bus until it reached its terminus on the left bank and headed back. It gave me a sense of the layout of the city, especially the differences between the old and new cities. Most expats work in the corporate sector and live in expensive high-rise apartments with names like Highville and Northern Lights on the left bank. Call me old-fashioned, but I have a soft spot for post-Soviet decay. I preferred to live on the right bank, preferably on a direct bus route to the university. The apartment blocks looked drab from the outside, but I had stayed in enough of them in other cities to know that they were often comfortable inside. On the right bank, I would be close to shops, restaurants, and markets. There, people actually walked on the streets rather than moved between mall levels.

My preferences did not impress my US embassy liaison. She informed me that because so many people were moving to Astana, apartments were scarce and rents high. She had been lucky to find me an apartment in the prestigious "Diplomat" complex, a new left bank development. The rent was $1,000 a month (utilities, cable TV, and Internet included). This was at the top of my price range, but I reluctantly agreed to take it. However, when she picked me up from the airport, we didn't go to the "Diplomat" but to another apartment block on the left bank. She said that this was temporary, and that I would be moving to the "Diplomat" in a few days when another American moved out. I slept on a pullout couch and found only one fork, knife, and spoon in the kitchen. As often happens, a family had moved out to make way for me. This was not what I had paid for, and I complained loudly when the landlady told me I would have to stay there for a month until the other apartment was available.

I was feeling disoriented on the left bank. The next evening, driving back from ENU with my interpreter, Diana Akizhanova, we got lost and had to call for directions. I'd e-mailed Irina about my housing problem, and when I got back to the temporary apartment, she had replied. "Why the hell are you putting up with this apartment?" she wrote. "There are vacant and cheaper apartments nearer the university." She sent me a link to an apartment rental website. I resolved to start searching for a new apartment in the morning. Then an e-mail from my friend, Hal Foster, a freelance journalist living in Astana, arrived. Hal had just received a job offer in Washington, DC. He was leaving in a week and wanted to see me before he left. And, by the way, did I need an apartment on the right bank? The next day we met for lunch, and I took the apartment. It was spacious, warm, a ten-minute bus ride from the university, and $200 a month cheaper than the "Diplomat" apartment to which I *might* be moving in a month. I moved the next day, and reclaimed rent from my landlady. She grumbled, telling me that I would not like living on the right bank and warning me about crime. I told her I wasn't planning to be out on the streets at night. It was just too cold.

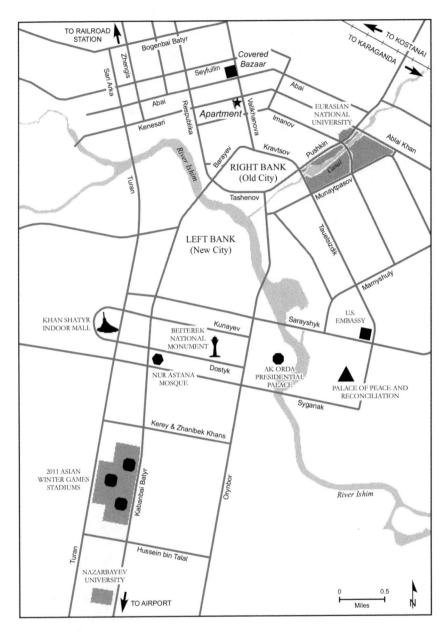

MAP 8.1 My Astana (map by Brian Edward Balsley, GISP)

One housewife to another: "I hear there'll be snow tomorrow."
"Well, I'm not queuing for that."

If you're looking for steady, seasonal work, try snow removal in Astana. In January and February, the city clears snow almost every day. It's an impressive operation. In some North American cities, snow piles up alongside roads and sidewalks. In Astana they literally remove it. Workers break up the snow and ice with pickaxes, and shovel it into front loaders that dump it into trucks that haul it out of town. I don't know where they dump it, but if some farmer's field is still under snow in May, we'll have a clue.

Astana is, according to climate data, the second coldest capital city in the world, with Ulaan Baatar in Mongolia (another city where I've shivered in April) in first place. It attained this dubious status when it became the capital in 1997, knocking Ottawa out of second spot. Understandably, the government and the tourist agencies don't talk much about temperatures in their promotional brochures. They'd prefer foreigners to think that other Northern Hemisphere capitals, such as Moscow, Helsinki, Reykjavik, and Pyongyang, are colder.

Of course, defining "coldest" raises methodological issues. Are we looking at average temperatures across the year, average winter temperatures, or just extreme conditions, when the temperature plunges to, say, minus 40 Celsius? I vote (with my cold feet) for average winter temperatures. Astana has an extreme continental climate with warm summers and long, cold, dry winters. Temperatures of minus 30 Celsius (minus 22 Fahrenheit) to minus 35 Celsius (minus 31 Fahrenheit) are common between mid-December and early March. The city also holds the record for the lowest air temperature ever recorded in Kazakhstan (minus 51 Celsius). Typically, the River Ishim freezes over between the second week of November and the beginning of April. It can feel even colder because of the wind chill.

My Fulbright began in mid-January, and I was prepared. Stephanie had bought me a warm down coat, an alpaca wool hat, gloves with liners, and two pairs of silk long johns. Unfortunately, United Airlines stored my checked luggage at Dulles Airport for three days before handing it over to Lufthansa for delivery. The long johns, of course, were in the luggage.

I ventured out the first morning wearing almost all the outer clothing I had, my legs yearning for those long johns. My first appointment was at the US embassy, a ten-minute bus ride from my temporary apartment. As I stood shivering at the bus stop, my liaison nonchalantly remarked that it was "not too cold today—only minus 30 Celsius."

Some parts of Astana are definitely colder than others. On the left bank among the high-rise apartments, government ministries, malls, parks, and public squares, the wind blows hard off the steppe, funneling along the boulevards and buffeting the few pedestrians brave enough to be outside. On the right bank in the older city, the buildings are closer together, providing shelter from the wind. Maybe it is partly psychological, but it feels warmer—or, in Astana terms, not as bone-chillingly cold—there.

On the streets, walking can be hazardous to your health. The snow may be only a few inches deep, but it is hard-packed. However, it's safer walking on the snow than on the sidewalk, which is often a sheet of pure ice. I moved slowly, looking for patches of snow that would give me a firmer footing. The locals seemed to be equipped with all-weather feet, walking briskly, some of the women in fashionable high heels. My complaints about the winter fell on deaf ears. Aleksandr, a taxi driver, told me the winter had so far been mild. He recalled that when he was growing up in a village in northern Kazakhstan, the snow reached almost to the roof (almost ten feet high) of the family's one-story home and they had to dig a passage through to the street. He said they never got too cold, because they had an ample wood supply and because the deep snow around the house had an igloo effect.

Even after my long johns arrived and my legs were reasonably warm, I didn't walk any further than I had to for fear of falling. Every day, I left my apartment, walked one block to the bus stop, and took the No. 9 or No. 11 along Kenesary Street to the Kazakhstan Supermarket stop. From there, it was another seven- to ten-minute walk to the journalism faculty. I went home by the same route, stopping at the supermarket in the apartment block. In almost three months, I left my apartment in the evening only three or four times to meet friends for dinner, and always took a taxi. On the weekends, I would walk fifteen to twenty minutes along Valikhanova Street to the covered market four blocks away. Sometimes I stopped at a coffee shop that doubled as an English-language library with books and DVDs. It also offered old newspapers and magazines donated by customers. You could learn that "Republicans Win 2010

Midterm U.S. Elections" six months after the fact in case you missed the story. I asked a British couple, Paul and Sarah, what they did for fun in Astana in winter. There was a brief silence. "Well, we often come here, have coffee, check out a DVD and go home and watch it," said Sarah. This was not encouraging news.

The government of Kazakhstan has spent lavishly to make its capital a city where people would want to live and work. It has worked hard to brand Astana as a business destination and as a host city for international conferences and sporting events. The city has a modern airport, five-star hotels, new conference and exhibition halls, upscale shopping malls, and the usual range of "international" cuisine—from sushi and tapas bars to the somewhat incongruous Irish pubs. It's now the sort of city that merits a glossy spread in an airline magazine, the writer gushing about his "24 Hours in Astana, Jewel of the Steppe," the architecture, museums, and nightlife. But neither government policy nor business investment can change the climate.

Winter Games

If you can't change the weather, make it an asset. That's what Kazakhstan did in its successful bid for the 2011 Asian Winter Games, although its offer to spend millions of dollars may have been more persuasive than the average daytime temperatures. It's estimated that the government spent over $1.4 billion building new stadiums or renovating existing ones in Astana and Almaty, upgrading Astana's airport and improving roads and transportation.

When I arrived in Astana in mid-January, preparations for the games were in full swing. A total of twenty-seven countries sent teams, and the organizing committee had scoured foreign-language departments across the country for student interpreters. The committee's headquarters, full of red track-suited volunteers, and the hotel where most of the athletes and officials were staying were just around the corner from my apartment. On my rare ventures along the snow-covered streets, I'd often see a busload of athletes heading out for the newly built stadiums on the left bank.

Fortunately for the organizers, Kazakhstan topped the medal table, with thirty-two gold, twenty-one silver, and seventeen bronze; Japan, South Korea, and China were the other major medal winners. Ticket prices starting at $100 deterred me (and other Astana residents) from attending events, but they were on TV every night and in seemingly endless reruns through the summer. The only live event I saw was a sideshow in a cavernous exhibition hall where organizers were showing off traditional Kazakh culture to foreign visitors.

I missed the horsemanship exhibition, in which cowboys raced around a small circus ring, performing daring acrobatics. What I did see were three traditional yurts, probably better appointed and furnished than your average out-on-the-steppe variety, and nice handicrafts (leather goods, ornaments, and carpets). The attempt to re-create the landscape was not as authentic, as I discovered when I leaned on a styrofoam rock and almost pushed over a small mountain. I drank *shubat* (camel's milk) and ate traditional snacks (salty or sweet, designed to give that extra burst of energy when you're rounding up the herd). And I listened to powerful singing from traditional musicians on a stage with a psychedelic light show going on behind. "What's she singing about?" I asked Diana, who had gamely accompanied me. "I've no idea. It's in Yakut [a Siberian language]," she said. Fortunately, the next performer sang in Kazakh. "What's she singing about?" I asked again. "Oh, about how to deal with life," said Diana, not very helpfully. "How much do you know about traditional Kazakh culture?" I asked her later. "Not much," she admitted. "I'm a city girl."

My Favorite City

It's time to take a virtual tour of the Astana that Nazarbayev, the government, and the business community would like the world to see. It is the modern business-friendly city where multinational companies have their headquarters, a center for higher education, technology, scientific research and innovation, a cultural hub with galleries and museums, and the host city for international conferences, sporting events, and festivals. As the posters proclaim, Astana is *Moy lubimyi gorod* (my beloved city). The posters look incongruous in other cities, which are presumably well enough liked by their own residents. But they are everywhere—on bus shelters in Karaganda, street kiosks in Semey, the megamall outside Almaty. Even if you haven't visited Astana, it must be your beloved city.

The image on the poster is of Bayterek, the monument and observation tower in the square opposite the Ministry of Foreign Affairs.

FIGURE 8.1 Bayterek monument, Astana (photo by Natalie Koch)

Bayterek represents a poplar tree holding a golden egg, a central symbol in Turkic mythology—the tree of life. Samruk, the magical bird of happiness, is said to have laid its egg in the branches of a poplar tree. Not coincidentally, Samruk is also the name given to Kazakhstan's sovereign wealth corporation which owns the government oil, gas, and mining companies, the railroad system, postal services, the national airline, and financial groups. In Astana, Samruk literally laid a golden egg. The *Economist* describes Bayterek, rather unkindly, as "a study in Asian authoritarian kitsch."[11]

It's definitely *not* kitsch to the thousands of domestic and foreign tourists who visit it every year. The observation deck is 97 meters (318 feet) above ground level, corresponding to 1997, the year Astana became the capital. One level offers 360-degree views of Astana and beyond, with a three-dimensional model of how the city will look in the future. The second and higher level features a wooden sculpture of a globe and a gilded print of Nazarbayev's right hand. Bayterek has an almost shrine-like quality. It is easy to see that, after Nazarbayev's death, it will likely become a place of pilgrimage, where citizens, cursing the latest set of scoundrels ruling the country, will solemnly place a hand in that of the Great Leader and ask him to return from the grave to restore national pride.

There is an echo of Karakorum at the pyramid-like Palace of Peace and Accord. Just as the Great Khan staged a debate at court among adherents of Islam, Christianity, and Buddhism, modern Kazakhstan sees itself as the cultural crossroads of Eurasia, where peoples, traditions, and religions meet. The palace was constructed (with an eye-popping price tag of $58 million) to host the triennial Congress of Leaders of World and Traditional Religions. Because of the extreme temperatures, engineers designed the steel frame to withstand expansion and contraction of up to 30 centimeters.

The pyramid is one of two signature designs in Astana by the British architect Sir Norman Foster. Although the idea of a pyramid originally came from a Kazakh architect, Western observers were quick to attribute it to the president. Writing in the *Sunday Times* in 2005, Hugh Pearman, editor of the Royal Institute of British Architects' monthly journal, was scathing: "Nothing [Foster] has done to date compares with

FIGURE 8.2 Palace of Peace and Accord, Astana (photo by Natalie Koch)

this latest job. Because nobody asks for buildings like this. Unless you happen to be President Nursultan Nazarbayev of Kazakhstan." Interviewed after it was opened, Pearman had not changed his view: "It's an unbelievable folly, in the sense that it's a grand monument by one man to himself."[12]

The central theme of media coverage, writes Koch, is that "the Pyramid, and indeed the whole Astana project, is a one-man show."[13] Nazarbayev is portrayed as a megalomaniac, an authoritarian ruler bent on adding his architectural imprint to his political and social control. The Pyramid, according to Michael Steen, "juts out into the barren plain" behind the president's palace, the Ak Orda. "Sounds odd? Astana, a Brasilia of the steppe, is like that."[14]

What is odder, Koch adds, is not the design of the Palace of Peace and Accord but the fact that it exists in a country where restrictions on religious freedom have been increasing. Although Kazakhstan portrays itself as a secular Muslim country and freedom of religion is protected by the constitution, proselytizing and missionary work are forbidden and so-called fringe groups—from fundamentalist Muslims to Jehovah's Witnesses and Hare Krishna—have complained of harassment, including police raids on places of worship. The government increased surveillance of Muslim sects and banned prayer rooms in public buildings after suicide bombings in the western oil cities of Aktobe and Atyrau. In 2011, a new law set stringent new criteria for the registration of religious denominations and faith-based civic associations, raising minimum membership thresholds, requiring official review of religious literature, and tightening guidelines for clergy training. In a year, the number of officially recognized faiths dropped from forty-six to seventeen. The Western media, writes Koch, have failed "to scrutinize the issue of religious intolerance—instead concentrating on the eccentricity of the Pyramid project."[15]

The left bank is bisected by a broad pedestrian mall. At one end, on the bank of the Ishim River, close to the Pyramid, is the presidential palace—the Ak Orda (White House), its blue-and-gold dome topped with a golden spire. There's more gold inside in the majestic halls used for state and ceremonial events, including the pessimistically named Hall of Extended Negotiations. Twenty-one types of marble were used for the floor patterns. According to the palace website, "Metaphorically, it reflects a steppe civilization in the mirror of the European culture, a

FIGURE 8.3 Ak Orda presidential palace, Astana (photo by Natalie Koch)

synthesis of arts of the planet's largest continent—Eurasia." I have no idea what that means, but it's typical of the lyrical descriptions of most of Astana's new buildings.

The Nur Astana mosque is the largest in Central Asia, with room for five thousand worshippers inside and another two thousand outside (presumably only in summer). The glass, concrete and granite structure is 40 meters (131 feet) high, symbolizing the age of the Prophet Muhammad when he received the revelations; the minarets are 63 meters (207 feet) high, the age of Muhammad when he died. Unlike other left-bank buildings, the government did not pay for construction. The mosque was a gift from the Emir of Qatar.

At the other end of the mall is a monument to consumerism. Foster's other major architectural contribution, Khan Shatyr, has been described as "the largest tent in the world." To compare it to something you can buy from an upscale outfitter or even to a large marquee is a gross understatement. The needle-tipped structure, 500 feet tall and with a floor area the size of ten football stadiums, is designed to evoke the traditional nomadic dwelling, the yurt. It leans sideways, as if blown by the wind from the steppe. Khan Shatyr is constructed from three translucent layers of a fabric called

FIGURE 8.4 Nur Astana Mosque, Astana (photo by Natalie Koch)

FIGURE 8.5 Khan Shatyr, Astana (photo by Natalie Koch)

ethylene tetrafluoroethylene suspended on a network of cables strung from a central spire. The transparent material allows sunlight through, which, in conjunction with air heating and cooling systems, is designed to maintain an internal temperature of 15–30 Celsius (59–86 Fahrenheit) in the main space and 19–24 Celsius (66–75 Fahrenheit) in the retail units.

Khan Shatyr roughly translates as the tent of the khan, or king, but it's all about business and entertainment, not politics. Koch admits that in this case, the "utopian or theme-park theme is unavoidable."[16] Underneath the tent is a huge shopping mall with squares and cobbled streets, movie theaters, a botanical garden, boating river, mini-golf, roller coaster, water park, and indoor beach resort, with sand, palm trees, and tropical plants shipped in from the Maldives. If Dubai can have its indoor ski slope, then Astana deserves its tropical beach.

Our left-bank tour is almost done. We've covered politics (Ak Orda), religion (Palace of Peace and Accord and Nur Astana Mosque), and commerce (Khan Shatyr). What's left, apart from government buildings, exhibition halls, museums, malls, and high-rise apartment blocks? Education—and the showpiece is the new Nazarbayev University.

University Dreamland

Most universities in Central Asia I've visited since the mid-1990s are in some state of disrepair—from the curriculum and academic management to the facilities and classrooms. On the outside at least, universities in Astana look in better shape. ENU has new, well-maintained academic buildings. Visitors to the glavni corpus enter through a huge foyer, leading to a museum on the history of Turkic languages and a large auditorium used for political rallies and public events.

ENU is ostentatious, but Nazarbayev University, the president's pet project, is almost surreal. I'd read about the heavy investment in construction and the contracts with leading universities in the United States, the UK, and Asia, but nothing prepared me for the view from the entrance portico. A long, wide mall, with fountains, palm trees, and carefully manicured shrubs, all enclosed under a huge atrium (palm trees don't do too well in an Astana winter). Lining the atrium are five-story blocks, each reserved for one of the international partners. When Koch showed pictures of the university's interior to focus groups in Almaty, most participants thought it was a shopping mall.

Why is Kazakhstan spending millions on Nazarbayev University when facilities and conditions at other universities are lacking, when teachers have to take two or three jobs to make ends meet, when there's no paper for the printer in the dean's office and sometimes no chalk for the chalkboard? It's about creating world-class education, of course, to provide the workforce for business and government. But it's also about Kazakhstan's image on the world stage.

Location is everything, and Nazarbayev University is the first complex you pass when you drive in on the airport road. I approached the university from the other direction on the Number 10 bus. Workers were planting flats of flowers in the newly cultivated beds. Vehicles rolled up for the start of the workday—Mercedes, BMWs, and SUVs, disgorging well-dressed administrators. A luxury bus arrived with what I assumed (by their more casual dress, balding heads, and laptops) were foreign faculty, bused in from the prestigious Highville apartment complex in the new city.

Will the investment succeed? Of course it will. The university has the president's name on it, so anything short of success is unthinkable. To help fund the project, money was diverted from what many in higher education agree had been one of Kazakhstan's success stories—the Boloshak program, which provided scholarships for outstanding students to do their undergraduate education abroad, mostly in the United States and Europe. Now there are no more undergraduate scholarships; only PhDs will be funded, and there won't be many.

How well Nazarbayev University creates the "international education on the steppe" experience remains to be seen. Although instruction is in English, most students are from Kazakhstan so they are not exposed to students from other countries and cultures. And the moment they leave the classroom and get on the bus back into the city they'll be speaking Kazakh and Russian again. Graduates will certainly have a competitive edge in the job market, but creating an elite group at the expense of improving general standards in higher education leaves other talented students, especially in the regions, at a disadvantage.

Welcome to the Eurasian Education Space

"Those are English words—but this is not English." The phrase, which I dutifully attribute to Stephanie, seemed apt when I opened a book presented to me by ENU on my first visit in September 2010. It was a hefty tome titled *Nursultan Nazarbayev and the Eurasian Education Space*, published to mark the country's advances and investments in higher education in the post-Soviet era and a higher education conference at ENU.

The introduction claims that Kazakhstan's trilingual policy in higher education (teaching in Kazakh, Russian, and English) has helped the country advance economically and promoted peace. There's some truth to that. However, if this book is any guide, the English part of trilingualism has still some way to go. Let's start with the title. Russian speakers often translate *prostranstvo* as space, but in this context it sounds silly; "sphere" is better. Not as silly, however, as the captions to the photos, most of which featured conference speakers, signing ceremonies, and group shots of participants. There are the "orderly rows of professors of natural sciences faculty," some of whom look as if they are quietly snoozing. A picture of four unidentified delegates is bizarrely captioned "In the cycle of supporters of the Eurasian integration." The group shot of university rectors is modestly titled "The memorable photograph." Then there's "The Eurasian vector of intercultural dialogue" (the ENU rector with delegates in national dress at the Palace of Peace and Accord). I don't know about the after-conference parties, but the daily activities apparently got pretty lively. A picture of a mildly enthusiastic standing ovation is titled "The wild audience applauds." And then there are "the wild discussions behind the scenes of the forum." I can imagine the conversation. "You know, Erlan, I'm just crazy about this Eurasian integration idea." "Me too. Another cup of tea?"

Of course, it's all too easy to poke fun. This was a significant conference, and the participants discussed serious issues. But if you're going to avoid the Borat make-benefit-glorious-nation-of-Kazakhstan tag and present the country (and university) as players on the world stage, the least you can do is hire a good English copy editor. This was a costly publication, with high-quality printing and glossy color photos, but the budget apparently did not include a close review of the text, which was probably translated word for word, the editor sometimes opting for the second or third dictionary meaning.

Unfortunately, literal translations are all too common in official communications. Irina, who has excellent English, told me that she once offered to correct the numerous errors in a coffee-table history book produced in her home city of Karaganda. Her offer was refused. The book, she was told, was translated by a "leading professor of English language and literature." Who was she to think she could improve the text?

Looking for Students

The student took the mobile phone call five minutes into my two-hour Saturday morning class at ENU on media and business. "That was the dean's office," she said. "We all have to go now. We're very sorry." I looked at my notes and the group exercise my interpreter had translated into Russian. "What is it this time?" I asked wearily. "We don't know. Maybe a forum or a rally to show support for our president. Can we go?" I shrugged. "Of course. Hope to see you next Saturday."

Halfway through the semester at ENU, I had learned to adjust to an unpredictable schedule. Sometimes the students were there. Sometimes they weren't. Occasionally, I knew why, but most of the time I had no idea what had happened to them. There were forums, conferences, university events, student talent shows, the March Nauruz celebration, and, in the weeks leading up to Kazakhstan's presidential election in April 2011, rallies in support of Nazarbayev. I felt sorry for the students. Some felt sorry for me. "You've come so far to teach us," they said.

Room assignments were switched without notice. Often Diana and I spent the first ten minutes of class searching for our student group. Every session was interrupted by students opening the door, in search of their own classes. At least we weren't the only ones who felt lost. Some days began with a frantic search for classroom keys.

Security makes sense only if there's something worth stealing, but the only movable objects in the classrooms were the heavy wooden desks. Anyone trying to carry one out would not have gotten far. A uniformed guard sat at the only entrance to the building. Occasionally he checked IDs, but most of the time he smiled and chatted with the students. It's another Soviet hangover. You need to have a building guard, even if there's nothing worth stealing.

The contrast between what I was trying to teach my students and their daily educational reality was palpable. I told them that knowledge gained through rote learning and repeated on tests and in oral examinations was not as important as the ability to think, analyze, and weigh evidence. My classes encouraged them to think, question data, challenge official sources of information. Yet when they left the classroom to attend a political rally, they became passive observers of changes in their country.

Passivity can make you sleepy, and apparently a few dozed off during speeches about Kazakhstan's Industrial-Innovative Plan for 2020 or the customs union with Russia and Belarus. I asked one student who sat for six hours in an auditorium what he remembered. He shook his head. "We were just bodies there—our minds were somewhere else," he said.

Can You Teach Russian Stylistics?

The faculty had a class schedule, of sorts, but apparently I wasn't a good fit for it. Although I had agreed on the classes I would teach with Dean Omashev at our meeting in September 2010, apparently he had forgotten to inform his staff, and my arrival took them by surprise. None of the classes were on the schedule. The assistant dean said the schedule had already been signed by the rector, and no changes were possible. I would have to teach classes already listed, substituting for other teachers.

We decided that my "Politics and Media" class was close enough to a political science class. My proposed class on reporting on business, environment, health, and education did not come close to anything on the schedule. Perhaps I could teach Russian style and stylistics? It seemed a surreal question, considering that I was working through an interpreter and planned to take Russian classes. Well, how about children's literature? We went through other approved classes before deciding that I would teach the reporting class, and they would call it children's literature. A teacher was sent to round up students. I introduced myself and asked the students if they had any questions. "What's this class about?" one asked.

My schedule was revised a month later after we discovered why more than half the students were not showing up for two of the three weekly sessions. It turned out that the dean's office had combined two groups, and one was already scheduled for a different class at two of the meeting times. We reduced this class to a single one-hour weekly session and I was given additional teaching—a first-year group for one hour a week, a second-year group for one hour a week, and another second-year group for two hours on Saturdays. I had no idea what the students were doing in the other sessions. I resigned myself to giving a series of guest classes, hoping the students learned something.

They probably did (or at least that's what they told me). However, my experience points to structural problems in a higher education system that still has to shake off its Soviet past.

The first is the group system. Students entering a university take most courses with the same group of fellow students throughout their college career. The system has benefits, especially for students who are struggling. There's always someone to help you outside class, or take notes if you miss a session. But it also encourages academic dishonesty, with students routinely signing attendance sheets for missing group members, and sometimes submitting assignments in their names. More worryingly, students who spend every day with the same group of peers are not exposed to the perspectives of other students.

The second is the rigid curriculum. Soviet-style central planning is still the norm, with ministries of education dictating curricula. Although elective courses are being introduced, most universities have little flexibility in adapting to the job market or to student interests.

The third is the teaching itself. Teachers who have earned graduate degrees in Europe or North America often adopt an informal, interactive style, building projects and discussion into class. But those who have spent their lives in the system teach the way they were taught—from behind the lectern. The teacher is the authority. Student questions are not welcome.

The fourth is assessment. At most universities, achievement is still largely measured by hours spent in the classroom or in so-called practical work (most of it unsupervised), not by learning outcomes or competencies. There is little or no time for outside work—reading, papers, projects, the independent research and critical thinking that are viewed as critical in Western education. Teachers are paid by the class hour, not by the course, so they have no incentive to reduce the number of hours they teach.

The fifth is financial. Most investments in higher education have been in new buildings and equipment. Pay rates for teachers have not significantly increased, and many work at two or three universities (or have part-time jobs outside teaching) to survive. Talented teachers have left for jobs in business, government, or international organizations. University teaching is still a prestige profession, but quality in some disciplines has declined.

Poor teacher pay contributes to the sixth problem—corruption. Despite high-profile attempts to root out the problem, bribery is common.

Prices range from several thousand dollars for admission to a top university (without even taking the entrance examination) to a few dollars for a pass on a course test. Students admit paying bribes; teachers admit soliciting them.

None of my ENU students offered me a bribe. Not because they knew I was earning six or eight times what their teachers were being paid. Or because they thought I had higher standards. They simply had no reason to try to bribe me because I was not allowed to assess their work. Despite the random teaching schedule, I gave a few tests and assignments. I was told they could not be included in the assessment. "The dean is afraid you'll fail some students and they'll complain," a colleague told me. "Just forget about it."

It's difficult to blame ENU, the journalism faculty, or the Soviet legacy for all my challenges. And maybe I could have pushed harder to make a difference. But there's one more culprit—a US embassy more interested in maintaining relations with a politically powerful university than in improving journalism education. "You're causing a lot of trouble," the embassy cultural affairs officer scolded me. "We need to maintain a good relationship with ENU."

I wanted to remind her that I was an academic, not an agent of US foreign policy, but I resisted. Instead, I said it would have helped if the embassy had explained the purpose of my six-month teaching fellowship to the ENU administration. "Well, I really don't know much about higher education," she replied. I could admire her honesty, but it did not bode well for US support of higher education in Central Asia.

nine

Coal and Steel

High Plains Country

Half an hour out of Astana by train heading southeast, the urban sprawl—factories, warehouses, shopping malls, apartment blocks, and residential subdivisions—peters out and the landscape opens out to the steppe. This is Kazakhstan's High Plains country—eastern Montana, Wyoming, or the Dakotas, but even more thinly populated. The grassland stretches as far as the eye can see.

When we think of the steppe, we usually think flat. But the Kazakh steppe is not flat, at least not in the way that the glaciated agricultural regions of Illinois, Indiana, and my adopted state of Ohio are flat. The steppe gently undulates, and in places is broken by low hills. Most is grazing country; the climate is too arid, the soil too thin and poor in most places to support crops. It is almost treeless, except for the scrubby bushes clinging to life on the banks of streams.

The villages also seem to cling to life along the railroad tracks, although the train passes by without stopping. Herding families live in small, single-story stone and brick houses, the whitewash and paint weathered by the summer sun and winter snows. The houses have dirt yards, animal sheds, hay piled on the roofs for winter feed, and small vegetable gardens. It's a world away from the high-rise architecture of Astana.

The train's final destination was Zhezkazgan in central Kazakhstan, a twenty-four-hour trip from Astana. Ten minutes after departure, the two attendants in my car were distributing sheets, pillows, and blankets to passengers. On this Soviet-era train, there were no sleeping compartments—just sections with lower and upper seats for beds, with mattresses. An hour into the trip, some passengers were already asleep. Others were eating. You don't go on a train journey in Kazakhstan, especially in winter, without bringing food because many trains don't have a restaurant car. It's customary to share food with fellow passengers. Hot water for tea and soup comes from a cistern heated by a coal stove.

The young couple sitting opposite offered me bread, sausage, and cookies. They both worked in Astana and were on their way to a village near Lake Balkash to visit relatives. We talked about travel. Train journeys across Kazakhstan can take as much as three or four days, and I asked them how they survived long trips. The question surprised them. Most people in Kazakhstan traveled by train, they said. "You are from the United States, another large country. Don't people travel by train there?"

I didn't need the bedding because I was getting off at Karaganda, 150 miles from the capital and almost four hours on the train. It's faster by bus or marshrutka, but some people prefer train travel in winter because icy conditions or snowdrifts make driving dangerous.

Half an hour from Karaganda, the landscape changed again. Lines of freight cars in railroad sidings. Trucks waiting at railroad crossings. Half-demolished factory buildings and warehouses with broken windows, rusty metal pipes, and abandoned heavy machinery. The air was cloudy with smoke from factories and coal-fired power plants. The land was dotted with artificial hills—coal tipples, partly covered by the snow. In the distance, mine elevator towers with conveyor belts extended like tentacles to the railroad tracks and service roads. The train stopped briefly at a way station, and attendants filled buckets with coal for the furnaces heating the cars and the hot water stoves. We were in coal country.

The Russians call it Karaganda, the Kazakhs Qaragandhy. However you spell it, no one—not even the most enthusiastic local booster—would claim that this blue-collar city of almost half a million in the northern industrial belt is a tourist destination. It has the economic base of an Akron or an Allentown, but without an inspiring industrial history of individual enterprise or collective struggle. The first edition of *The Lonely Planet Guide* uncharitably described the city, halfway between Moscow and Beijing, as "a bleak place on the steppe surrounded by iron and steel works and microregions of apartment blocks, and beset by the typical problems of a post-Soviet industrial city. No one comes here who doesn't have to."[1] Its reputation as a remote, inhospitable, and polluted place, honeycombed with mine tunnels, surrounded by coal tipples and inhabited by convict labor, made it the punch line in Soviet jokes. In the prepositional case, *ver Karaganday* (in Karaganda) rhymes with a different Russian word and the final syllable with the word for where (*gde*). Depending on the context, it can mean "in the middle of nowhere," "in a bad place," or something much too rude to print here.

Coal mining began in 1857 to supply a copper smelter, but the industry remained small until the late 1920s when the bituminous coal reserves of the Karaganda basin were developed to supply industrial plants in the Urals. Mine labor initially came from the kulaks, peasant landowners who had resisted the forced collectivization of agriculture. Dispossessed and disenfranchised, they were sent to the northern forests or industrial areas of Central Asia. The first wave of prisoners arrived in Karaganda in 1930–31. Many more from all over the Soviet Union were to follow. The city became the center of a vast penal colony, much of it directly controlled by the NKVD secret police (officially the People's Commissariat for Internal Affairs) in Moscow.

In its early years, Karaganda consisted of several dozen mining settlements, scattered over an area of about 300 square miles. Soviet planners wanted to build an administrative and cultural center, with wide streets, parks, and monumental public buildings, but it was too risky to start construction over mine tunnels. No apparatchik wanted to report to Moscow that the local Communist Party headquarters had suddenly disappeared into a big hole in the ground. A site south of the mining area was selected for the "New Town" with construction beginning in 1934.

The city expanded during World War II when the Soviets moved factories, machinery, and workers east to prevent them from being captured by the Germans. Karaganda's prizes included the giant Parkhomenko coal-mining machinery works from the Donets basin of Ukraine. New iron and steel works supplied munitions for the front. Cement plants and food-processing industries were established. Kazakhstan has the largest coal reserves in Central Asia. In the late 1980s, it was supplying 25 percent of the Soviet Union's coal and generating 27 percent of its electricity from coal-fired power stations. Kazakhstan's growing economy has increased demand for electricity, and new coal-fired power plants have opened or are under construction.

Although many of the public symbols of Soviet ideology have been quietly removed since independence, those to mining and miners have been preserved. The Miners Palace of Culture is a major landmark in Karaganda's "New Town." The Russian word for mine is *shakhta*, and it's the root of the name of several districts—Shakhtan, Shakhtinsk and Shakhtersky—a homage to industry rivaled only by the less picturesque name of the Tsemzavod (cement factory) district. Fans of the city's Premier League football team, Shaktyor Karaganda (the Karaganda Coalminers), are as loyal as any from Manchester or Glasgow. The coal miner is still a symbolic worker-hero. A billboard on the highway to Astana proclaims, "All honor and glory to coal miners." Another shows a miner peering into a misty (and noticeably unpolluted) future, with the slogan "From the energy dream—to the energy reality."

Like all industrial cities, Karaganda has its seamy side. When the economy tanked after independence, industrial cities were hit hardest. Factories and mines closed, throwing thousands in Karaganda out of work, with little prospect of new jobs. Some left for Russia or Germany. Some who stayed turned to private enterprise, which, at least in the early to mid-1990s, was sometimes indistinguishable from organized crime.

As a major road and rail transshipment point, Karaganda was well placed to participate in the underground economy. If you were making money at that time in Central Asia, you were probably in the import-export business, bringing in truckloads of cheap Chinese clothes, electronics, and kitchenware, and better-quality goods from Europe. Your retail outlet was the bazaar or often literally the back of a truck parked at the bazaar.

In the mid-1990s, Karaganda's ethnic German population briefly opened a new branch of the Silk Road to Germany, using their contacts, relatives, and language skills. The big-ticket items were used autos purchased (or sometimes stolen) in Germany, driven more than 4,000 miles across several borders (with bribes to customs officials) and then resold on the used-car lots of Karaganda. No certificate of title required. At that time, most cars in Central Asian cities were Soviet-era Ladas, Moskviches, and Nivas. Most of the foreign-made cars were German—Audi, BMW, Mercedes. "Where did you buy your car?" I would ask a driver. More often than not, the answer was Karaganda.

Today, most business in Karaganda (including the auto business) is aboveboard, although the underground economy chugs along, petty corruption persists, and tax evasion is common. The same could be said of every city in Central Asia, so Karaganda is by regional standards a pretty normal place. But some locals take perverse pride in the city's criminal record, just as Boston, Chicago, and New York residents boast about the rough, tough neighborhoods where they were raised.

"Igor is from the ghetto," my interpreter Irina Velska told me with almost a straight face as she introduced her boyfriend. The word seemed out of place in Karaganda, an ethnically mixed city with no discernible residential segregation or ethnic enclaves. In Russian, the word has largely lost its ethnic associations and simply refers to an economically depressed, high-crime urban area. In Karaganda, the "ghetto" is Mikhailovka, a district of dreary, Soviet-era apartment blocks with a high incidence of street crime and drug use.

Igor nodded solemnly in agreement, informing me that Mikhailovka was well known in criminal circles in Moscow. Then his face broke into a broad smile. If I ever wanted to visit Mikhailovka, he would come along and provide protection. He knew the mean streets of the 'hood.

Igor is no street thug. He has a university degree and works as a graphic designer for a company producing magazines and brochures. But he's stocky in build and looks as if he'd be on the winning side in a street or bar brawl. I made a mental note to take him along if I ever needed to go to Mikhailovka.

Karaganda may never be able to shake off its reputation for crime and grime, but by 2009 Lonely Planet had revised its "bleak place" description. Karaganda was "a pleasant city, with avenues of trees and a large central park providing greenery, and the downtown revived with shopping malls, cafes and restaurants."[2] That's the Karaganda I know. I like the city partly because it's so different from Astana. In its made-for-government-and-business new city, Astana's modern architecture seems to serve only two purposes—to house government ministries and their staffs, and to impress foreign visitors. By contrast, the factories and mines of Karaganda produce stuff, even if they create dirt and smoke doing so. Karaganda is a working city. It has a reason to be.

TV Star of the Hostel Cafeteria

My first visit was in mid-March. Karaganda was still firmly in the grip of winter—deep snow, average temperatures minus 10 to minus 20 Celsius and a bitter wind blowing off the steppe. It may be a few degrees warmer than in January or February, but it doesn't feel that way.

I had come to teach at the journalism *kafedra* (department) of Karaganda State University (KarGU). My hosts had booked me a room at the *gostinitsa universiteta* (university hotel). It turned out not to be a hotel but the hostel where new students stay for a few days while they look for permanent housing. The building doubled as the student medical center (*sanatoria*), so at least it was clean, but it reminded me of the dreary *obsh'ezhitiyi* (dormitories) where most university students live. I had a small single room with a short bed, a chest of drawers, a rickety writing desk, and one electrical outlet that hung dangerously out of the wall. At least there was hot water in the shared bathroom. I stuffed a sock in the hole in the window frame to keep out the cold and slept in my long johns.

At least I didn't go hungry, because my hostel package included breakfast and lunch. Breakfast was always kasha and tea. It's a challenge to make porridge look appealing, but the cooks did their best with the aid of food coloring. Each day, the kasha was a different color, albeit within a limited chromatic range from beige to yellow. The taste did not change with the color, but it was satisfying and warming—the right stuff to prepare me to tramp through the snow to class. Most days, I returned for lunch, which was almost always mutton and noodles. It did not vary in color.

Foreign professors are a rare sight in the hostel cafeteria, and the cooks were friendly and curious. "I saw you on TV last night, Channel 5 News," one said, as she served me. I asked if she remembered what I said in the interview about journalism education. She said she didn't, but that I looked very nice on TV. I guess this supports media research studies that suggest it's the image that's recalled—not the content of the message. The next morning (after another TV interview), another cook said she had seen me on Channel 7. I figured it wasn't worth asking the same question again so I just made a joke about doing too many TV interviews and thanked her for the kasha.

The journalism department at KarGU has the third-largest enrollment in the country with about 120 students in a four-year program. The teachers were worried about a proposal from the Minister of Education to close all journalism departments at regional universities. Only KazNU in Almaty and ENU in Astana (where I was officially assigned) would offer journalism majors. It was presented as a fiscally responsible plan to avoid duplication of programs and reduce costs. Given the government's reputation for unnecessary spending, no one bought that line. The teachers saw it for what it was—a thinly disguised attempt to seize control of journalism education. In the view of some officials, the goal of journalism education should be to prepare students to work in government media and corporate public relations. The rectors of regional universities, most of whom are political appointees with lobbying clout, opposed the proposal, and most people I talked to thought it lacked the support to be implemented. Still, I got a round of applause from students and teachers when I said that centralizing journalism education would be a disaster—both for higher education and the profession.

Meiran Zhumabekov, the young chair of the department, invited me home for dinner. Meiran, his wife, and two young boys lived in a new apartment in a sprawling high-rise development, partly financed by government subsidies to keep prices affordable. Until they bought the apartment, they had lived with his mother and other relatives—eight people in an apartment with two bedrooms and a living room. Many other families in Central Asian cities live with relatives because of the housing shortage and the cost of rents and mortgages. Meiran apologized for the lack of furniture but explained that, even with two incomes and a subsidized mortgage, the family was struggling to make ends meet.

The meal was traditional Kazakh—besh barmak (boiled lamb and noodles) with salads. Meiran said the meat was from a freshly slaughtered sheep from his wife's village near Lake Balkash. We also enjoyed fresh, sweet butter made by her mother. As is customary, Meiran offered me vodka and cognac but did not seem offended when I limited myself to one glass.

QUESTION TO ARMENIAN RADIO: Is it true that conditions in our labor camps are excellent?

ANSWER: It is true. Five years ago a listener of ours raised the same question and was sent to one, reportedly to investigate the issue. He hasn't returned yet. We are told he liked it there.

Although the Soviet Union claimed to protect the rights and cultures of ethnic minorities, in practice the leadership feared ethnic and religious unrest. In the 1930s and during World War II, thousands from Karelia to the Caucasus were deported to labor camps (gulags) in Siberia and Kazakhstan. Collectively, the deportees were known as the Trudarmiya (Labor Army). The *zeks* (convicts) were forced to work in agriculture, factories, and mines.

The word *gulag* has come to signify isolation, back-breaking labor, and systematic physical and mental oppression, connotations that are largely absent in its original etymological form. The Soviets had the habit of using long, pretentious (and sometime innocuous-sounding) bureaucratic phrases for state institutions. In ordinary speech, no one wanted to use the full phrase (even if they could remember it) so acronyms and compound words were developed. GULAG is short for Glavnoye Upravleniye Ispravitel'no-trudovykh Lagerey (Main Administration for Corrective Labor Camps). "Lager" was imported (in a minor historical irony) from the German, where it also means "camp." KARLAG, the collective name for the prison labor camps of the Karaganda region, has a similar etymology—the Karagandinskiy Ispravitel'no-trudovoy Lager' (Karaganda Corrective Labor Camp). It's not difficult to imagine how the term Karlag carried other, more sinister, overtones. In Russian, the verb *karat'* means "to punish." In Kazakh, *kara* simply means "black."

Volga Germans made up the largest ethnic group in the Karlag, and their descendants have documented the experiences of those who survived and died in written and oral testimonies. The Karlag system consisted of about seventy-five camps, some designated for specific groups or purposes. Intellectuals, scientists, and artists were sent to the Dolinka (little valley) camp, thirty miles from Karaganda. Ajir, thirty miles from Astana, was reserved for "The Wives of Traitors of the Motherland," housing women and children after their husbands were executed as "enemies of the people." The most notorious camp was Spassk, known as the Camp of Death because of its high execution rate and large population of sick prisoners.

The most famous zek, Aleksandr Solzhenitsyn, was arrested in 1945 while serving as an artillery captain for reportedly expressing skepticism about Stalin. After serving time in a Moscow prison, he was sent to Ekibastuz in northern Kazakhstan, where he worked eleven-hour days in subzero conditions as a bricklayer at the power station. Solzhenitsyn's novels, *One Day in the Life of Ivan Denisovich* and *The Gulag Archipelago,* provided the first graphic accounts of conditions in the camps for Western readers. Every day, the zeks were awakened at 5:00 a.m., pulled on their ragged, frozen uniforms, and stumbled out of their barracks to the mess hall to eat cold kasha. After the morning roll call, they filed silently to work, "half dead men strung along the ice in a grey line." The routine was unrelenting. "The days rolled by in the camp," wrote Solzhenitsyn, "but the years they never rolled by: they never moved by a second."[3]

No one knows for sure how many were sent to the Karlag, although some sources claim it was as many as 1.2 million. Prisoners were housed in rough barracks, surrounded by barbed-wire fences and watchtowers with armed guards. Food and water were strictly rationed. In crowded conditions, sickness and disease spread quickly, but perhaps the biggest killer was the climate. In 1943, the NKVD reported: "The death rate among prisoners has increased sharply in Karlag. . . . Having spent a work shift in the frost many are unable to warm up in the cold barracks . . . and die without receiving any medical help."[4]

At the Wiedergeburt center in Karaganda, I met eighty-six-year-old Maria Litke. She was fourteen when her family was deported by cattle car from the Donetsk region of Ukraine. "There were eighteen in our family, including the children, and about a dozen more people in the car," she told me. "The journey took almost a month. My grandfather killed and cooked a pig to feed the family, and we shared the meat with the others."

Maria's grandfather was a vet, so the family was sent to work on a kolkhoz near Semipalatinsk. After two years on the farm, at the age of sixteen, Maria was sent to the Kirova coal mine near Karaganda where she tended horses pulling the coal cars. Food was scarce, and when her ration card was stolen, she sneaked out of the camp to a village to trade firewood for food. She was caught, beaten, and placed in solitary confinement.

FIGURE 9.1 *Trudarmiya* survivor Maria Litke in Karaganda

Freedom for many of the zeks did not come until after Stalin's death in 1953. In 1952, prisoners at several camps rioted. A larger revolt in 1954, centered on the Samarka and Kengir camps, was brutally suppressed; the Soviet army was sent in with tanks, and more than seven hundred prisoners were killed. Realizing that unrest would continue, the government closed the camps a few months later, and the prisoners were released.

After she was freed, Maria married a miner and raised three children. Now a widow, she lives with her daughter in a small apartment in Karaganda. At one time, she thought of joining the exodus of ethnic Germans to Germany. "I have many relatives living there, and I speak good German," she said. "But when I was deported, I lost my passport and birth certificate. I applied for a new passport from Ukraine. I was told the archives had burned and no records were left, so I could not prove I was ethnic German. Now I'm too old to leave."

Maria's story is repeated a thousand times by other former zeks of other nationalities. In one sense, Maria was more fortunate than most because she lived to tell it. Over half a century after the end of the Karlag, Russian authorities still refuse to release some official records, perhaps because the descendants of the camp guards still live in Karaganda and surrounding communities.

Outside Karaganda, one former camp has been converted into a prison for modern criminals. In Dolinka, one row of abandoned barracks is now a waste dump, and others have been converted into homes. Scraps of metal and barbed wire litter the steppe. Many prisoners are buried in unmarked graves, and some local residents describe the surrounding steppe as "one big mass grave." One field is dotted with crosses, a place where hundreds of children, "the offspring of the enemies of the people," were buried. It is known as Mamochinko—or Mommy's—cemetery.

The Karlag, like the Nazi concentration camps, presents a historical and moral dilemma for a country trying to define its identity. Do you bulldoze the camps in an effort to erase memories of the darkest chapter in the history of the Soviet Union, and gloss over the deportations in the school textbooks? Or do you preserve the camps, build visitor centers, and offer tours to school groups with interpretive guides?

Kazakhstan is still struggling with this troubled past. May 31 is on the official calendar as the Day of Remembrance of the Victims of Soviet Oppression. On that day in 2011, government officials, representatives of political parties and NGOs, foreign diplomats, and the children and grandchildren of former Karlag prisoners attended a ceremony in Dolinka to mark the opening of a Museum for Commemoration of Victims of Political Oppression. The museum is housed in the camp's former processing center, its facade bearing a picture of hands clutching barbed wire. The exhibition rooms are lined with the photos and case files of zeks. One hall maps the systematic program of deportation of nationalities—the Poles, Koreans, Volga Germans, Crimean Tatars and Greeks, Chechens, Ingush, Balkars, Kalmyks, Karachays, Meskhetian Turks, and Armenians. Another display documents the famine of the 1930s, in which an estimated 1.5 million, a quarter of the Kazakh SSR's population, died. The disaster was precipitated by the forced collectivization of agriculture when herders slaughtered their livestock rather than hand them over to the state. They were pastoralists, not arable farmers; deprived of their herds and ancestral pastures, they struggled to survive on the kolkhozes.

The symbolism of a new museum fails to satisfy those who claim that the Nazarbayev government downplays the Soviet legacy for fear of jeopardizing relations with Russia—the most powerful military power in the region and Kazakhstan's largest trading partner. In the apartment blocks of Karaganda and in villages such as Dolinka, descendants of prisoners and their former guards are neighbors. The painful memories of the Karlag are rarely discussed, in public or private.

Space Junk

Just across from the Lenin statue on Karaganda's main drag, Bukhar Zhirov (formerly Sovietsky Prospekt), the EcoMuseum is housed on the first floor of a local government administration building. You have to know it's there because there's no sign on the street and only a small one on the door.

The museum features an eclectic mix of artifacts and interpretive exhibits from central and northeastern Kazakhstan, a region rich with environmental problems. There are exhibits on mining, manufacturing, pollution, water resources, and the environmental wasteland of the Semipalatinsk Polygon, where the Soviets conducted above- and below-ground nuclear tests for more than forty years. The museum is also in the ecotourism business, offering guided tours of central Kazakhstan's mountain and desert regions and Lake Balkhash, the largest lake in Central Asia, as well as the signature "Back in the USSR" tour, an 1,125-mile circuit that takes visitors back in time to Dolinka and the Karlag, the Polygon, and the village of Aksu, whose claim to fame is its alley of Soviet monuments with many busts and statues of Lenin.

The museum's flashiest exhibit is the space center, a mock-up of the Mir space station control room, with banks of monitors, flashing lights, control levers and dials, and a throbbing, techno soundtrack. On both sides of the space station, the museum floor looks like a junkyard with misshapen chunks of metal, some partly burned, with barely distinguishable Cyrillic markings. Most of the items were salvaged from the military base at Lake Balkash. When the Soviet Army left Kazakhstan, it abandoned tons of military hardware—trucks, artillery, mortars, ammunition, and communications equipment. Economic times were hard, and local people moved in to salvage and sell what they could. Most of the metal went for scrap, but some items ended up at the EcoMuseum.

Credit for the collection goes to Dmitry Kalmykov, the museum director and a trained scientist. As a child growing up in Ukraine, he loved to collect scrap metal and bring it home. "When I moved to Karaganda and discovered there was all this stuff from the military and the nuclear test site, it reawakened my childhood interest," he said. Dmitry started picking up metal debris during a 1992 scientific investigation at the Polygon nuclear test site and hasn't stopped.

The gems of the collection are parts of rockets launched from the Baikonur Cosmodrome, 550 miles away in the semidesert of southwestern Kazakhstan. For the Soviet Union, the remote location—far away from population centers and, presumably, the long lenses of US spy planes—was ideal for its military space program. Since the first human space mission in 1961, when the cosmonaut Yuri Gagarin's brief jaunt stunned the United States into kick-starting its own manned space program, Baikonur has been the launch site for all Soviet- and Russian-crewed space missions and for rockets carrying satellites.

After the Soviet Union collapsed, Russia's space program faced a problem—its launch site was in a foreign country. Although Russia claimed it should still control the cosmodrome, the military installations and forces guarding them, Kazakhstan insisted that Russia not only agree to joint control but start paying rent. In 1994, Kazakhstan agreed to lease the complex to Russia for about $120 million a year. The new spirit of cooperation was marked when the Kazakh Talgat Musabayev and the Russian Yuri Malenchenko blasted off together on a visit to the Mir space station.

The deal has turned out well for both countries. Baikonur is a commercial success—the preferred launch site for most countries and private companies that want to get stuff (mostly communication satellites) into space. More than 35,000 people work there. It's the no-frills discount store of space launch sites, easily beating the European and Asian competition for price. Most launches use the cheap and well-tested Proton rocket, the workhorse of the Soviet space program since its first launch in 1965. The Proton has gone through several model changes but remains one of the most successful heavy boosters in the history of space flight.

The people of central and northeastern Kazakhstan don't see much from Kazakhstan's $120-million-a-year rocket revenue. But they sometimes see the rockets, or parts of them, out on the steppe. Rockets are launched in a northeasterly direction, with the first stage burning off over an area that can range from six to sixty miles wide, depending on the size of the rocket and its payload. A large region of the steppe from Zhezkazgan in the south to Pavlodar in the north is within the ellipse of the rocket flight path.

What doesn't burn up in the atmosphere falls to earth, usually on the uninhabited steppe but sometimes near populated areas. In 1999, a rocket carrying a communications satellite blew up soon after lift-off, scattering debris and fuel over a wide area. A large section fell into the backyard of a house in a village near Karkaralinsk. "This is dangerous material," said Dmitry. "The nose of the first stage has an engine with rocket fuel. It's like a bomb, and the fuel is highly toxic."

Although there have been no reports of death or injuries, Dmitry worries about the authorities' lack of preparedness and emergency plans. He pulls out a map of the rocket ellipse. "The *akimat* [local government] doesn't have such a map. If you ask the authorities where the danger area is, they don't know. Maybe it's here, maybe it's there. We need to inform the people of the dangers. If you're informed, you're aware. Information is protection."

Dmitry says the rent paid by Russia is supposed to cover the cost of safety measures—equipment and training for emergency personnel, medical staff, and disposal teams, as well as safety precautions for the general population. In 2001, a parliamentary committee held hearings on safety at Baikonur, and issued a report with about thirty recommendations. These included low-cost technical fixes, such as installing radio beacons on rockets so that they can be more easily located on the steppe. If radio beacons had been used, says Dmitry, it would not have taken three days in 2006 to locate a rocket that spun out of control and crashed soon after lift-off, causing widespread ecological damage.

The next year, a Proton-M rocket carrying a Japanese TV satellite crashed in flames two minutes after lift-off. Talgat Musabayev, the Kazakh space agency chief who thirteen years earlier had blasted off on the joint mission with the Russian cosmonaut, said that almost 219 tons of rocket fuel "either fell to the ground, or burned up in the air. This is rather a lot of poisonous substance." In terms of diplomatic relations, it didn't help that Nazarbayev was visiting the region at the time. "This is absolutely outrageous," said Prime Minister Karim Masimov. "If the president's visit is taking place and a rocket is being launched, we must have the right to stop everything." Kazakhstan suspended launches and promised tougher rules. An official from the ecology ministry said there had been six accidents in ten years. "It just happens too often," he said.

Public statements have not been matched by action. A decade after the parliamentary commission issued its report, few recommendations have been implemented. In July 2103, an unmanned rocket carrying three navigation satellites veered off course shortly after lift-off and crashed in a ball of fire near the launch pad, spreading toxic fuel in the area. There were no casualties, but the estimated loss from the three satellites was $200 million.

Despite the dangers, rural residents have resourcefully recycled the space junk dropping from the sky. Rocket bodies have been turned into garages, animal sheds, and outhouses, metal panels used for fencing for livestock, and smaller sections sold for scrap. Dmitry showed me photos taken on tours of the steppe. Half a section of an aluminum rocket body makes a pretty good Quonset hut. There's an old Moskvich, parked in a garage built from mud bricks, with a rocket body for the roof. Part of a rocket body converted into a summer kitchen, with shelves stacked with canned goods and a cookstove.

I asked Dmitry which government agency was responsible for safety. "That's a prohibited question because nobody knows. The space agency says the space industry is responsible. The industry says the local akimat is responsible. The akimat says it's the Ministry for Emergency Situations. The ministry says it's responsible after an explosion or accident, but not before. In Kazakhstan, no one takes responsibility."

Iron Mountain

After my teaching stint at KarGU, I escaped from the hostel, the kasha, and the affable cooks to spend the weekend with Irina, Igor, and Irina's grandmother Tonya at the apartment they shared in Temirtau, a city of 180,000 nine miles northeast of Karaganda. In Kazakh, *temir* means iron and *tau* mountain. The mountain is actually no more than a hill, but the "Iron Mountain" city was built on steel.

Its origins were modest. In 1905, about forty families from the Samara region of southern Russia settled on the left bank of the Nura River. The Samarkandsky settlement remained small until the development of the Karaganda Basin coalfield in the 1930s when the first steel plant and a coal-fired power station were built on the left bank of the river. The plant, which recycled scrap metal in furnaces fueled by coal from the Karlag, was refitted to produce munitions in World War II. In 1945, the Samarkandsky settlement was granted city status and renamed Temirtau.

FIGURE 9.2 Temirtau, city of metallurgy

By the 1950s, the steel plant was out of date, and authorities undertook construction of a new plant on the other side of the river. It was to be one of the largest in the Soviet Union. In 1958, the call went out for workers and their families to come to the steppe to build the Karaganda Magnitka plant, its roads and railroads, and a modern city that would be the pride of the Kazakh SSR.

One young man who heeded the call was a herder's son from Chemolgan, a village in the foothills of the Zailiskiy Ala Too twenty-five miles east of Almaty. Nursultan Nazarbayev was born in 1940 and grew up on a kolkhoz helping with the farm chores. According to his Western biographer, Jonathan Aitken, young Nazarbayev was a serious student, excelling in math and science. His primary education was in Kazakh, but he quickly became fluent in Russian, the language of government and the Communist Party. He was an avid reader—the Kazakh literary greats such as Qunanbayev but also the Russian classics of Tolstoy, Chekhov, and Pushkin and Russian translations of European authors. Everyone (including Nazarbayev himself) expected him to go to university in Moscow to study chemistry. He had been inspired by radio broadcasts of Khrushchev's speeches on the need for scientific research to improve the productivity of agriculture.

Aitken writes that three factors changed Nazarbayev's career path. His parents, though illiterate, had supported him in his desire to gain an education. After a lifetime of work on the kolkhoz, they still lived in relative poverty, and their health was failing; Nazarbayev did not want to go off to Moscow for three or four years, leaving them to cope without his help. Second, conversations with a young Ukrainian geologist from a village family sparked his interest in metallurgy. The geologist described the process by which iron ore is melted in a blast furnace until it becomes molten metal, after which it is shaped into steel pipes, rails, and sheets. Finally, according to Aitken, Nazarbayev was inspired by a piece of Soviet propaganda pulp fiction, *How the Steel Was Forged,* in which the hero overcomes all kinds of physical and human obstacles to build a steel railroad through challenging terrain.

In 1958, Nazarbayev read the newspaper advertisement for workers for the Karaganda Magnitka plant. Members of the Komsomol (Young Communist League) were invited to enroll in training courses in metallurgy at the Temirtau Technical School to prepare for jobs in the steel works. They would join "a noble and proud profession." The job of a steelworker was one "for real men who will earn the highest wages."

In Aitken's broad narrative sweep, Nazarbayev's rise from poor herder's son to president becomes an ideologically and socially conscious Soviet version of the Horatio Alger myth. Nazarbayev is a loyal son, a hard-working, intellectually curious student, admired by his teachers, who gives up the opportunity to join the Moscow elite. Instead, out of devotion to communism and to care for his family, he takes a dangerous, physically demanding industrial job, and becomes an inspiration to his fellow workers. His dedication is rewarded when his leadership qualities are recognized, and he rises in the party hierarchy.

The settings are pure Soviet—the kolkhoz, the Komsomol meetings, the floor of the blast furnace, the May Day parades and party rallies, the meeting rooms and hallways of Communist Party headquarters—but the plot is universal. The moral is that anyone can overcome their humble beginnings and make their way in the world. Much of Nazarbayev's enduring popular appeal and political longevity rests on the fact that he did not come from wealth and privilege. It is the classic poor-boy-makes-good story.

Of course, it wasn't as simple as that. When Nazarbayev arrived in Temirtau in September 1958, construction of the plant had not yet begun. He found, according to Aitken, "a small town, surrounded by a vast construction site with cranes and tractors." His first job was as a laborer, mixing concrete to build the approach roads to the site. He then joined a group of three hundred young recruits sent to a technical institute in Ukraine for eighteen months to be trained in steelmaking.

Despite Soviet restrictions on media, Nazarbayev and his fellow students learned about the riots that swept through Temirtau in August 1959. Construction workers assembled to protest about working conditions, food shortages, contaminated drinking water, and inadequate winter clothing. When the management refused to negotiate, they looted the food shops. Soviet troops and police brutally suppressed the riots. Sixteen workers were shot and killed, twenty-seven wounded, and more than seventy arrested; twenty-eight police officers were wounded. Leonid Brezhnev, the future Soviet leader, flew in to show Moscow's support for the local authorities' repression.

The plant's first blast furnace went on line in July 1960 with hand-picked workers, including twenty-year-old Nazarbayev, on the first shift. Archival photos in the city's museum show Nazarbayev and coworkers, wearing broad, floppy felt hats to protect their heads and necks from sparks from the furnaces where temperatures reached over 2,000 degrees Celsius. Nazarbayev rose quickly in the steelworker hierarchy—from junior to senior blast furnace attendant, then from deputy to senior gas man. By the time he was twenty-one, he was earning 400 rubles a month and sending half of his paycheck home to his parents.

Nazarbayev had a strong work ethic. After an eight-hour shift, he took the bus to Karaganda to attend four hours of evening classes in metallurgy. On weekends, he organized social activities and enlisted fellow workers to join the subbotnik (Saturday activity), the Soviet equivalent of community service, planting trees on a desolate hilly area that had been designated for a park.

As production expanded, more workers were needed. Nazarbayev became a poster boy in a marketing campaign. *Kazakhstanskaya Pravda,* the official newspaper of the Kazakh SSR, published a picture of the smiling, handsome Nazarbayev dressed in the uniform of a blast furnace attendant, his wide-brimmed felt hat tilted backward at what Aitken calls "a slightly rakish angle." The photograph was reproduced in newspapers all over the Soviet Union with captions suggesting that Karaganda Magnitka was a great place to work.[5]

The workforce grew rapidly, from 2,000 in 1960 to 30,000 three years later. Local authorities struggled to provide housing for workers and their families, but by the end of the decade Temirtau had become a Soviet

industrial showplace, with boulevards, apartment blocks, schools, theaters, parks, a 15,000-seat sports stadium, and monuments to industrial
workers. Karaganda Magnitka's production from its seven coke ovens and
four blast furnaces accounted for 10 percent of the Kazakh SSR's GDP.

In many ways, Temirtau was similar to the American company
town (although the "company" was the state) but with better housing,
transportation, schools, medical care, and recreational facilities. In the
same decade, Americans were shocked by media reports showing the
desperate economic and social conditions of Appalachian communities,
and the scars left by a century of exploitation of the region's coal and
forests. President Lyndon B. Johnson's War on Poverty put Appalachia
on the political and media map, and brought funds, volunteers, and resources to the region to combat its generational poverty.

I wonder if some who lived in the coal camps would have exchanged
their wood-frame shacks for a heated apartment in Temirtau, a steady
paycheck, free education and medical care, parks and recreation facilities, even if it meant having to "live under communism."

Saving Temirtau

Steel brought Tonya (Antonietta) Golubsova, Irina's grandmother, to
Temirtau. She and her steelworker husband moved from a town near Moscow in the early 1960s, joining the stream of industrial workers who resettled in Temirtau. At the plant, her husband worked shifts with Nazarbayev.
Tonya thinks Nazarbayev's modest, working-class background helps account for his popularity. "He didn't come from a rich or well-connected
family," she said. "People feel that he understands their problems."

Nazarbayev was soon elected secretary of the Komsomol section,
representing young workers at the plant. He gained a reputation as an
orator, able to motivate fellow workers, and as an effective organizer.
He married Sara Kunukayeva, an electrical worker at the plant, became
a Communist Party member—the ticket to political advancement—and
in 1968 took a job as a local party official. Over the next thirty years, he
worked his way up through the Communist Party hierarchy, positioning
himself for the presidency in 1991.

Tonya says she admires Nazarbayev's personal achievements but
does not like policies that she feels discriminated against ethnic Russians
and Germans. Like other Russians, she resents Kazakhstan opening its

borders to all those who claimed Kazakh ethnicity—the oralmans—offering them apartments, jobs, and a relocation allowance. Tonya claimed this resulted in an influx of unskilled workers, especially from Mongolia and Uzbekistan, who did not have the same work ethic as the industrial workers who had left.

The collapse of the Soviet Union sealed the fate of many single-industry cities. Without investment to modernize equipment and a sales force to market products, factories closed their gates, throwing thousands out of work. Many feared that Temirtau would suffer the same fate. The steel plant went through tough times in the early 1990s, and many of its top managers and engineers left for Russia. City authorities struggled to cope with unemployment, crime and drug abuse, and to provide services for an aging population.

Temirtau was saved by the Indian billionaire steel magnate Lakshmi Mittal. In 1995, his London-based LMN Group purchased the plant for $250 million. With a $450 million loan from the European Bank for Reconstruction and Development and $250 million of its own money, the company modernized the plant. When workers from the coal mines in Karaganda threatened to cut off supplies because they had not been paid, the company bought the mines and put the miners on its payroll. After Temirtau's electricity generating plant failed sixteen times in 1996, interrupting steel production, it bought the plant and its distribution network, making the steel company the supplier of the city's heat and electricity. With new iron deposits being exploited in Karaganda and Kostanai provinces, new Asian markets, especially in China, and world prices for construction materials rising, the plant was expanded. In 1999, it turned its first profit.

The company, now renamed ArcelorMittal, employs almost 30,000 people in its steel plant and coal mines, almost as many as Karaganda Magnitka at the height of production. The company has put money back into the city. It renovated the aging water system, bought a textile factory to manufacture uniforms for workers, refurbished the run-down Steel Hotel, provides health services, subsidizes teachers' salaries, started a TV station, and made the trolley buses run on time. At the Mittal football stadium, the Mittal-sponsored Temirtau Steelworkers play local derbies against the Karaganda Coalminers. Temirtau is, to all intents and purposes, a company town again.

Despite large investments and an image-building campaign, local officials and environmental groups complain about the company's safety and environmental record. More than one hundred miners died in accidents at mines between 2004 and 2010. Temirtau is one of the most polluted cities in Kazakhstan. In 2010, the regional prosecutor's office fined Mittal for air pollution and poor documentation on the environmental effects of its operations. Still, the company refuses to disclose the results of its air and water quality tests or discuss its environmental record at public forums. Irina says that local residents have become used to pollution, and the company has worked to convince them that the environmental and health effects are minimal. On many days, a thick pall of smoke from the blast furnaces hangs over the city. "Sometimes the smoke is grey, sometimes yellow, sometimes pink," she said. "We have no idea what's in the air."

Steel is still the lifeblood of Temirtau. The historical signs and symbols are everywhere, from Soviet-era monuments of heroic steel-workers to the Metallurgists' Palace of Culture. Fittingly, the newest landmark, dwarfing the steelworkers' monument at the north end of the main drag, Prospekt Mettalurg, is a museum dedicated to Temirtau's most famous steelworker. Although other construction projects in Kazakhstan were delayed or abandoned after the global economic crisis, the museum opened in time to mark the twentieth anniversary of Kazakhstan's independence in December 2011 and twenty years of Nazarbayev's presidency.

Some local businessmen had proposed something even more striking—carving Nazarbayev's into the face of the iron mountain. "Mount Rushmore is a well-known national monument," the group's leader told the *akim* (governor) of Karaganda oblast. "Why can't our country pay a similar tribute to the first president of Kazakhstan?" The akimat promised to study the proposal, but did not sound too positive. "The president has never been in favor of such type of recognition," a spokesman said.[6]

Steel and Strawberries

Tonya isn't too interested in rock carvings, museums, or independence celebrations. Like many older residents, she impatiently awaits the first days of spring when she can escape from her apartment to her two-room dacha, nestled in the low hills on the right bank of the Nura River. Far away from the noise and pollution, she raises potatoes, carrots, cabbages, beans, cucumbers, peppers, tomatoes, apples, cherries, raspberries, gooseberries, and other fruits. She makes some money selling her produce. In the winter, the vegetables and canned fruit are kept in a root cellar under a garage near the apartment. She had given Stephanie tomato seeds from plants she has grown; on a return trip, I brought envelopes with seeds from three of Stephanie's favorite varieties.

Tonya's pride and joy are her strawberries. "I can pick strawberries from April to October," she claimed, as she showed me her carefully cultivated beds.

"Babushka, what are we going to do with all these strawberries?" asked Irina, as she stacked banki (jars—or, in this case, cut-off plastic water bottles) brimming with fruit on the porch. *"Prosto kushayte, kushayte* [just eat, eat]," said Tonya. On a sunny day in late June, we picked and ate, picked and ate, until night fell. Then we drove back to Temirtau, the trunk full of banki of strawberries. In the fall, Tonya will fill the refrigerator with jars of home-made strawberry jam, and Irina will ask, "Babushka, what are we going to do with all this jam?" And Tonya will probably answer, *"Prosto kushayte, kushayte."*

FIGURE 9.3
Tonya Golubsova at her dacha (photo by Irina Velska)

ten

No Polygon, No Problem

Open Steppe and Open Minds

By temperament and academic training, Magda Stawkowski does not rush to judgment. She's a medical anthropologist, schooled in the classics—Margaret Mead, Bronisław Malinowski. She knows first impressions of a place, a community, or a culture can be misleading, maybe even downright wrong.

Yet when she and Robert Kopack, a geographer, arrived in a remote village in northeastern Kazakhstan to study how people live near a former nuclear test site, they had the same initial reaction. Cattle, horses, sheep, and people move freely throughout the so-called Polygon region, where for forty years the Soviet Union conducted above- and below-ground nuclear tests. "Nothing is marked—you may be in a very radioactive area and not know it," said Magda.

"I thought there's no way people should be living there," said Robert. "They should get out—right now." The couple considered getting out themselves after they took Geiger counter readings in the house where they stayed for a few days after arriving. "It was scary," said Robert. "I said, 'We don't have to stay. There's a nuclear test site here.' But that view changed, oh my god, so fast."

When I met Magda in March 2011, she was working with Dmitry Kalmykov at Karaganda's EcoMuseum, plowing through a stack of data and reports for her dissertation at the University of Colorado. She spotted me, looking perplexed, in front of the museum exhibit on the Polygon. I don't have a science background, so understanding data on nuclear tests and radioactive levels is difficult enough in English; even with a dictionary, I had little chance with the Russian version. Magda gave me a quick primer on Russian nuclear terminology. Then we started talking about her experiences living in the village.

Two months later, on my next visit to Karaganda, I met her and Robert to learn about the journey they had taken from fear and doubt to the conviction that the people of the Polygon should be left to control their own lives.[1]

The region is significant to the history of the Kazakh people. The writer, poet, and educator Abay Qunanbayev, whose works are required reading in schools and whose statue stands in city and town squares all over the country, was born in a village in the region and traveled through it. Other famous artists, writers, and political leaders had their roots there. Some families have lived in the region for seven generations, and their ancestors are buried there.

"The people have a strong relationship to the land," said Robert, whose research project was to draw maps with overlapping layers showing indigenous names, radiation zones, and grazing areas. "People have been living here for 150 years and they talk about the landscape in specific ways. They have names for mountains, caves, and rivers, names that help them avoid getting lost, even in the winter. These names mean something—a name may signify a type of face, such as a wrinkled morning face."

Villagers told Magda and Robert that if they were relocated, they would lose their connection to the land, family, and community. Instead, they needed doctors, access to social services, better roads, and assistance in developing livestock raising.

"It's a beautiful place," said Magda. "It's not just the flat steppe. There are hills and valleys, lakes with wildlife. People feel free, and they live their own way without the laws that apply in the city. There are no police. The social fabric is the structure that holds the community together. Yes, life is tough, especially in winter. But the people are kings of their own domain; they're self-sufficient. Some people want to move them. I'd be the first to say that's a crazy idea. In the city, they're dead, they don't have the skills. Make their lives better where they are. It's a very simple thing."

For the authorities, deciding what to do with the vast nuclear test site and the people who live there is far from simple. If there was scientific consensus on the levels of radioactivity and the dangers to public health and the food chain, policy decisions could be made. But there is no consensus. Although everyone agrees a cleanup is needed, Kazakhstan's regulatory authority, the National Nuclear Center (NNC), claims that research by foreign scientists and environmental groups exaggerates the dangers. Although other test sites around the world have been closed off, the NNC wants to open almost all the Polygon to commercial mining and livestock grazing. And, as is too often the case in Kazakhstan, no one is sure which government agency is responsible for cleanup.

Forty Years of Nuclear Tests

On the map of Kazakhstan, the Polygon looks like a small area. But it's a question of scale. The 7,000-square-mile region, southwest of the city of Semipalatinsk, is almost as large as Israel, about half the size of the Netherlands or Taiwan. The site was selected in 1947 by Lavrentiy Beria, the political head of the Soviet atomic bomb project. He falsely claimed the region was uninhabited, although at the time about 3,000 people lived in villages and kolkhozes.

Labor from the Karlag was used to build the test facilities, including a laboratory complex on the southern bank of the Irtysh River, named for Igor Vasilyevich Kurchatov, the nuclear physicist who, along with Georgy Flyorov and Andrei Sakharov, directed the secret Soviet effort to develop nuclear weapons during World War II and headed the postwar program. The first successful bomb test, Operation First Lightning (nicknamed "Joe One" by the Americans in reference to Stalin), was conducted by Kurchatov's team in 1949, scattering grey radioactive dust on nearby villages which Beria had neglected to evacuate. The shock waves

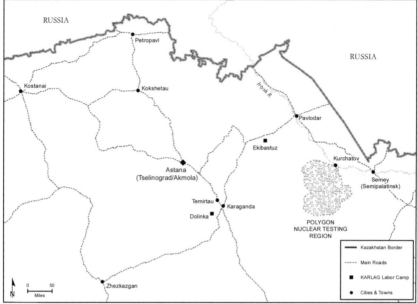

MAP 10.1 Northeastern Kazakhstan and Polygon (map by Brian Edward Balsley, GISP)

were felt as far away as Karaganda where coal miners working underground feared the tunnels and roofs would collapse.

The nuclear program included research on the effects of radiation on humans and animals. In later tests, groups of people of all ages were given cash and cases of vodka, dropped off at sites near ground zero, and picked up after the explosion. They were examined for the effects of radiation at a secret hospital in Semipalatinsk, and the results were sent to Moscow. Sheep, horses, and dogs were also tested.

Official figures claim that 161 tests were conducted from 1949 until 1963, when aboveground testing was banned, but the number could be higher because some controlled explosions were not classified as tests. Up to 1989, 295 devices were detonated in mountain tunnels, according to a 2010 study by Kazakhstan's Institute of Radiation Security and Ecology.

In Soviet times, the region was a restricted zone, guarded by 20,000 troops. Kurchatov (known only by its postal code, Semipalatinsk-16) was a closed city, one of the most secretive and restricted places in the Soviet Union. Villagers did not know that they were living near a test site. "People couldn't enter or leave—this place was not even on the map," said Magda.

Many died or suffered from radiation-induced diseases. According to government statistics, the number of stillbirths in the region rose from 6.1 per thousand in 1960 to 12.2 in 1988. Human birth defects were at least six and a half times the Soviet average, mental retardation and diseases of the nervous system two and a half times greater, and cancer rates significantly higher. In total, as many as half a million people may have suffered from the effects of radiation.

With the reforms of the perestroika era, the Communist Party's grip on politics and society began to loosen. In 1988, Gorbachev's government decided to allow the formation of informal political and social groups outside the party, which had previously sponsored all organizations. The most prominent environmental group to emerge was the Nevada-Semipalatinsk movement, founded by the writer Olzhas Suleimenov in 1989 to halt nuclear testing. More than a million people signed petitions demanding a test ban on Kazakhstan's territory, and huge crowds turned out at the group's rallies. Nazarbayev's support for the movement reinforced his political position and nationalist credentials as he prepared for the country's independence.

Although nuclear tests were halted in 1989, Kazakhstan was left with the fourth-largest nuclear arsenal in the world (after the United States, Russia, and Ukraine). More than one hundred missiles, each with ten nuclear warheads, were housed in deep bunkers across the steppe. There were fears in the West that the country would not be able to guard the missiles and the stockpile of weapons-grade uranium and plutonium, or—in a nightmare scenario—would sell them to the highest bidder. The CIA claimed Iranian intelligence agents were visiting nuclear installations throughout the former Soviet Union, shopping for deals.

Whether or not the CIA was right, Kazakhstan wanted to get rid of its nuclear stockpile. In August 1991, Nazarbayev signed a decree officially closing the Polygon and declared that Kazakhstan had no interest in remaining a nuclear state. The United States paid for the transfer of missiles to Russia to be dismantled, and compensated Kazakhstan for the weapons-grade uranium in the warheads. In 1994, a specialist US team embarked on a secret mission to the closed city of Ust-Kamenogorsk to recover half a ton of enriched uranium from a vault at the Ulba Metallurgical Plant, the largest lead-zinc smelter in the country. Over a six-week period, using a mobile nuclear laboratory, the team opened a thousand canisters of uranium, measured the contents, and transferred them to stainless steel containers, which were packed into special 55-gallon drums for shipment to the US nuclear facility at Oak Ridge, Tennessee. The elaborate and dangerous mission, code-named Operation Sapphire, signaled a new level of cooperation and trust between the United States and Kazakhstan.

You're in the Polygon, but You Wouldn't Know It

Although the tests, bombs, and missiles were gone, "nuclear-free" Kazakhstan faced the formidable task of dealing with the environmental legacy of forty years of nuclear tests—the equivalent of the explosion of twenty thousand Hiroshima bombs. In the 1990s, with the economy in tatters and the government strapped for cash, progress was slow. Although some tunnels were sealed and detectors installed on others to keep out scrap-metal scavengers, open areas of steppe remained largely unguarded. Barbed-wire fences rusted. Signs marking radioactive areas faded or were stolen. People swam and fished in water-filled nuclear craters.

"The Polygon has been fully open, ever since it was closed," said Magda. "It's astonishing how unprotected, how unmarked the site is. You don't know if you're in the test site or out of it." Villagers drive through the Polygon to the cities of Kurchatov, Semipalatinsk (now renamed Semey), Pavlodar, and Karaganda. Alternative routes outside the nuclear test zone add many hours to travel time. In summer, drivers stop on the dusty roads to change flat tires; in spring, they push their cars out of the mud.

In an attempt to show that the Polygon is safe, the government has invited foreign journalists and "disaster tourists" to visit Ground Zero. There haven't been many takers. Louise Gray of the *Telegraph*, who took the tour in August 2011, didn't find it reassuring:

> The point of detonation . . . is now a small lake in the heart of the steppe. With the quivering rushes and endless sky, it looks almost pretty. . . . But the Geiger counter is racing and so is my heart. My stomach is churning as radioactive dust rises, even though we are wearing gas masks and protective covers on our feet. The Soviets filled the area with apartments, bridges and roads, to resemble a town; now, all that is left are burnt lumps of concrete. . . . Our guides, dressed in camouflage gear and

disarmingly casual, pick up rocks of melted soil wearing just surgical gloves. The Geiger counter is reading three micro-sieverts per hour, which is considerably more than you might expect of natural background radiation. Yet the NNC tells us that, during our 10-minute visit, our group of seven received less radiation than on a transatlantic flight. Its director, Dr. Sergey Lukashenko, claims to have swum in an "atomic lake" created by another explosion.[2]

For local herders, convoys of off-road vehicles with tourists and jour-nalists are just the latest unwelcome visitors to their traditional grazing lands. They kick up the dust, make noise, and sometimes leave litter, but they never stay long. For those whose homes are on the steppe, life and work go on. "People simply accept that they are living near a nuclear test site, and get on with their lives," said Magda. "There's still a belief that a shot of vodka will protect you from radiation. If you drive through the Polygon, you take a bottle of vodka in the car."

With or without vodka, it's almost 250 miles from Karaganda to the village where Magda and Robert lived. On a good day, it's a six-hour journey; when the weather is bad, it can take up to fifteen hours. After two hundred miles on the main highway, a gravel road branches north-east into the Polygon. "It's an awful road," said Robert. "The whole car shakes. After almost every trip, we had to tighten down the screws." The couple say they changed at least thirty flat tires. "We used inner tubes so the tires wouldn't fall apart. We carried a spare but on one trip we had two flats. We just pumped up the tire and kept driving until we had to pump it up again."

The final seventeen miles is on a dirt track, euphemistically called a steppe road. There are few landmarks; as tracks intersect, it's easy to get lost. "You just have to go by memory," said Robert. "We got used to it—by the end we could drive at night."

The road is closed by snow from late December to late March, leaving the village isolated. Spring rains make driving hazardous. "On one trip in April, we got stuck in the mud," said Magda. "We ended up sleeping in the steppe. We did not walk at night because there are wolves in the region. In the morning, we walked to the village to find someone to pull the car out. It was April Fool's Day. You know they celebrate that in Kazakhstan?"

Magda didn't set out to do her dissertation on a village in the Polygon. When she first came to Kazakhstan in 2007, she was planning research on the Polish diaspora—descendants of Poles exiled by Stalin in the 1930s. She had a personal stake in the history. "My family is from Poland, and they were deported to Siberia in that period," she said.

As she traveled north from Astana to Polish villages, she heard a "passing comment" about the Polygon, and decided to investigate. The next year, she returned, rented a car, traveled through the region, and decided to change her research topic. "As a medical anthropologist, I study illness in its social and cultural contexts," she said. "How do people perceive illness? How do they heal themselves? How do they assess risk?"

She learned about the village from a 1999 study on the effects of radiation on health and the environment conducted by Karaganda State Medical University. The study compared the health of people in two villages with similar economic and social conditions—one six miles from the aboveground test site and one outside the nuclear zone. Through a chemical analysis of meat and milk products, bone, and animal and human waste, the team, led by Dr. Naila Dusembayeva, a geneticist, found that levels of five radioactive elements, including the highly toxic Caesium-137 and Strontium-90, were significantly higher in the village near the test site. Dusembayeva's team compiled family trees and health histories, recording stillbirths, infant mortality, and a range of physical and psychological diseases. Again, the rates for the village in the nuclear zone were significantly higher than for those in the other village.

"In villages in the Polygon, people are dying because of disease, not because of age," Dusembayeva told me. She says the herders' diet of meat and milk products is the main cause. Radioactive elements enter the food chain because animals graze on contaminated pastures. Few villagers grow vegetables "because they know the ground is not healthy."

"Some scientists argue that the people aren't hygienic enough, that they live in squalor," said Magda. "I say that's bullshit. Look at other villages in Kazakhstan. People live the same way, and they don't die as quickly."

In the Soviet era, the village had a population of about 400. It was part of a *sovkhoz* (state farm), with tractors, machinery, and warehouses, raising grain and livestock. It was a multinational community with

Kazakhs, Russians, Ukrainians, Volga Germans, Poles, and Tatars. Since 1991, the village has gone into a steady decline as people leave to seek jobs in the cities, and now has only about fifty inhabitants, almost all Kazakh. Many farm buildings are in disrepair, and organized agriculture has been replaced by pastoralism, with herds of cattle, sheep, and horses grazing freely on the unfenced steppe. Herders enjoy common grazing rights, and no land is privately owned. "You follow your animals," said Magda. "You don't enclose them—you take them to food."

The herding families rely on livestock for income, and meat prices in Kazakhstan have been rising. Sheep, cattle, and horses from the Polygon are slaughtered and sold on markets throughout northeastern Kazakhstan. The carcasses are inspected for animal diseases such as brucellosis, but not tested for radiation because the analysis is too expensive. According to Dusembayeva, the health risks of radiation have spread from those who raise livestock in the Polygon to urban residents. "There are no restrictions," she said. "No one tells the villagers where it's dangerous to graze animals. We have enough land in Kazakhstan that people should not have to use dirty ground."

Magda agrees with Dusembayeva that no area of the Polygon can be given a clean bill of health, but she questions whether the medical research told the whole story, particularly about personal health histories. "The health study was done by doctors, and they compiled data by handing out surveys. The survey had questions such as 'Do women smoke?' People answered 'No.' 'Do women drink?' 'No.' Women don't do anything. They are totally healthy. The reality is that if you're there long enough you realize that the surveys are completely meaningless."

As an anthropologist, Magda knew that the best way to understand how people in a nuclear test zone view their health was to live among them—to do interviews, collect medical histories, and observe how they lived and worked.

Telling No Lies

Villages in Kazakhstan are close-knit communities, where strangers are often regarded with suspicion. A colleague in Karaganda put Magda in contact with the akima (mayor) of the village, who agreed to make introductions. It wasn't easy. Why would two educated Westerners want to live there for four months?

"I explained what I could [about my research]," said Magda. "For about a month, everyone thought we were spies and didn't want to talk with us. You have to establish rapport and that takes time and willingness to participate and become part of the daily life of the village."

Magda and Robert moved into one half of a house with a stove and a few furnishings. Their closest neighbors were in the other half, and they often shared meals. They started to work. Robert did *chabaning* (herding) and helped slaughter animals. Magda cooked and helped neighbors with chores. They painted the house, chopped wood, and collected animal dung for fuel. In winter, animals are kept in barns beside houses, and fed with hay stacked on the roofs. "We put up huge stacks of hay," said Robert. "There was just a lot of physical labor."

In Soviet times, villagers in the Polygon were routinely submitted to medical tests to determine the effects of radiation. Results were sent to labs in Moscow, and the people tested were never told about their conditions. Overcoming suspicion about researchers is difficult. "They think people lie to them," said Magda. "They come in and take their blood without giving a reason, and they get no results. That's been a consistent pattern—they are used for someone else's needs. That was my biggest concern—not to exploit, even unknowingly, a population that is vulnerable. We didn't lie to them."

Magda and Robert had seen the data from the 1999 study about the radioactive elements in meat and dairy products, but decided that the health risk was outweighed by the issue of trust. "We ate the meat; we drank the milk," said Robert. "What are you going to do? Make these people feel as if there's something wrong with them? Not eat their food? Wear a mask around them?"

"People believe they are sick from radiation," said Magda, "but they accept it. Life is hard, anything can kill you—that's their attitude. They have accepted a very difficult life and they are survivors."

No Polygon, No Problem

US, Australian, and Canadian mining companies already operate in the region, exploiting reserves of gold, copper, manganese, and coal. In 2010, the director of Kazakhstan's National Nuclear Center (NNC), Kairat Kadyrzhanov, claimed that only 5 percent of the region was "heavily contaminated" and proposed a ten-year program to open up the rest to commercial agriculture, primarily livestock raising. "We will guarantee that it's possible to work there safely—to raise cattle and build houses," said Kadyrzhanov. "Some politicians are irritated with our suggestion to open part of the Polygon for agriculture. But we are talking like scientists, not like politicians."[3]

Environmental activists such as Kaisha Atakhanova think it's the other way around: the government scientists are talking (and acting) like politicians. A veteran of environmental politics, Atakhanova has seen it all before. In 2001, Kazatomprom, a state enterprise, introduced legislation to allow Kazakhstan to import and dispose of low- and medium-grade radioactive waste. Kazatomprom said it would be a major boost to an economy that was still struggling and forecast revenues of up to $40 billion over a twenty-five-year period. And where would the waste be dumped? At old uranium mines in western Kazakhstan or, in a cruel historical irony, in the Polygon, where new storage facilities could be created.

Supporters claimed that the revenue would be used to help Kazakhstan clean up its own nuclear waste. Atakhanova was not the only one to question how importing more nuclear waste would reduce levels of radioactive contamination. The *Economist* wryly noted that at the same time that Nazarbayev marked the tenth anniversary of the closure of the Polygon test site to appeal for more foreign aid to deal with cleanup and the long-term effects of radiation, a state enterprise was proposing turning the country into "a nuclear dustbin."[4]

Atakhanova led a coalition of more than sixty NGOs that lobbied parliament to defeat the legislation. They argued that a country rich in oil, gas, and other natural resources did not need revenue from radioactive waste imports. The scheme would damage Kazakhstan's international reputation and scare off tourists. Besides, because of government corruption, there was no guarantee how the revenue would be spent. The legislation was stopped, and the environmental network formed went on to campaign on other issues.

Atakhanova says the NNC wants to turn over the Polygon so that it is no longer legally liable for monitoring and cleanup. With land in private ownership, local authorities will be responsible, but they lack funds and expertise. "It's a pragmatic approach by the national government," she told me. "They tell the local authorities: it's your responsibility and it's your budget. No Polygon, no problem."

Gulsum Kakimzhanova, who heads an environmental NGO based in Semey, says reclassifying land as suitable for agriculture means that radiation-control regulations, including the removal of a layer of soil and the wearing of protective clothing, no longer apply. "Why will people follow regulations if they don't have to? They'll do whatever they want," she said. She doubts the NNC's claim that off-limits areas will be clearly marked. "What are you going to do?" she asked an NNC official at a meeting. "Give a cow a map so it can decide whether it can eat the grass or not?"

Atakhanova and Kakimzhanova dispute the NNC's claim that more land is needed for agriculture. Much of the land in the Polygon is of poor quality, and water is scarce. At community meetings in 2011, only a handful of farmers said they needed more grazing land. "We lost this land many years ago, and we don't need it now," one local official told them. Instead, villagers told them that they needed social and medical services, including special programs for radiation victims, better schools, and economic opportunities, including microcredit to develop small businesses. Local authorities have proposed moving people from villages to regional centers, where jobs and services are better. "We should think not only about economic interests," said Atakhanova. "The government should ask these people what they need and then do it. We are not a poor country. We can improve the quality of life for people in the Polygon."

In 2005, Karaganda's EcoMuseum sent a formal request to more than twenty government agencies, asking them to outline their areas of responsibility for public health and safety in the Polygon. Most did not respond, but those that did were not reassuring. The pattern was familiar to EcoMuseum director Kalmykov, who had asked similar questions about the Baikonur cosmodrome, and received a similar runaround. "On the Polygon, the Ministry of Health Protection said that the local akimat was responsible, the akimat said that the Ministry of Emergency Situations was responsible, and the ministry said that the NNC was responsible. That's the situation in Kazakhstan. Nobody is responsible."

"There's no process for taking a decision," said Atakhanova. "No ministry is willing to take responsibility. What are the legal requirements and criteria for returning this land to agriculture? No one knows. I told the NNC, 'You are scientists. It's not your job to push government to make this decision. Please organize an open discussion of stakeholders.' No other country has returned a nuclear test site to agriculture. Will Kazakhstan be the first in the world to do so?"

Magda says she's surprised that the issues are even being discussed. "In the US, no one would ever argue whether or not it was safe to graze animals on a nuclear test site or swim in nuclear craters. We wouldn't ask these questions. For whatever reason this is up for debate in Kazakhstan."

The Seven Palaces

Since the beginning of the Soviet nuclear test program, the city of Semipalatinsk has been linked—economically, politically, and, not least, semantically—with the Polygon. Most historical accounts refer simply to the "Semipalatinsk Polygon" as if the nuclear test site was, if not part of the city itself, then at least an outer suburb. In fact, the test site is almost one hundred miles southwest of the city. Even so, residents remember the force of explosions shaking the ground and rattling apartment windows. No one knows how much fallout drifted over the city when the wind was from the west.

In 2007, the city name underwent cosmetic surgery when its name was officially changed from the Russian Semipalatinsk to the Kazakh Semey. However, it's difficult for the city to shake off its dark historical associations. Although the headquarters of the nuclear testing program was at Kurchatov, Semipalatinsk was the regional administrative center and economic and transportation hub, with medical facilities for radiation testing. Many families have members who worked for the nuclear program as scientists, technicians, teachers, medical staff, and laborers. Some were exposed to radiation, and the city has high rates of cancer and birth defects. Since independence, the city has built a monument to the victims of testing—a giant stone mushroom cloud.

If you can ever forget about the Polygon, Semipalatinsk ranks as one of the more attractive cities in Kazakhstan's northern industrial belt. The first settlement was a Russian fort built in 1718 on the Irtysh River near a ruined Buddhist monastery—a lonely outpost where the Russians faced off against the warlike Oyrats from Mongolia. The fort was named Semipalatinsk for the monastery's seven buildings (*palata* can mean a hall, chamber, house, or palace). Because of frequent flooding, the fort was moved eleven miles upstream in 1778, and a small city grew up around it, based on the river trade between China and Russia. Its commercial importance increased with the construction of the Turkestan-Siberia Railway (the Turksib), making it a major point of transit between Central Asia and Siberia.

During the civil war, the Kazakh nationalists of the Alash Orda movement renamed the city Alash-qala and made it the capital of their short-lived independent state; it was recaptured by the Red Army in 1920. As a manufacturing city, its population grew during the Soviet period, and after World War II the nuclear testing program brought in scientists, engineers, and skilled workers. After 1991, Semipalatinsk joined the rust belt of industrial cities stretching across northern Kazakhstan from Ust-Kamenogorsk to Uralsk. However, unlike single-industry cities, its economy was more broadly based, with universities, medical facilities, retail outlets, and service industries. It's also a cultural center, with galleries and museums. Nevertheless, its population has declined from about 350,000 in 1991 to under 300,000, with many young, educated people leaving for jobs in Astana and Almaty.

I flew from Astana to Semey in February—a two-hour trip across the snow-covered steppe. As you approach the city, the steppe gives way to forests of pine, fir, and birch. The landscape looks more like southern Siberia than Kazakhstan; indeed, Semey is only just over sixty miles from the Russian border, close enough for weekend shopping. Prices for almost everything—meat, vegetables, bread, vodka, Chinese clothes, and other imports—are higher in Russia, so it's worth the trip.

Semey has the usual rows of drab apartment blocks and triumphal public architecture—a large central square with government buildings, parks, and a war memorial. There's more activity around the Tsum central department store, where streets are lined with shops and some trendy, if rather out-of-place hangouts—the London Pub, with a large photo of Tower Bridge at night, an Irish pub, and the distinctly retro SSSR Café, with reprints of Soviet-era posters and newspaper headlines from *Pravda* and *Izvestiya* announcing Yuri Gagarin's April 1961 pioneer space flight.

A few blocks from the city center, you enter an older, pre-Soviet era—small one- and two-story log houses, some faced with stucco, with brightly painted windows and carved ornamental woodwork. Most have small gardens. These are the traditional homes found throughout Siberia and northern Central Asia, with logs cut from the great birch and fir forests. On some streets, they sit awkwardly between modern concrete commercial buildings, but in other places they line both sides of the street. Although many old, single-story houses have been bulldozed in Astana's real estate boom, much of Semey's nineteenth-century architecture survives.

FIGURE 10.1 Traditional Russian house, Semey

FIGURE 10.2 Traditional Russian house, Semey

Literary Semey

One of the best preserved nineteenth-century homes is now a museum dedicated to its most famous resident, Fyodor Dostoyevsky. In 1849, the writer, then aged twenty-eight, was one of a group of intellectuals in St. Petersburg arrested for attending meetings of the Petrashevsky Society, a socialist utopian group that called for emancipation of the serfs, judicial reform, and, more dangerously, the end of the monarchy. A military court found fifteen of the accused, including Dostoyevsky, guilty of a "conspiracy of ideas." On a December morning, they were taken to a square and lined up before a firing squad. At the last moment, a messenger rode up with an order from Tsar Nicholas I. Their sentences had been commuted to hard labor and exile in the East—the favorite destination for aristocratic opponents of the tsars.

Dostoyevsky spent the next four years in iron shackles on a labor crew at a prison in Omsk in southern Siberia, an experience that inspired his first major novel, *Notes from the House of the Dead*. In 1854, he began five years of enforced military service as a private in the First Siberian Company of the Seventh Line Battalion, garrisoned in Semipalatinsk. Although the officers were regular army, the regiment was composed mostly of released prisoners and exiles.

Despite the rigors of army life, Dostoyevsky greeted his arrival in Semipalatinsk as a liberating experience. "When I left my melancholy prison, I arrived here with happiness and hope. I resembled a sick person who is beginning to recover after a long illness, and having been at death's door, even more strongly feels the pleasure of living during the first days of his recovery." The writer was waiting for an amnesty, hoping that soon he would be able to return from exile to European Russia.

Soon after his arrival, Dostoevsky met the young Baron Aleksandr Wrangel, a German-Russian aristocrat sent from St. Petersburg to become the new district prosecutor. Wrangel had read Dostoevsky's novel *Poor Folk,* and the two became close friends, with the young prosecutor helping and supporting the writer and introducing him to Semipalatinsk society. Dostoyevsky returned to writing in earnest. "There is clarity in my soul," he wrote. "It's as though I have my whole future and everything that I'll do right before my eyes."

Brief sketches of Semipalatinsk are found in his works. *Notes from the House of the Dead* begins with a description of the city: "In the remote regions of Siberia, amidst the steppes, mountains and impassable forests, one sometimes comes across little, plainly built wooden towns of one or often two thousand inhabitants, with two churches—one in the town itself, and the other in the cemetery outside—towns that are more like the good-sized villages of the Moscow district than they are like towns." A scene in the story "Uncle's Dream," set in Semipalatinsk, is similar: "In the streets, with their rows of little houses sunk into the earth, there was a savage barking of dogs which abound in provincial towns in alarming numbers."

Dostoyevsky spent the spring and summer of 1855 with Wrangel at a dacha on the banks of the Irtysh where they went swimming, fishing, and riding, tended a flower garden, and read books sent from Moscow. By now he had fallen in love with Maria Dmitrievna, the wife of a local customs officer, Aleksandr Isayev. It was a tortured relationship, with Maria callously playing on the writer's jealousy and insecurity. When Isayev's alcoholism cost him his position, the couple fell on hard times and moved north to Kuznetsk in Siberia. Isayev died a few months later, leaving Maria penniless. Dostoyevsky borrowed money from Wrangel to pay for the funeral. Meanwhile, Wrangel used his connections in St. Petersburg to obtain an officer's commission for Dostoyevsky and to have his hereditary title restored. Maria eventually agreed to marry Dostoyevsky, and they rented the second floor of the house of the city postmaster in Semipalatinsk. It was an unhappy match, with Maria now jealous of her husband. Dostoyevsky was experiencing frequent epileptic seizures, and was discharged from the military. After eighteen months, word finally came that his exile was over, and the couple returned to European Russia. The marriage continued on its turbulent course. Maria's health declined, but her death left Dostoyevsky devastated. Maria, attractive, fickle, and manipulative, became the model for the tragic character of Katerina Ivanovna Marmeladova in *Crime and Punishment*.

FIGURE 10.3 Dostoyevsky Museum, Semey

In 1971, the house where the couple lived was reopened as the Dostoyevsky Museum, and in 1976 a modern annex was added to the original building. Next to the museum, in a small garden, a statue of Dostoevsky stands beside that of another of his friends, the army officer, explorer, folklorist, and artist Chokan Valikhanov.

The two had met in Omsk, and renewed their friendship in Semipalatinsk. Valikhanov, a grandson of the last khan of the Kazakh Middle Horde, was educated in the prestigious Orenburg Cadet Corps and rose to the rank of captain in the Imperial Army. In Central Asia, he served as an intelligence agent among the Kazakhs and Kyrgyz. In 1858, disguised as a merchant's son, he arrived in the city of Kashgar in western China, a region where the Qing Dynasty faced unrest and sporadic revolts from its Muslim subjects. Valikhanov lived undercover in Kashgar for five months, gathering intelligence, before traveling to St. Petersburg to report to the government and write about his adventures.

Valikhanov's historical reputation—and the reason he is a national hero in Kazakhstan, with streets in many cities named after him—rests on his written accounts of expeditions to explore Kashgaria and the "seven rivers" or "seven waters" region (*Semireche* in Russian or *Zhetysu* in Kazakh) of what today is southeastern Kazakhstan. Like all nineteenth-century explorers, Valikhanov painstakingly recorded everything he saw and learned. His notebooks are crammed with observations on the landscape, animals, plant life, history, folklore, language, literature, and politics. He was the first person to reportedly write down a fragment of the *Manas* epic from a Kyrgyz bard.

Dostoyevsky realized Valikhanov's significance as one of the few educated Central Asians who could educate Russians about the region. "Isn't it a great goal, isn't it a sacred mission," he wrote him, "to be practically the first of one's people who would explain in Russian what the steppe is, its significance and that of your people in regard to Russia, and at the same time to serve your homeland by means of enlightened intercession for her among the Russians?"

Intercession had its limits as the Russian army pushed eastward and southward into Central Asia in the 1860s. Torn between his duties as an officer and his sympathies for his fellow Kazakhs and Muslims, Valikhanov protested at the army's brutal conquest. Nevertheless, he continued intelligence work until his early death in 1865 at the age of thirty, either from tuberculosis or syphilis contracted in Kashgar.

While downplaying his ethnic sympathies, the Soviets found Valikhanov to be a ready-made hero for the Kazakh people—an intrepid explorer, a scholar, artist, man of the people. In heroic status, his nineteenth-century literary counterpart was the poet, translator, and educator Abay Qunanbayev. Just as Valikhanov had, in the service of the Russian army, recorded the traditional culture of Central Asia, Qunanbayev used his literary talents to draw connections between Kazakh and Western traditions.

Qunanbayev was born in 1845 in the village of Qasqabulaq in the Chingistau hills, south of Semipalatinsk. The family was reasonably well off by local standards, so there was money to send the bright boy to school—first to a madrassa and then to Russian school in Semipalatinsk. At school, he read and admired the works of Mikhail Lermontov, Aleksandr Pushkin, and other nineteenth-century writers, and determined to pursue a literary career.

Qunanbayev was a contemporary and friend of several leading nineteenth-century Russian literary figures, and translated their work into Kazakh; he also translated Byron, Goethe, and other European writers. Qunanbayev's major original work is *The Book of Words,* a philosophical treatise and collection of poems in which he encourages his fellow Kazakhs to embrace education, literacy, and moral character to escape poverty, enslavement, and corruption.

> If you honor God and have any shame, if you want your son to be a real man, send him to school! Don't begrudge the expense! For if he remains an unlettered scoundrel, who will benefit? Will he be a solace to you? Will he be happy himself? And will he be able to do any good for his own people?

Although Qunanbayev is celebrated as a national hero for writing in the Kazakh language, he knew the importance of learning Russian. The nomadic life that had supported his people for centuries was already changing, and he urged them to broaden their horizons.

> One should learn to read and write Russian. The Russian language is a key to spiritual riches and knowledge, the arts and many other treasures. If we wish to avoid the vices of the Russians while adopting their achievements, we should learn their language and study their scholarship and science, for it was by

learning foreign tongues and assimilating world culture that the Russians have become what they are. Russian opens our eyes to the world. By studying the language and culture of other nations, a person becomes their equal and will not need to make humble requests.

Qunanbayev's main contribution is his poetry, which expresses nationalism and grew out of Kazakh folk culture. Before him, Kazakh literature had consisted chiefly of long oral poems. Qunanbayev's public readings of his translations as well as his own work were the beginnings of Kazakh as a literary language. He wrote in the Arabic script that was used until the early twentieth century, when the Roman alphabet was adopted, only to be replaced by Cyrillic when the Soviets took over the region after the civil war.

Today Qunanbayev is universally revered as one of the first Kazakh folk heroes. Almaty State University, public schools, and streets and boulevards in Almaty, Astana, and almost every city in the country are named after him. Statues, generally depicting him in full traditional dress holding a dombyra, stand in squares in many cities as well as in Moscow. Semey's Abay museum opened in 1995, the 150th anniversary of the writer's birth.

Qunanbayev died in 1904. In the early Soviet era, despite his pro-Russian leanings, his works were suppressed because his accounts of traditional culture were regarded as backward and antiproletarian. After the Stalinist purges of the 1930s and 1940s, the authorities realized that each republic needed a few acceptable ethnic heroes. The batyrs, the Alash Orda nationalist leaders, and other regime opponents were not considered appropriate. Writers, artists, musicians, scientists, and teachers fit the bill. Qunanbayev's reputation was restored, and his literary works (especially his pro-Russian writings) officially licensed by Moscow.

Although it's impossible to forget the dark side of Semey's history, I prefer to think of the city as a cultural and educational center. Apart from Qunanbayev, who spent most of his life in the region, other Kazakh literary greats were raised in the Chingistau hills—his nephew and student, the historian, philosopher, and poet Shakarim Qudayberdiuli (1858–1931), for whom Semey State University is officially named (though the formal name is rarely used in everyday speech); the writer and social activist Mukhtar Auezov (1897–1961); and others. Dostoyevsky,

Valikhanov, and others spent time in the city, and wrote about it. This is what sets Semey apart from other cities in Kazakhstan's rust belt.

Meals on Wheels and Sheep's Heads

One thing that does not set it apart is the city services. In Astana, the snow is cleared; in Semey it just piles up. In Astana, city workers have modern snowplows and front-end loaders. In Semey, they have old Soviet trucks and shovels. They try to clear the main roads, but the side streets, even in the center of the city, don't get much attention. You are almost always walking on snow, over ice, over hard-packed snow. This makes the habit of holding onto your companion not only culturally acceptable but vital to personal safety. I felt most secure when my two assistants/interpreters from the university—Togzhan and Natasha—were to my left and right, their arms locked in mine.

I stayed at the official university guest apartment. It was more than I needed—two bedrooms and a formal dining room with chandeliers, an ornate dining table with eight chairs and the largest red-leather sofa and armchairs I've ever seen. None of the three TVs worked, but the place was comfortable. There was even room (or at least apartment) service. Each morning, an unsmiling staff member from the university canteen drove over to deliver my breakfast. In the evening, my driver (who smiled even less) stopped at the canteen to pick up dinner. By the end of the second day, the small refrigerator was almost full and I had to insist that no more deliveries be made for a couple of days. I said I hoped my request was not culturally offensive and that I genuinely appreciated the university meals-on-wheels service.

After years of travel in Central Asia, I have learned that you refuse food at your peril. Central Asians pride themselves on their hospitality, and even the poorest families feel both the duty and pleasure of entertaining guests, even if they do not have enough food for their own needs. Although it was acceptable to halt the supply of bread, cheese, sausage, and kasha from the canteen, I could not refuse food at a more formal occasion. And Semey State had apparently planned several for me. On the first day, I joined Yerlan Sydykov, the rector, and his five vice-rectors for a traditional Kazakh feast, with besh barmak, potatoes, and carrots, soup, salads, *balkhash* (a traditional fried dough), fruits, and sweets. The vice-rector sitting to my right kept loading my plate with another traditional delicacy—horsemeat. When I protested mildly, he explained that there were several varieties, each with a different taste and texture, and I surely had to try them all. The eight people at the table ate a fraction of the food served. But that's not the point. In Kazakh culture, you dishonor your guest if you do not prepare a huge spread. Sydykov told me that this tradition came from the days when his people were nomads, and visitors, bringing news from other places, were rare and welcomed.

I expected a farewell lunch on my final day, so I did my best not to think too much about it, particularly about the part of the sheep, which (according to tradition) is presented to the guest of honor. The head duly arrived—very well cooked—along with a kitchen knife and instructions to cut pieces for all the guests. I'm not much good at carving the Thanksgiving turkey, and this was a more formidable task. I struggled for a few minutes while the vice-rectors looked on nervously. "Ot sebya! [away from you]," one urged, as the knife slipped. Fearing that my next trip would be to the hospital, they passed the task on to another guest who expertly extracted the meat. I was expecting to be offered the eye (as I had been at Issyk Kul), but I guess they've had dinner with enough Westerners to know that may be asking for too much cultural sensitivity.

Lunch was in the university's formal dining room. The decor was 1970s Las Vegas—walls painted in red, blue, and black, making the place look more like a night club than a dining room. It's probably the right atmosphere because few evening affairs go by without karaoke, dancing to loud music, and vodka. Fortunately, my lunchtime send-off was more sedate, with the usual series of toasts and short speeches. I was touched by the warmth and hospitality of everyone I met, and the vice-rectors were generous in their thanks. They also felt warmly about the United States, which several had visited. One spoke about his stay at the University of Nebraska agriculture college. "Sredniy zapad—nastoyashaya Amerika [the Midwest is the real America]," he said several times. After many toasts and pledges of friendship, I was presented with gifts—a basket in the shape of a yurt, Kazakh-language books about the university and its symbolic founder, Shakarim Qudayberdiuli, a T-shirt, cap, and pen. The most impressive gift was a crimson velvet coat with yellow embroidery, the traditional dress of a Kazakh nobleman, and the pointed felt hat, called a kolpak (also found in Kyrgyzstan).

I posed for pictures, packed up the coat and hat, and then set off by car to the next event—a concert by the Kazakh tenor Shakhimardan Abilov at the Semey Pedagogical Institute. As a foreign guest, I was expected to sit in the front row. I wasn't expecting to sit in the front row dressed as a Kazakh nobleman, but my hosts insisted that I show up in my formal dress. I felt pretty conspicuous, but no one seemed to pay much attention. There are people in traditional dress at every cultural event.

Shakhimardan is a national hero, who has toured internationally and devoted himself to teaching younger singers. He sang mostly in Kazakh, serious songs about Qunanbayev and funny songs about village life and courtship. He also sang in Ukrainian and Italian. The rector of the institute presented him with an honorary degree, and then there were more group photos with the recently minted Kazakh nobleman trying to hide behind the tallest person in the shot.

I had met Shakhimardan the previous evening at a dinner given by Rector Sydykov at the university resort. He was an engaging character—"Just call me shark," he said, baring his teeth. As the guest of honor (this time, he got the sheep's head), he sat at the head of the table, and I was seated next to him. After a couple of toasts, he was invited to sing. I've never been that close to an opera singer before, and it was a powerful, moving experience. One of his protégés, sitting at the opposite end of the table, also sang and played the dombyra.

The guest list—it was a strictly all-male affair—was a who's who of the power brokers of Semey. Besides Sydykov, there was the rector of the pedagogical institute, a former minister of health (now rector of the Semey Medical Institute), a two-time mayor, the current mayor, and two leading local businessmen. The former mayor, who had once served as Nazarbayev's security chief, kept wagging his finger at me. "You are CIA, you are CIA," he jested. "Well, I guess that makes you KGB," I answered. In the corner, the DJ cranked up the music every time a toast was made, while the staff filled the glasses with vodka and whisky. About two hours into the evening, Sydykov announced that it was time for a break. This was the cue for karaoke and billiards. The sport is popular in Semey, with many cafés and bars advertising billiards, but that night (after many toasts) no one was shooting very straight.

Strong Leader, Successful Country

On the drive out of town, I had asked Sydykov about his life. He grew up in a village in the Polygon and worked as miner before going to college and on to a career in academia and national politics. Sydykov said that almost every family in his village had at least one member who contracted sickness from radiation; his own brother died. He said one aboveground test took place less than twenty miles away. Along the road, he pointed out the secret clinic where Soviet doctors conducted tests of local residents for radiation.

I had not expected to find much in common with Sydykov. He had recently gained less-than-positive Western news coverage for leading the campaign for a referendum to abolish presidential elections and make Nazarbayev president for life. The referendum initiative was thrown out by Kazakhstan's Constitutional Court, but it earned Sydykov a national political profile. I had expected to meet a rabid nationalist and party loyalist, but instead I found a smart, urbane, and open-minded man who genuinely believes Nazarbayev's continued presidency is best for the country's economy and political stability.

In some ways, it's difficult to argue with that position. Kazakhstan is the most stable and prosperous country in Central Asia, with the highest average standard of living. No wonder the opposition parties are small, weak, and divided. Most people seem to accept that Nazarbayev will be in power for a long time, and they put their economic well-being and safety ahead of their political rights. A large banner in Semey's central square summed up public opinion. Nazarbayev is shown in the archetypal leader-at-work pose, with his jacket slung over his shoulder. The slogan reads "*Sil'niy lider—uspeshnaya strana* [Strong leader—successful country]."

Sydykov genuinely shares Nazarbayev's vision of Kazakhstan as a modern nation, where peace, stability, and economic growth are more important than individual rights or democracy. His support also doesn't hurt his career prospects. We said good-bye at the regional headquarters of Nazarbayev's Nur Otan political party. He had taken time off from his duties as rector to head up Nazarbayev's presidential campaign in Eastern Kazakhstan oblast. "*Moy otpusk* [my vacation]," Sydykov joked. Nazarbayev won the April election by the usual landslide, and Sydykov's star has continued to rise. In 2012, Nazarbayev promoted him to be rector of ENU in Astana.

You Are Kazakh, No Matter Where You Were Born

I had one more cultural experience in Semey—an invitation to the traditional Russian *banya*. In the sauna, a large fire heats stones in a fireplace.

Your companion douses the stones with water, creating hot steam. As you lay on the bench, he beats you with the leaves of birch branches to help the steam circulate through your body. Then you either go roll in the snow—not recommended, in this case, because of pedestrians and traffic—or jump into a small pool. Then you eat horsemeat, chicken wings, nuts, and fruit, drink vodka, play billiards, and do it all over again. If you're a regular at the banya, you keep going back for more steam and beatings. I could do it only twice because the steam was incredibly hot. I finished with a massage and slept very well.

I talked with my banya hosts about our lives and families. When I explained that I was born in the UK, have lived in the United States for more than half my life, have dual citizenship, and do not feel a strong sense of identity, one looked puzzled. "If your father was Kazakh, you are Kazakh, no matter where you were born or where you live," he said.

Even as society changes in Central Asia, family membership continues to carry both rights and responsibilities. One of my hosts told me that five hundred people (almost all family members) were expected at his father's upcoming sixtieth birthday party, and that he and his brother each had to commit $1,000 as a birthday present. On the other hand, if he had financial or personal difficulties, all family members would help as much as they could.

In the traditional herding economy, people traveled as a family unit and lived in a yurt. In the modern economy, based on oil, gas, natural resources, and commerce, more people move away from their families to find work. As the percentage of the population living in urban areas and working for salaries and wages increases, maintaining the ties of tribe, clan, and family is becoming ever more difficult.

eleven

Wheat and Oil

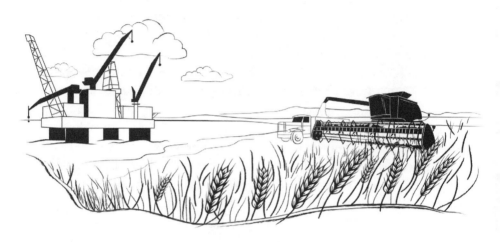

Is This How Russians Live?

As the train pulled out of Astana, Valery opened the first bottle of cognac and was figuring out how much alcohol our compartment would need for the fifteen-hour overnight trip to Kostanai. It was only 4:30 p.m., and, with several hours of daylight left, I wanted to look out the window, not drink. But to be sociable, I agreed to a couple of shots.

Half an hour later, I escaped to the corridor for an hour before returning to the compartment. Valery and his friend Igor were already almost through bottle number two and had bought another bottle of vodka from the drinks trolley. The restaurant car served vodka and cognac by the glass, but for those who want to drink in compartments, a vendor plies the corridors.

Sensibly, Valery and Igor were also eating—dark bread, cheese, sausage, piroshky, and strong Russian mustard. Valery slapped mustard on a slice of bread and cheese and passed it to me. I felt as if my head was going to explode. "Good for your health—you won't get a cold," Valery laughed as I gasped and turned red. "Here, have more vodka."

As the evening wore on and the alcohol took its toll, the conversation became more animated and difficult to follow. Valery and Igor were on their way to Kostanai oblast in northern Kazakhstan for a hunting and fishing trip. I must have skipped the chapter on winter outdoor sports in the Russian textbook because most of the vocabulary was new to me. There was a lot of extending of arms and simulated "boom boom" gunshot noises as virtual ducks fell to earth.

Valery, who said he loved all sports and was wearing a David Beckham T-shirt, wanted to know why I had never served in the military. He was reluctant to accept my explanation that there was no military service requirement in the UK and that I had arrived in the United States too late to be drafted for the Vietnam War. Military service was compulsory in the Soviet Union, and Valery served in Afghanistan. "A useless war," he admitted, yet he still seemed to resent those who, in his opinion, had not served in the military. My argument that there are other ways to serve one's country did not impress him.

By 10 p.m., everyone had settled down for the night. Then the snoring started. It didn't bother me while we were moving because it was drowned out by the sound of the train, but it woke me when we stopped at stations, as we did four or five times after midnight. At 3 a.m. at an isolated town on the frozen steppe, there's no traffic and no people. Only snoring.

At 6 a.m., the attendants knocked on the doors to tell passengers we'd be arriving in Kostanai in an hour. Valery swung down from the top bunk, opened a bottle of beer and offered me another. I politely refused. He smiled. "Now you know *kak russkiye zhivut* [how Russians live]," he said, with a smile. I wanted to say I hoped not all Russians lived that way but recognized the sincerity of the hospitality. It was another warm memory of a cold winter.

On the Northern Border

The city of Kostanai (population 215,000) is on the northern edge of the steppe where it meets the pine and birch forests that stretch for thousands of miles across northern Kazakhstan and southern Siberia. Kostanai is 90 miles from the Russian border, and about 220 from the industrial city of Chelyabinsk, which grabbed world attention in February 2013 when an

11,000-ton largest meteor, the largest to fall to earth since 1908, exploded overhead. Almost 1,500 people sustained injuries, mostly from shattered glass, and 3,000 buildings were damaged. The meteor was seen by Kostanai residents, with one of the most widely circulated photos taken from a dashboard camera in a car on the Kostanai-Chelyabinsk highway.

Within a few hours Russian bloggers and tweeters were offering their own spins on the phenomenon—that the Americans were testing a new weapon, that it was a Kremlin or opposition plot, or that it was "the lighting of the Olympic flame—space giving its blessing to the 2014 Sochi Winter Olympics." In Russia, Chelyabinsk is often the butt of jokes for its pollution and harsh living conditions. One blogger commented: "The asteroid's inhabitants watched in horror as they approached Chelyabinsk."

Although there were no injuries or damage in Kostanai, its majority ethnic Russian population sympathized with Chelyabinsk residents. The two cities have close ties. Because food and other items are cheaper in Kazakhstan, many Russian citizens cross the border to shop. For most residents, Russian is their first language, and little Kazakh is heard on the streets.

The city was founded on a trading route on the Tobol River which runs north to the Irtysh, and then joins the Ob, the second-longest river in Asia, at the Russian river port of Omsk, flowing north to the Arctic Sea. Since the 1950s when Khrushchev launched the Virgin Lands program, Kostanai has been a center of the northern wheat belt, storing and shipping grains. The region has large deposits of iron ore and other minerals, including bauxite, gold, silver, and nickel. As the administrative capital of the province, Kostanai has a diversified economic base, with universities and technical institutes, hospitals, government offices, and cultural and sports facilities. It's a quiet, friendly, and clean city, with boulevards, parks, theaters, and museums.

Kostanai State University, a former teachers' college, has about 12,000 students. Like other universities, it is officially named for a national hero—Akhmet Baitursynov, a writer, translator, and teacher, noted for his adaptation of Arabic script for the Kazakh alphabet. Like many Kazakh intellectuals, he was active in politics and a fervent nationalist. In 1909, he was arrested and exiled, returning after the 1917 revolution to join the Alash Orda political party. After the Soviets reasserted control, he worked on education reform but was arrested in 1937 for harboring "bourgeois nationalist sentiments" and summarily executed. He is not some distant historical figure; his writings are part of the national high school curriculum; university administrators in Kostanai mention him in almost every discussion; an annual conference is held in his honor; and most students seem to know who he was and the values he represented.

The rector, Askar Nametov, told me he was under pressure from the Ministry of Education and Science to meet "international standards." Nametov was most concerned about research productivity. In its effort to establish itself as a leader in science and technology, Kazakhstan wants its academic researchers to publish in Western peer-reviewed journals. Kostanai State University has strong departments of agronomy and veterinary science and is doing research on algae as biofuels, reckoning that the more than five thousand lakes in the province can be an important future source of energy. It will be an uphill battle. In the Soviet era, research in most disciplines was published in slim, cheaply produced paperbacks, often without outside review. At regional universities, scientific researchers lack equipment and funding, contacts with Western colleagues, and English-language skills. "We are traveling in a plane but we need a rocket," said Nametov. Or maybe a meteor.

Don't Mess with the Restaurant Critic

The deputy editor of Kostanai's *Nasha Gazyeta* (Our Newspaper), Timur Gafurov, had attended my curriculum workshop in Astana in 2010. *Nasha Gazyeta,* which is about as independent a newspaper as the local authorities will tolerate, was doing pretty well, judging by the number of advertising column inches and its coverage of business and social issues. It has to be cautious in its political coverage, but still manages edgy, sometimes critical, tongue-in-cheek reporting. In Kazakhstan, all regional officials are appointed, and the 2011 presidential election provided an opportunity for Nazarbayev to shake up subordinates and build alliances. When Prime Minister Karim Masimov showed up to announce the appointment of the next akim (governor) of the oblast, *Nasha Gazyeta* ran a front-page picture showing the current akim, Sergey Kulganin, and Masimov, seated at a table with an empty chair, with the headline, "The Secret of the Third Chair." "Only Nazarbayev knows who the next akim will be," Timur told me. "It's always a big secret." However, no one was really surprised when Kulganin was reappointed, making him one of the country's longest-serving akims. He's not that popular in Kostanai, but evidently Nazarbayev was happy with his performance. He was just made to sweat for a few weeks and no doubt reaffirm his loyalty.

Nasha Gazyeta certainly faces government pressure. The KNB, the national security service (successor to the KGB), once claimed that the newspaper was supported by the CIA, probably because its publisher had taken a State Department–funded tour of US newspapers. The more present danger may come from the business sector because of its critical reporting of agribusiness. Actually, its criticism goes all the way through the food chain. The newspaper's restaurant critic has never awarded any establishment more than a three-star rating, and she has given some scathing reviews. She writes under a pseudonym, a sensible precaution because on at least two occasions leather-jacketed men with short-cropped hair have shown up at the newspaper office demanding to know the identity of its restaurant critic. Timur and his colleagues refuse to disclose her identity. However, if she is ever named, the restaurant gang may want to think twice about confronting her. Under a male pseudonym, she is also the newspaper's outdoors reporter, specializing in fishing and hunting. She probably shoots as straight as she writes.

Kazakhstan Needs Its Vegetables

Kostanai oblast—twice the size of Hungary or Portugal and almost as large as Kyrgyzstan—is the country's top wheat-producing region. Its economy is dominated by large enterprises farming thousands of hectares. Over 40 percent of farmland is controlled by four holding companies, with one farming 900,000 hectares (an area the size of Cyprus or Puerto Rico). The companies own grain elevators, trucks, and freight cars, essentially controlling the market.

In this land of megafarms, Viktor Simanenko's operation on the bank of the Tobol River is tiny—just 350 hectares. But unlike some farmers who have endured several tough years, he is making money. The clue to Simanenko's success is in the name of his farm, *Sadovod* (gardener). While most farmers depend on a single crop, wheat, Simanenko grows potatoes, carrots, cabbages, beets, onions, tomatoes, cucumbers, and watermelons. He raises plants from seeds in greenhouses and uses river water to irrigate fields. He owns a local wholesale outlet that sells to retailers in Kostanai and other cities in northern and western Kazakhstan.

FIGURE 11.1 Viktor Simanenko knows his vegetables.

Simanenko portrays himself as a rebel with a cause. "In the Brezhnev period, I almost went to jail for eight years for commercial activity and hiring labor," he boasts. He started farming in 1989, two years before Kazakhstan's independence, "because I knew the country needed vegetables, and the local authorities weren't doing anything to encourage entrepreneurship."[1]

Wheat has been central to the economy of northern Kazakhstan for more than half a century. Under the Virgin Lands program, thousands of people were resettled on large kolkhozes, where the flat, open land was judged suitable for large-scale agriculture. The kolkhozes have been replaced by private farms, and Soviet tractors and combines by high-tech John Deeres with air-conditioned cabs, stereos, and GPS, but the agricultural economy of Kostanai oblast is still almost completely dependent on a single crop. More than 90 percent of farmland is planted for wheat. In good years, Kostanai produces as much wheat as Kansas, although yields per hectare are lower. However, climate, government policy, and fluctuating prices have left the region in a precarious boom-and-bust cycle.

Northern Kazakhstan is arid, with an average rainfall of twenty inches a year. Fields are not irrigated, and the region suffers from severe drought an average of two out of five seasons. In 2009, for example, above-average rainfall produced high yields, but the abundant harvest depressed prices. The next summer was hot and dry with low yields and high prices. Some farmers lost money both years and could not repay bank loans for seed, fertilizer, and equipment.

"Small and medium-sized wheat farmers are in a tough position," Shaurab Zhempisov, a Kostanai State University agronomy professor, told me. "Last year's debt is left for this year and they don't know when they can repay." Farmers will keep on borrowing because the government requires banks to make low-interest loans. The state also subsidizes seeds, pesticides, fertilizer, and diesel fuel. "It's not a gift," he said. "The farmers have to sell a portion of their wheat to Prodkorporatsia [the state grain corporation] at a fixed price that's lower than they can earn if they export it."

After independence, Kazakhstan's wheat output declined. Production increased after 2000 when the government restored subsidies and encouraged wheat exports. Today, Kazakhstan is the world's seventh-largest wheat producer, with major export markets in Russia, Ukraine, Central Asia, Europe, and North Africa.

Dependence on wheat has left Kostanai farmers vulnerable to swings in world prices. In recent years, the government has encouraged farmers to diversify. With prices rising for meat and dairy products, cattle-raising is the most profitable option. The megafarms have the capital and resources to diversify, but small farmers are stuck. "All their machinery and storage facilities are designed for wheat," said Zhempisov. "They don't have the money to buy new technology. They need the profit from wheat."

"A single crop like wheat exhausts the soil, especially in a region of low rainfall," said Almabek Nugmanov, deputy director of Kostanai State University's Agricultural Research Institute. "For the rational and efficient use of soil, we need to rotate crops." His institute is developing strains of rape, linseed, and sunflowers suitable for the soil and climate of the region. With irrigation, potatoes and other root crops also grow well. "There's a big market for chips in Kazakhstan," Nugmanov said.

For Nugmanov, farmers like Simanenko are pioneers in an agricultural revolution in the wheat belt. Zhempisov is not as optimistic. Only farms near rivers, like Simanenko's, have access to enough water for irrigation, and farmers lack the capital to invest in equipment and storage for vegetables. As world wheat prices fluctuate, Kostanai's farmers keep hoping that a good harvest and high prices for exports will make the next year the one when they can repay their loans. They are not counting on potatoes for profit.

Simanenko is proud of his potatoes, but the title he really relishes is that of onion king. Until his first harvest in 2007, onions—used in many dishes, including the popular shashlyk—were imported by truck from southern Kazakhstan and Uzbekistan. His locally produced onions were an instant hit, fresher and cheaper than the imports.

Simanenko does not rely on market forces alone. Every year, he asks the Russian Orthodox bishop to bless the Sadovod fields before planting. "One year, we missed a field," he recalled. "It was hit by hail that cut the potato plants, and we lost the whole harvest." Now each spring, full divine coverage is on his to-do list.

Oil, Guns, and Roses

It's Kazakhstan's equivalent of a booming Gulf Coast oil town. Atyrau, on the northern coast of the Caspian Sea, sprawls for miles across a flat, sandy landscape, with scrub grass and the occasional dried-up creek bed. New roads push out in all directions, lined with office towers, high-rise apartments, and storage and service facilities for the oil industry. Roadside billboards show President Nazarbayev mingling with oil workers or sitting in a high-tech classroom, demonstrating the government's commitment to education. Energy company billboards trumpet their investments in the local economy and corporate social responsibility. One shows a peaceful, meandering river with the slogan "Care for the Environment." It didn't look like any river near Atyrau.

Atyrau's main claim to fame, apart from oil, is that it is a transcontinental city, situated on both banks of the Ural River (formerly the Yaik) which forms the boundary between Asia and Europe. The region was conquered by the Russians from the Golden Horde in the late sixteenth century, and became home to the Yaik Cossacks. Since the ninth century, the Volga River, which enters the Caspian Sea below Astrakhan, had served as the main trading artery between Russia, Central Asia, the Caucasus and Persia. The 1,500-mile-long Yaik, rising in the southern Urals, offered another trade route. In 1645, the Russian merchant Guryev Nazarov built a wooden fort on the delta to trade with the khanates of Khiva and Bukhara. The Yaik Cossacks resisted attempts by the central government to impose rules and regulations, and in 1773–75 joined other Cossacks in the Pugachev Rebellion, taking control of much of southeastern Russia. After it was suppressed, Catherine the Great issued a decree renaming most of the places involved. The Yaik River and the fort city of Yaitsk, north of Guryev, became the Ural River and Uralsk, respectively, and the Yaik Cossacks became the Ural Cossacks.

For centuries, the local economy depended mainly on fishing, most profitably for sturgeon whose roe are processed into caviar for export. In recent years, overfishing has depleted the sturgeon population, leading some environmentalists to call for a complete ban. However, with caviar prices high, profit trumps penalties. Local authorities lack the manpower to enforce fishing regulations, and fishermen sometimes bribe inspectors to look the other way. Other fish include carp, white fish, trout, roach, and bream, but the industry is in slow decline. The real undersea wealth of the region lies in its immense oil and gas reserves.

The world's first offshore oil wells were drilled in the Caspian Sea near Baku, the capital of Azerbaijan, in 1873. By 1900, Baku had more than three thousand wells, and by World War II the region was supplying almost 75 percent of the Soviet Union's oil needs. Although geological surveys indicated that the western region of the Kazakh SSR and the eastern shore of the Caspian Sea had reserves of oil and gas, exploitation did not begin until the 1980s. In 1979, the vast Karachaganak gas condensate field was discovered about one hundred miles east of Uralsk. It is estimated to contain 1.2 trillion cubic meters (42 trillion cubic feet) of gas and one billion tons of liquid condensate and crude oil. In 1997, Texaco (now Chevron) and the Russian state company Lukoil signed a forty-year production-sharing agreement with ENI (formerly AGIP) and the BG Group (formerly British Gas), the original two operators. The government holds a 10 percent stake through its state corporation KazMunayGaz (KMG). Local villagers complain about air, ground and water pollution from the wells and oil refinery, including emissions of hydrogen sulfide gas and high levels of cadmium and nitrates in the soil. They claim the toxic chemicals cause migraines, dizziness, hair loss, deterioration of vision and hearing, and skin diseases. They'd like the oil and gas consortium to pack up and go away, but most would settle for being moved to a safer place.

The Tengiz field (*tengiz* is Turkic for "sea"), also discovered in 1979, is located in low-lying wetlands along the northeastern shore of the Caspian Sea, about 220 miles south of Atyrau, which serves as its main supply and transportation base. Its development featured a battle between energy companies, with the government holding most of the cards. The name of the production consortium, Tengizchevroil (TCO), indicates

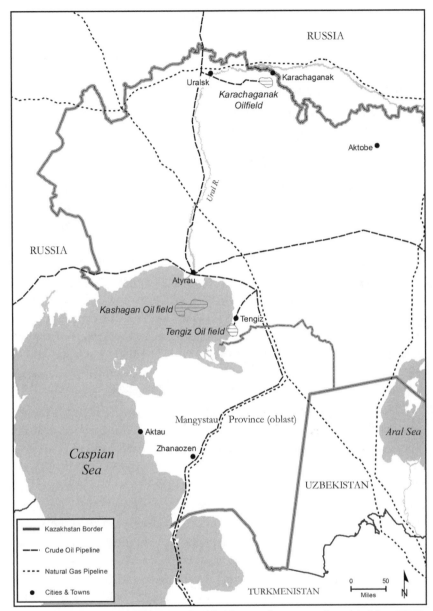

MAP 11.1 Western Kazakhstan and oil fields (map by Brian Edward Balsley, GISP)

the big winner—Chevron, with a 50 percent stake. Exxon Mobil has 25 percent; the government 20 percent; and Lukoil 5 percent. In 2001, the partners opened a US$2.7 billion, 935-mile pipeline to export Tengiz oil to the Russian Black Sea port of Novorossiysk.

The biggest prize is fifty miles west of Tengiz. When the offshore Kashagan field was discovered in 2000, it was hailed as the world's largest oil strike since Alaska's Prudhoe Bay in 1969, with estimated recoverable reserves of 8–12 billion barrels of oil. It is not easy to extract, and early forecasts of when the oil would flow proved hopelessly optimistic. So was the cost estimate of developing the field, which has spiraled from $57 billion to at least $136 billion, and may go higher. The oil lies 2.5 miles below the seabed under shallow waters that freeze for five months of the year. In winter, temperatures can drop to minus 30 Celsius, and icebreakers can take thirty-six hours to reach Kashagan. Conventional rigs could not be used because of the harsh conditions; instead, the developers built an archipelago of artificial islands out of local limestone, encased in an impermeable membrane. Twelve oil wells have been constructed with a fifty-seven-mile-long pipeline to the shore. The field, which began commercial production in 2013, is operated by a consortium of seven companies, including KMG. In 2013, the Chinese government struck a $5 billion deal for a stake in the field. It's expected to be the main source of supply for the Kazakhstan-China oil pipeline, a joint project completed in 2009 to carry oil from northern Kazakhstan and the Caspian Sea to Xinjiang. Kazakhstan hopes that oil from Kashagan will push the country into the top ten of world oil producers.

The pipeline's Caspian Sea terminus is at Atyrau. With the Tengiz field in production, the Kashagan field coming online and the third-largest oil refinery in the country, the once sleepy fishing port and regional administrative center is experiencing a population boom. The oil industry is a magnet for poor migrants, mostly from rural areas, and for the oralmans, ethnic Kazakhs from other countries. Since the early 1990s, the government has offered them start-up cash payments and housing assistance to resettle in Kazakhstan. The oil boom has made moving more attractive. With Aktau, the other major oil port to the south, Atyrau is the fastest-growing city in the country.

Atyrau evidently has more oil than it needs. My plane from Astana parked literally twenty yards from the arrivals hall, an easy walk from the gangway. Instead, we boarded buses that drove out onto the tarmac and followed a circuitous route, depositing us several minutes later a few feet from where we had started. "They need to show they have plenty of petrol," said Sasha. "I wonder which route they will choose for the luggage."

Sasha was Aleksandr Peytchev, a Bulgarian career diplomat who is now the economic and environmental officer for the Organization for Security and Cooperation in Europe (OSCE) Center in Astana. I was traveling with him for a workshop for journalists from western Kazakhstan on covering environmental issues. That evening, we walked along the bank of the Ural River, talking about his career and the diplomatic cocktail-party circuit in Ghana and Kenya in the 1970s and 1980s. Our turnaround point was the Halliburton headquarters, which occupies a prominent riverside location. I'm not sure exactly what Halliburton is doing in Atyrau, but I suppose it's providing, among other things, logistics and security for the oil industry. And it has a sizable staff. We stayed at the Ak Zhaik Hotel. With its stained, threadbare carpets and rickety, pressed-wood furniture, it was not the best hotel in town (despite the shop in the lobby claiming to sell "Elite Haute Couture"), although it was probably not the worst. It's where oil companies accommodate their non-European and non–North American staff, the Pakistanis, Indians, and Filipinos. A sign on the breakfast bar—just past the "Potatoes—at home" and "Skramlet with vegetables" (a combination of "scrambled eggs" and "omelet," I assume)—read: "All quests [*sic*] except Petrofax and Halliburton must pay for soft drinks and juice." In the evenings the workers picked up their meals (and free soft drinks) and took them to their rooms to eat.

The main draw for the higher-paid energy company staff at the Ak Zhaik was the Guns and Roses Pub and Grille (that last "e" on grill is de rigueur, indicating that it's not a greasy spoon such as the Burger House a few blocks away). Wood paneling, fake oak barrels, dim lighting, black and white photos of rock groups, English-speaking staff, and the usual pretentious signs: "Fine beer. Fine food. Fine music. Fine service." The central motif is the Doors, with a large artistic rendering of Jim Morrison and a quote from him about spirituality and music or something like that. The food and drinks are pricey, but the place is filled with expats and well-heeled locals every night, with a large crowd at happy hour. And it's one of several watering holes in Atyrau. Along the river, where many expats live in gated communities, I passed by Atyrau's Irish pub row where O'Neills and The Celtic Dragon vie for customers. I usually try to avoid expat hangouts where they speak English even when you're trying to practice your Russian, but Sasha wanted a beer, so I complied. Fortunately, we left town on Friday morning, missing "Rockin' at Guns with the Jakies," where a local band attempted covers of the Doors and Led Zepellin.

The oil and gas reserves of Karachaganak, Tengiz, and Kashagan are the major prizes in the energy stakes, but more than twenty other fields are scattered throughout western Kazakhstan. Near Aktobe in the north, the Umit oil field, on the pipeline to Xinjiang, is owned and operated by the China National Oil Corporation. In Kyzylorda oblast in the south, a state company runs the Kumkol field. There are two more large off-shore reserves in the Caspian Sea—the Kurmangazy oil field and the Khvalynskoye gas field. The other major fields are in the sparsely populated Mangystau province in the far southwest.

North and west of the great environmental disaster that is the Aral Sea, the desert stretches for hundreds of miles, the monotony of sand and scrub occasionally broken by ridges, canyons, and rock outcrops. The only livestock that can survive in this barren terrain are camels; apart from a few oases along streams, the land cannot support sheep or cattle grazing. However, the region is rich in minerals—phosphates, iron ore, manganese, salts, uranium, and oil and gas. The first oil fields in Mangystau were developed in the 1960s, and by the mid-1990s the province was producing about 70 percent of Kazakhstan's crude oil. Even as the northern oil fields have come online, Mangystau remains a major producer with more than a dozen fields, owned and operated by KMG and multinational energy companies.

The commercial and logistics center is the port of Aktau on the Mangyshlak Peninsula. In the early 1960s, the Soviets discovered uranium deposits nearby and established a secret mining settlement, code-named (in a backhanded compliment to the founder of Atyrau) Guryev-20. The planners laid out a town of broad, straight streets, numbering the residential districts and apartment blocks. The city is distinguished—or undistinguished, depending on your view—for having no street names. An address consists of just three numbers—the microraion, house, and apartment. It was Soviet central planning at its most sterile. At least they didn't number the city. After it was clear that it wasn't a secret anymore, it was named Shevchenko for the nineteenth-century Ukrainian poet and artist Taras Shevchenko, who was exiled to Kazakhstan for his nationalist views.

A nuclear power station was opened in 1973 to produce plutonium and supply power to the city and the desalination plants that were its only source of fresh water. Despite its remote location, it became a vacation spot for the Soviet elite, who enjoyed the sandy beaches and hotel nightlife. With independence, and Kazakhstan's abandonment of its nuclear arsenal, the tourism and uranium industries went into decline. From the mid-1990s, the recovery began as oil exploration and development picked up.

Mangystau province is bordered by western Uzbekistan and northern Turkmenistan where many ethnic Kazakhs live. With jobs scarce, they were attracted by the government's open-door immigration policy and the prospects of work in the oil industry. According to government statistics, of the estimated 860,000 ethnic Kazakhs, the oralmans, who migrated in the twenty years since independence—not only from Uzbekistan and Turkmenistan but also from Russia, Mongolia, and Xinjiang—over 100,000 settled in Mangystau. The province's population grew by over two-thirds in a decade—to over 440,000 in 2009—with half of that growth attributed to oralmans; Aktau's grew by 32 percent in the same period.

The migration created inflationary pressures. Housing is scarce and expensive because Soviet-era apartments are deteriorating and new construction has not kept up with demand. Many migrants, lacking education, have struggled to find work, and some end up hawking goods at the bazaar. The global economic crisis of 2008 halted oil field development and eliminated low-skilled jobs, especially in construction, making the housing shortage even worse. Oralmans competed with poor migrants from rural regions for jobs and government resources, leading to social tensions and rising crime. Nate Schenkkan, a journalist, wrote that "the fundamental catalyst for tension is economic—tens of thousands of un- and underemployed people, many of them recent migrants, . . . see vast resource wealth being extracted but live in crowded, dilapidated, yet expensive conditions." Although the government has been aware of tensions for several years, "it has not fundamentally changed its approach. It is funding more and bigger development schemes, appointing new leaders answerable only to Astana to run the regions, and intensifying repression."[2]

The social tensions are largely invisible to the energy company engineers, accountants, and tax lawyers who frequent Aktau's upscale hotels, restaurants, and bars. Like Atyrau, Aktau is a poster city for the oil industry, touted in government campaigns to attract foreign investors. The brochures and business reports portray a modern, dynamic, business-friendly city where energy revenues are contributing to better medical care, social services, and education. The oil workers and their families in the pictures look healthy and happy, and volunteer quotations on how their companies have given them good pay, housing, and a secure future. No doubt some enjoy such benefits. For those who do not, it's dangerous to speak up or protest about pay and working conditions.

Occupy Zhanaozen

Zhanaozen, with a population of over 60,000, is the second largest city in Mangystau, but it's a world away from Aktau. Unemployment, poverty, and crime rates are high. Oil workers from the Uzen field and their families live in broken-down apartment blocks and tenement houses along dusty, pot-holed roads. Schools and medical services are inadequate.

The Uzen field, opened in 1961, was one of the first to be developed in Mangystau. It is owned and operated by KMG. In May 2011, workers went on strike for higher wages, unpaid danger money, and better working conditions. The strike was declared illegal by local courts, and KMG sacked more than two thousand employees. Some occupied the Zhanaozen town square, demanding union representation and recognition of workers' rights. Strikers were periodically hauled into court and fined or given short jail terms. In August, Natalia Sokolova, a lawyer advising the strikers, received a six-year prison sentence for inciting social discord. By mid-December, some workers in the square began calling for the right to form independent political parties.

On December 16, the twentieth anniversary of Kazakhstan's independence, clashes broke out between protesters and police who were attempting to clear the square in preparation for Independence Day celebrations. Activists claimed police opened fire on unarmed demonstrators, but the authorities said the casualties were caused by ricocheting bullets when the police fired into the air. These assertions were undermined by a YouTube video that showed police shooting fleeing demonstrators and beating the fallen. Protesters set fire to the town hall, a hotel, supermarket and the local KMG office. The government claimed that fifteen people (workers and police officers) were killed, although opposition sources put the death toll much higher. More than one hundred were injured. Due to a shortage of hospital beds in Zhanaozen, many were taken to Aktau, almost a hundred miles away, to be treated.

On December 17, a state of emergency was declared, roads into Zhanaozen were blocked, and the local airport closed. Mobile phone coverage and Internet connections were cut off. However, reports of the violence had reached Almaty, where police arrested opposition activists protesting against the deaths. Workers at two other oil fields went on strike, and unrest was reported at other towns in Mangystau. In his first statement, President Nazarbayev hinted at outside agitators, urging people not to confuse the protest with "the actions of bandit elements which wanted to use the situation for their criminal designs."

The government worried about escalating violence and damage to its image and business confidence. On December 22, Nazarbayev flew to Aktau to try to calm the situation. Police officers charged with shooting at protesters were arrested. Nazarbayev fired several local government and KMG officials. The provincial governor resigned. Zhanaozen claimed its most high-profile official victim when Nazarbayev fired his son-in-law, Timur Kulibayev, as head of Kazakhstan's sovereign-wealth fund, Samruk, which manages KMG. Nazarbayev's actions were welcomed by many citizens and foreign observers, who noted that he had not tried to protect officials he had appointed, and had even taken action against a close relative, widely tipped to be his successor as president. It was not clear at this stage that the government would use the investigations into the Zhanaozen massacre to launch a far-reaching clampdown on the opposition and the press.

A trial of thirty-seven protesters began in Aktau in late March 2012. Many complained that they had been physically abused, and some even tortured, while in police custody. Some witnesses also claimed they had been threatened by police into giving false testimony. In June, thirty-four were found guilty of criminal behavior. Thirteen were given jail terms ranging from three to seven years: sixteen were given suspended sentences; and five were amnestied. There was uproar in the courtroom when the verdicts were announced. The judge had to duck out as enraged relatives hurled shoes and plastic bottles at him. In another trial, five police officers received jail terms of between five and seven years for abuse of office, and the former head of the police detention center in Zhanaozen received five years for the death of a detainee who was beaten while in custody.

The government widened its net. Several opposition figures, including politicians and journalists, were arrested, although none had been in Zhanaozen on December 16. The authorities did not accuse them of violence but instead used a vaguely defined article in the criminal code about "inciting social discord." The most high-profile trial began in August in Almaty. Vladimir Kozlov, leader of the unregistered Alga opposition party, and Akzhanat Aminov, a former Zhanaozen oil worker, were accused of fomenting social unrest, calling for the overthrow of the state, and setting up a criminal group. The political activist Serik Sapargaly faced the first two counts. The prosecution's case closely followed the official narrative that outside agitators were responsible for inciting the violence. Nazarbayev, while acknowledging the grievances of oil workers and police wrongdoing, maintained that "political opponents have tried to destabilize the country by taking advantage of existing grievances." The chief villain was a former political ally and energy minister, the exiled oligarch and media baron Mukhtar Ablyazov. Accused by Kazakhstan's BTA Bank of embezzlement, Ablyazov was on the run from British authorities after a London court handed him a twenty-two-month prison sentence for contempt of court. Prosecutors alleged that Ablyazov and a Kazakh associate in the UK used Kozlov, Sapargaly, and their political organizations to funnel money and print propaganda to the strikers, charges they both denied. In October, Kozlov was found guilty on all charges; he was sentenced to seven and a half years in jail, and his property was confiscated; Sapargaly and Aminov were given suspended sentences of four and three years, respectively. The verdict on Kozlov was roundly condemned by human rights groups. The United States, which, to this point, had simply called for a fair and open trial, denounced the "apparent use of the criminal system to silence opposition voices."

The US State Department's 2013 human rights report criticized severe limits "on citizens' rights to change their government" and "restrictions on freedom of speech, press, assembly, religion, and association," dating the crackdown to the Zhanaozen massacre. The European Parliament passed a resolution expressing concern at the "dramatic worsening" of the human rights situation, and called on the government to revise the clause in the criminal code on inciting social, ethnic, or religious discord—the catchall charge used to prosecute Kozlov and others. Activists in Kazakhstan had heard it all before and said that the criticism had no teeth because no penalties or sanctions were attached. Kazakhstan was simply too important to the West as a source of oil and minerals for criticism to be followed by action.

Domestic opinion is a more serious matter. The government has been pouring money into the rebuilding of Zhanaozen. In February 2012, it pledged $29 million for redevelopment over the next three years. Two new oil production units were created, one in Zhanaozen and one in Aktau, to provide jobs for most of the two thousand workers who had been dismissed. And the workers received another bonus—improved

TV service. While families throughout western Kazakhstan fiddle with rabbit ear antennas to pick up grainy images, Zhanaozen viewers were among the first to receive digital TV. Under the three-year switchover plan announced by Kazteleradio in 2012, digital TV was offered first in the urban areas of Almaty, Astana, Karaganda/Temirtau, Zhezkazgan—and Zhanaozen. The larger western cities of Aktau, Atyrau, and Uralsk would have to wait for digital TV. The decision clearly had more to do with politics than technology. According to Seytkazy Matayev of the Kazakhstan Union of Journalists, the isolated town had been off the broadcast map, not even reached by the national channels; local residents received their information from K-Plus, an opposition channel that showed how the protest in the square turned ugly. The new multichannel digital package is dominated by government and government-allied stations, and K-Plus is not included. The gift of digital TV to Zhanaozen came at a price: no opposition voices.[3]

Although some government officials fired in the aftermath of Zhanaozen are in jail, for others it was a minor career hiccup. Kulibayev, sacked with much fanfare by his father-in-law as head of the Samruk sovereign wealth fund, remains a powerful political figure and is still the odds-on favorite to be named as the next president. In 2013, he returned to the ranks of the Forbes list of billionaires, with an estimated net worth of $1.3 billion, making him the fourth richest man in Kazakhstan. He owns the national Halyk Bank and holds several key positions in the energy sector.

How do you make Zhanaozen go away? Well, one way is to simply remove it from the map. At independence, many towns and cities in Kazakhstan shed their Soviet names in favor of Kazakh ones, including Zhanaozen, which was formerly called Novi Uzen. In November 2012, the Council of Elders of Mangystau province proposed that Zhanaozen be renamed for Beket-Ata, an eighteenth-century Sufi philosopher and scholar from the region. The council insisted the proposal had nothing to do with the upcoming anniversary of the massacre but was intended to immortalize a prominent person from the area. Local opinion on social media was divided: some pointed to Beket-Ata's historical significance, while others sensed a conspiracy to erase historical memory. "You can give a different name to a city, but the problems will stay the same," wrote one Facebook user. "I am afraid our Beket-Ata would be turning in his grave now. May he rest in peace."[4]

Since independence, Kazakhstan has built a generally well-deserved reputation as the most peaceful and stable country in Central Asia. Its economy, fueled largely by the energy sector, has grown rapidly, and although the gap between the rich and poor has widened, many citizens feel they are better off today than they were in the 1990s or in Soviet times. The country's record on human rights, press freedom, and religious tolerance is spotty, but opinion polls suggest that for many people these issues are less important than public safety, jobs, housing, education, and medical care. Nazarbayev has consistently argued that stability is needed to allow the economy to grow and for living standards to rise, and that too much freedom can undermine progress. He points to the example of the so-called Asian Tigers of South Korea and Taiwan that developed economically under authoritarian rule before making a transition to multiparty democracy. In an April 2013 speech, he suggested that Kazakhstan was following this model: "The democracy and freedom that exist in the West . . . are for us the final goal, and not the start of the path." Lacking native tigers or lions, Nazarbayev had to find another large indigenous cat to serve as the economic growth metaphor. By 2030, he promised, "Kazakhstan will become the Central Asian snow leopard."

Even those who gripe about Nazarbayev's autocratic style, rigged elections, suppression of opposition voices, and muzzling of the press, or about profligate spending to make Astana a world-class city, admit that he worked hard to take the country through the difficult times of the 1990s, trod a careful diplomatic path between the United States and Europe, Russia and China, and has kept a lid on ethnic and religious unrest. In another country—or in one with presidential term limits—it would be time for him to retire from public office, open a presidential library, start a foundation, and write books. But the man who has headed the country since independence shows no sign of leaving its top post.

Nazarbayev has been reelected four times since 1991, and his current term runs until 2016. In 2007, the country's two-term presidential limit was suspended to allow him to run again, so legally he could be president for the rest of his life. In 2010, he was declared Leader of the Nation, a title which grants immunity from prosecution and allows him to have a say in policymaking even after he steps down. That is reassuring to citizens who fear a power struggle among the political elite. They would prefer a smooth transition in which Nazarbayev groomed his successor. Some regard the post-Zhanaozen trials, the clampdown on opposition parties, and the closure of more than forty media outlets, including the well-known *Vzglyad* and *Respublika* newspapers, as a strategy to reduce debate and social tension ahead of a political transition. There are also signs that Nazarbayev is burnishing his historical legacy. In 2012, December 1 was declared as a new public holiday—President's Day. Across the country, concerts, exhibitions, and competitions were held. In Astana, the climax was a show titled "One Country! One Destiny! One Leader!" featuring a mass singalong and the waving of banners depicting Nazarbayev. The president is the subject of flattering books, movies, and theater productions, and even appears in a children's fairy tale. A movie trilogy called *Way of the Leader*, based on Nazarbayev's memoirs, was completed in 2013. The Museum of the First President of the Republic of Kazakhstan in Astana depicts the humble home of his parents in Chemolgan, with a spinning wheel, soup bowls, and wooden spoons. It also includes Nazarbayev's first typewriter, his first reception room with its six phones, and the graduation gowns he has worn when receiving honorary doctorates abroad. A street in Jordan's capital, Amman, has been named for him, and a statue built in Turkey's capital Ankara.

Citizens like to compare Kazakhstan with other Central Asian republics. Kyrgyzstan is certainly more democratic, with the parliament balancing the power of the president, but it remains a poor country, heavily dependent on foreign aid, and has experienced two revolutions and ethnic violence in the south. Tajikistan is as poor as Kyrgyzstan and is beset by ethnic and regional power struggles that led to a five-year civil war in the 1990s. In Uzbekistan, a Soviet police state has been replaced by a domestic one; the economy is stifled by bureaucracy, and the country's human rights record is worse than Kazakhstan's. There were hopes that Turkmenistan would open itself up after the death of the so-called Turkmenbashi, Sapamurat Niyazov, in 2006, but his successor as president, Gurnanguly Berdymukhammedov, has done little to change the most closed and policed society in Central Asia, replacing one personality cult with another. By comparison with its neighbors, Kazakhstan looks like a leader on almost all counts.

twelve

The Seven Lessons of Stanland

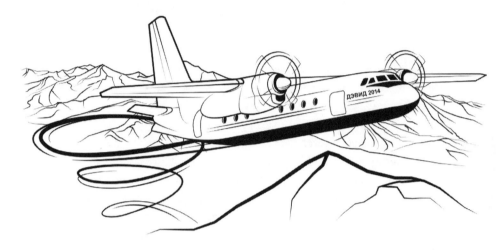

The more I've learned about Central Asia, the less inclined I am to accept broad-brushstroke analyses by governments, international organizations, scholars, and journalists. How can we talk about Kyrgyzstan as a country without considering the north-south divide? In Kazakhstan, oil, gas, clan loyalties, ethnicity, language, the wealth gap, and the sheer size of the country make any conclusions tentative. It would be comforting to come up with key points—the "Things we all need to know about Central Asia" list—but it would not do justice to such a complex region. The best I can do is offer seven lessons learned.

#1: Oil, Afghanistan and Democracy

In 1999, I was hired by USAID to travel through the region to interview journalists, media owners, and human rights activists. My job was to find out why journalists were not working together in professional associations to raise standards and battle for press freedom. For an academic, it was a dream assignment. I was working for the Central Asia

278

Office of Democratic Transition (ODT), whose modest mission was to jump-start democracy, political pluralism, and the free press. Yet just down the corridor at the US embassy, a larger and better-paid group of consultants was busy promoting economic development, helping US companies negotiate for oil, gas, and minerals leases, and pushing for legislation to protect foreign investors. For them, political stability and law and order were essential, even if they came at the expense of human rights and press freedoms. The court of USAID was divided into two factions. I always knew which was stronger.

After the fall of the Soviet Union, Americans "plunged headlong" into Central Asia, writes Karl Meyer, "the way led before 9/11 by high-minded nongovernmental organizations and profit-minded energy executives, followed after 9/11 by convoys of Pentagon officials, special White House emissaries and eager members of Congress."[1] As long as only US economic interests were at stake, the democracy and human rights faction had a fighting chance, but once military and security considerations were in the mix, all it could do was shoot off critical reports on rigged elections, human rights abuses, restrictive media legislation, and dismal press freedom rankings. Although the United States and other Western governments sometimes added their voices, most criticism was ignored because it came without penalties or sanctions.

Western governments hoped that the honor of chairing the OSCE in 2010 would convince Kazakhstan to mend its ways, open up politics to opposition parties, and repeal restrictions on press and Internet freedom. The hopes were in vain. Kazakhstan took the carrot, ate it, and boasted about eating it; the stick was never wielded. In November 2012, less than a year after the massacre of striking oil workers in Zhanaozen and a month after the jailing of Vladimir Kozlov for "inciting social discord," Kazakhstan was elected to a seat on the UN Human Rights Council, winning support from all but 10 of the UN's 193 members. There was no penalty for bad behavior. Not only did Kazakhstan's government not get sent to its room, it continued to be invited to all the best international parties.

The paradox has played out on a broad canvas since 9/11. The leaders of Kyrgyzstan, Kazakhstan, and Uzbekistan opened up their roads, railroads, air corridors, and military bases for the campaign in Afghanistan, and were rewarded with aid and diplomatic cover. In 2002, the United States promised to triple annual aid to Uzbekistan to $160 million, despite rigged elections, President Karimov's crackdown on opposition and media, and the routine torture of political prisoners. In 2005, Karimov ordered troops to fire on demonstrators in Andijan in the Fergana Valley. At least 187 were killed (some put the death toll at over 1,000), and thousands fled over the border to southern Kyrgyzstan. While the US State Department condemned the crackdown and reduced aid, US Central Command quietly continued to fund the Uzbek military. Since 2009, the NATO-led coalition has used the so-called Northern Distribution Network (NDN) of road and rail routes through Kazakhstan, Kyrgyzstan, Tajikistan, and Uzbekistan to ship supplies to Afghanistan; the Central Asian states have reaped an estimated $500 million a year in "access fees" for the NDN. As NATO withdraws, they will continue to benefit not only from the fees but from "excess defense articles," such as military vehicles and hardware, either donated or sold at yard-sale prices. The NATO allies are not going to fuss about human rights violations in the Central Asian republics while extricating themselves from Afghanistan.

However, to shrug off "creeping authoritarianism as a price worth paying in the bigger geopolitical and financial game" is a mistake, says the *Economist*. "Tyrannies with unhappy subjects are unlikely to be reliable economic or strategic partners."[2] Such realpolitik, writes Meyer, amounts to abandoning Central Asians "who have taken seriously America's oft repeated pledges to promote human rights and genuine elections, as well as to succor freedom of speech and worship." The task facing Washington, he adds, "is to deal fairly and effectively with Central Asia's rulers without becoming their accessories in abusing human rights, creating dynastic oligarchies and funneling unearned increments into Swiss bank accounts."[3]

#2: The New Great Game

If you want to leave Kazakhstan, learn English. If you want to stay, learn Chinese.

What started as a joke in business and government circles in Astana and Almaty has taken on a serious tone as China's economic, military, and political clout has increased. In the nineteenth century, China watched from the sidelines as Russian and British explorers, envoys, and spies wandered around its western provinces and Tibet, mapping trade routes, building alliances with local leaders, and hatching plots. The Chinese empire, weakened by internal discord and rebellion, could not play in the Great Game. By the end of the twentieth century, the roles were, if not reversed, at least rebalanced, with China vying with Russia and the United States in a new Great Game. Hungry for oil, gas, and natural resources, China has invested heavily in Kazakhstan's energy sector. It built the pipeline to carry oil from the Caspian Sea east to Xinjiang, and is financing construction of a gas pipeline and a 1,700-mile stretch of highway to connect China with Europe. Russia, Europe, and the United States support pipelines running west to the Black Sea and Turkey. For now, there's plenty of oil to flow both ways, but the supply will not last forever. Analysts worry about population pressures: if its cities cannot accommodate more people, will China look west to the sparsely populated steppe?

The end of the Soviet Union briefly revived the dream of the Uighurs of Xinjiang of uniting with their fellow Muslims in a Greater Turkestan or caliphate. China leaned heavily on Kazakhstan, Kyrgyzstan, and Tajikistan to restrict Uighur political activity and settled the border disputes that had plagued Chinese-Soviet relations. China has reduced the demographic power of the Uighurs by resettling Han Chinese in Xinjiang. With oil from Kazakhstan and gas from Turkmenistan, China no longer has to rely on sea routes that can be disrupted by the United States. China brought the Central Asian republics into the Shanghai Cooperation Organization and exploited new export markets.

Russia has long-standing economic ties with Kazakhstan. It's also the economic magnet for thousands of migrant workers from Kyrgyzstan and Tajikistan, the two poorest countries in the region. Remittances from migrant workers in Russia account for about 29 percent of Kyrgyzstan's GDP and 47 percent of Tajikistan's. Russia provides aid and loans and maintains military bases in both countries. With the withdrawal of NATO forces from Afghanistan and the handover of the Manas air base in Bishkek, the United States no longer has a significant military presence in Central Asia, but its economic interests, particularly in Kazakhstan's oil, gas, and mining sectors and in banking, make it the other major player. Iran and Turkey are also in the game, although only Turkey has so far invested heavily in the Central Asian economies and sought influence through education and social programs.

It may be too much to revive Sir Halford Mackinder's theory and claim that Central Asia is once again the "geographical pivot of history." It's a complicated world, and other regions—notably the Middle East and East Asia—will vie for the title. Central Asia is more of a paradox than a pivot, but what happens there as China, Russia, the United States, Turkey, and Iran—and possibly India, making a late entry to the game—compete will affect the world balance of economic and political power. As the journalist Ahmed Rashid, author of two books on Central Asia, remarks: "One of the great dangers for the U.S. and other Western powers will be continuing ignorance and neglect of what is happening there."[4]

#3: Mind the Gap

The Arab Spring of 2011 sent shock waves through the presidential palaces of Central Asia. If the rulers of Tunisia and Egypt could be overthrown so quickly by popular demonstrations, what could happen if crowds rallied in Ashgabat, Astana, Dushanbe, and Tashkent? Memories of the protests that toppled Kyrgyzstan's President Bakiyev and the ethnic violence in the south less than a year earlier were still vivid. Central Asian governments were quick to draw contrasts between conditions in their countries and those in the Middle East. At the same time, they stepped up surveillance on opposition groups and media and tightened restrictions on the Internet and social media. It was a case of blaming the messenger; although social media and text messages were the organizing tools of the Arab Spring, the protests were caused by political, social, and economic conditions, not by communication technology.

Among those weighing in with a "We're not Egypt" message was Nazarbayev, in an op-ed for the *Washington Post*. After independence, when Kazakhstan's economy "lay in ruins," he wrote, most of the world "dismissed us as a remote former Soviet republic." Now, twenty years later, "The Kazakh people's hard work and unity have led to a stable, multicultural nation with a strong economy and rapidly improving living standards and public services." He listed a series of achievements—a twelvefold increase in GDP per capita since 1991, a thriving private sector, a fast-growing middle class, ethnic and religious tolerance, and reforms to protect human rights, promote press freedom, and strengthen the independence of the judiciary. "We are not going to become a fully developed democracy overnight," he wrote. "But we have proved that we can deliver on our big ambitions."[5]

Nazarbayev's economic statistics were correct. At the same time, the gap between the rich and the poor has been widening. According to *Forbes*

Kazakhstan, the fifty richest people in the country are worth a combined $24 billion. They include Nazarbayev's daughter Dinara Nazarbayeva and her husband Timur Kulibayev (both billionaires), daughter Dariga Nazarbayeva and grandson Nurali Aliyev (millionaires). Taken alone, the Nazarbayev clan's wealth is estimated at about $7 billion, according to the Russian magazine the *New Times.*

High unemployment and poor living conditions in rural areas have fueled migration to the cities. The urban underclass is growing and with it fears of social unrest. Many unskilled migrants end up in low-paid jobs, struggling to pay for rent and food. In the shadow of corporate office blocks, condominiums and five-star hotels, people live in broken-down khrushchevkas or shacks built from rough lumber and scrap metal, without safe water or reliable heating. For the journalist Joshua Kucera, the paradox of wealth and poverty in the oil city of Atyrau was palpable. Most people, he wrote, "may not care much about the finer points of democracy and human rights, but they do resent their politically well-connected compatriots getting rich while their lives go nowhere. . . . If there is any challenge facing [Nazarbayev], it's not resentment over repression or authoritarianism, but inequality and corruption."[6]

In 2010, according to a report by the World Health Organization and UNICEF, three-quarters of Kazakhstan's rural population did not have access to safe running water. The poverty, education, and health indicators for rural populations in Kyrgyzstan, Tajikistan, and Uzbekistan are just as bad, if not worse, but at least these countries do not boast of "rapidly improving living standards and public services."

#4: Nation Building

Over lunch at ENU, I asked my colleague Zhas Sabitov, a political scientist, for a rundown of Kazakhstan's political demographics. "There are three groups," he said, with a smile. "The Kazakh-speaking Kazakhs vote for nationalist parties. They think Nazarbayev is a traitor to his people for working with the Russians and the West. The Russian-speaking Kazakhs are doing well in the economy. They vote for Nazarbayev to maintain stability. And the Russians who don't speak Kazakh vote for Nazarbayev because they are afraid the first group is going to kill them."

It's not as simple as that, of course, but Zhas's wry summary points to the intersection of ethnicity, language, economy, and politics. Most

Kazakh speakers live in rural areas, where jobs and services are lacking. Some feel as poor and neglected as in the Soviet era, but now the pain is more deeply felt because it is ethnic Kazakhs, not Russians, who are running the show. Russian-speaking Kazakhs make up most of the urban middle class. Their incomes and living standards have been improving, and they credit Nazarbayev with developing the economy and maintaining social stability. Russians may resent the preference given to Kazakhs in government jobs and higher education, and the increasing use of the Kazakh language in schools and for official business. They may grumble that Russia's contribution to Kazakhstan's development has been written out of the history books and that the street names have been changed. Through the 1990s, some voted with their feet, moving to a Russia most had never known. Those who stayed admit that things could have turned out worse if a rabid nationalist, not Nazarbayev, had been in power. They worry what will happen when he is gone.

For Nazarbayev, another message is as persuasive as "We're not Egypt." It's "We're not Kyrgyzstan." The so-called island of democracy has experienced two revolutions, violent ethnic clashes, and political turmoil, while the economy has tanked, poverty levels have risen, and education and social services have declined. Are these the fruits of democracy? It's tempting to attribute the problems to a weak and divided government that was unable to maintain control, and to an open political system that allowed extremists to garner support. This interpretation overlooks the social and economic conditions—poverty and lack of housing and social services—that breed protest, but it is readily accepted by those who believe the dangers of democracy, political pluralism, and press freedom outweigh the benefits. They fear that granting too much freedom will unleash divisive ethnic, religious, and political forces. What is the point of liberty, they argue, if it destroys the nation?

#5: Reinventing History

Each Central Asian republic has tried to create a usable past—a collective narrative with a timeline and gallery of heroes to build national unity. Everywhere, this has involved renaming cities, towns, and streets, erecting statues and monuments, creating museum displays, and rewriting school textbooks. In Uzbekistan, historians have adopted a "history of the territory" approach. That means that anything that ever happened within the borders of present-day Uzbekistan becomes the country's historical property, making it possible to depict thousands of years of "Uzbek" history. The texts and artifacts of ancient civilizations living between the Amu Darya and Syr Darya rivers? Definitely Uzbek. The fourteenth-century warlord, Tamerlane (Timur), who gives his name to a street in almost every city and has a whole museum in Tashkent dedicated to him? Also Uzbek (although he wasn't). Timur's capital of Samarkand, and Bukhara, the great centers of Tajik culture? Centers of Uzbek culture. By contrast, Tajik historians have had to adopt a geographically elastic approach, focusing on historical periods when Tajik culture was dominant in Central Asia. That allows them to reclaim Samarkand and Bukhara, at least in their writings.

Historians in Kazakhstan can focus on the three hordes and the eighteenth-century batyrs and bis, and then skip to Abai Qunanbayev and other Kazakh writers, and finally to the Alash Orda movement. In Kyrgyzstan, which has almost no written history, there are more gaps to fill. That did not prevent the government from celebrating "2,200 years of Kyrgyz statehood" in 2003. The claim was based on Chinese annals from the first century BCE that describe a tribe known as the Yenisei Kyrgyz living in what today is southern Siberia. They did not start moving south to the Tian Shan until the tenth century, so "statehood" seems a stretch. The national epic is the *Manas,* which may be the world's longest praise poem; with more than half a million lines, it's about thirty times as long as *The Odyssey* and can take three weeks to recite. It recounts the exploits of an ancient hero, with superhuman powers, who vowed at the age of twelve to free the Kyrgyz people from oppression and establish a homeland. The epic is preserved and delivered by *manaschis,* masters of recitation who chant it at festivals and other gatherings. Some Kyrgyz claim that the epic is more than a thousand years old—a leap of time-travel proportions, considering that most events described took place in the sixteenth and seventeenth centuries. Like other praise poems, the content was shaped by the prevailing political climate. In nineteenth-century versions, Manas is the leader of the Nogay people, a Turkic tribe from the north Caucasus. In versions dating from 1920, when the Soviets were constructing a distinct Kyrgyz nationality, Manas becomes a leader of the Kyrgyz.

Each nation reconstructs history to suit its present purposes, but in Central Asia, where the republics did not exist until the Soviets created the SSRs, the reinvention of a usable past along with national heroes has become an academic cottage industry. In the Uzbek narrative, the bloodthirsty Tamerlane is repackaged as a wise philosopher-king and national role model. All the Kazakh batyrs are noble, patriotic warriors. It's no different in nationalistic Russia where Stalin usually finishes in the top five in the list of most-admired historical figures. You can do wonderful things with history if you try.

#6: The Dead Dog of Press Freedom

In May 2002, Irina Petrushka, editor of the independent newspaper *Respublika*, found the headless body of a dog tied to the door of the newspaper's offices in Almaty with a note that read, "This is the last warning." The newspaper had been a thorn in the side of the authorities for exposing official corruption and supporting an opposition party. Several days later the office was burned down. Petrushka, who was under police surveillance and feared for her life, fled the country.

The dead dog was a warning not only to *Respublika* but to all journalists to toe the line and not probe too deeply into the murky doings of Kazakhstan's political and business elite. It was simply the latest, and most gruesome, incident in an ongoing war against independent media. In 2012, the media monitoring group Adil Soz recorded 19 assaults on journalists, 17 criminal cases (including 11 of criminal libel), more than 100 civil libel suits, and more than 180 cases where access to websites, online forums, and blogs was denied. Many journalists put personal survival ahead of principles and adopt self-censorship. They know which topics are safe to cover, which are not, and for those on the borderline, how far they can go.

The paradox is that some refuse to bow to pressure. For more than a decade, *Respublika* dodged and weaved but managed to keep publishing. Banned from printing in Almaty, it moved its operation to Bishkek and shipped copies across the border. In 2009, faced with a $400,000 fine for an opinion piece critical of the government-owned BTA bank, staff started publishing using office equipment. Banned from street newsstands, the newspaper was circulated privately. When the authorities filed legal papers against *Respublika*, it changed its name; when papers were filed against the new name, it was changed again. Today, it relies primarily on the Internet and social media, playing a cat-and-mouse game of proxy servers and domains as the authorities try to block it. The government uses a range of legal and extralegal weapons, including pressure on advertisers and bureaucratic regulations, to stifle opposition voices. As an Almaty radio station director put it to me, "The government has many gears."

The government accuses media outlets of the vague crime of "inciting social discord." Despite a constitution and media law that proclaim press freedom and lots of fine words about democracy and international best practices, Kazakhstan has less press freedom than at any time in its postindependence history, and most of the time its Western allies don't seem to care.

#7: The Virtues of Slow Travel

I have two travel heroes. The first is the Muslim legal scholar Ibn Battuta who in 1325 set out from Tangier (on the north coast of present-day Morocco) for his once-in-a-lifetime haj to Mecca. Then he just kept on going. He traversed the Mediterranean, Middle East, and Persia; he spent twelve years in the Indian subcontinent and traveled to Southeast Asia and China before returning to North Africa. In 1351, he was back on the road, across the Sahara to Mali. Finally, he sat down in Fez with another Muslim scholar to record thirty years of travel experiences.

Battuta, who has been compared to the most famous medieval Christian traveler, Marco Polo, was an eagle-eyed observer of the world around him, making notes on landscape, people, religion, politics, trade, and many other topics. He was able to do so because, like all travelers of his age, he moved slowly. Most of the 75,000 miles he logged was by camel. Renting camels isn't as easy as it once was, so it's impossible to match the pace of Battuta's travels. That's a pity because as travelers we could learn much from Battuta's patient observations.

My second travel hero is the cultural geographer Hubert Wilhelm, who traveled faster than Battuta but still pretty slowly. He was always frustrating family and friends by refusing to drive on the interstates, instead taking state highways, county and township roads, stopping as often as possible to inspect houses, barns, and farm buildings, and wandering through cemeteries with German gravestones. It took him hours to get anywhere, but he saw patterns in the landscape that are invisible from highways that flatten the landscape into a reassuring sameness and where the journey is marked only by exit numbers and rest areas.

You need to slow down to understand any place, and certainly Central Asia. The region often presents two contrasting images to the outside world. I'll call them the new and old yurt images. The first is epitomized by Astana, the Dubai of the steppe, the modern, business-friendly city with five-star hotels, upscale malls, and sushi bars; there the yurt is that monument to conspicuous consumption and presidential excess, the Khan Shatyr. The second is an idyllic scene of traditional culture, a mountain valley dotted with spring wildflowers, horses, falcons, traditional crafts, and shashlyk roasting on the spit; tourists sit cross-legged on brightly colored shirdaks in a real yurt listening to a manaschi reciting lines from the *Manas* while young women in national dress serve herder fast food, tea, and kumys before performing a traditional dance.

Both these scenes exist, and are often presented in dramatic counterpoint in tourist brochures: "From mountain pastures and endless steppe to modern cities, from the ancient Silk Road to international airports, from traditional food to European and Asian cuisine, from horseback games to rock concerts, Central Asia brings together . . . ." And so on. However, everyday life for most citizens has little to do with either. Most people live in khrushchevkas and brezhnevkas, not in condos or yurts; they travel by train and bus, not by horse or in business class; for entertainment, they usually watch TV. These less exciting images are the Central Asia I know.

I feel privileged to have traveled in Central Asia before interstates are built. I have not had a Battuta experience, of course, but I've tried to follow Hubert's advice and travel slowly. Most times when I hail down a car in Almaty, Astana, or Bishkek, the driver has something to tell me; in a train, long-distance bus or marshrutka, passengers share food, jokes, and rumors. Even with air travel, my trips in old Soviet puddle-jumpers—the Antonov-24 and the Yak-40—have been more revealing than faster, higher-altitude flights in Airbuses and Boeings. And, of course, I've walked in all sorts of weather—to the bazaar, to the university, to restaurants, to shiver at the bus stop, to get my shoes repaired, to get a haircut, to pay a $2.50 phone bill. For me, slow travel is the only way to grasp the paradoxes of places and people, and to start telling their stories. I'll always be writing postcards.

Notes

Chapter 1: Travels in "Kyrzakhstan"

1. Lee Moran, "John Kerry Gaffe: In New Role as Secretary of State, He Mistakenly Creates a New Country—Kyrzakhstan—during Speech," *New York Daily News*, February 26, 2013.

2. Jonathan Earle, "John Kerry Invents Country of Kyrzakhstan," *Telegraph*, February 25, 2013.

3. Cheryl K. Chumley, "John Kerry Defends Americans' 'Right to Be Stupid' a Day after Inventing Country Named Kyrzakhstan," *Washington Times*, February 26, 2013; "John Kerry's Dumb Talk," http://thecolbertreport.cc.com/videos/r7gapm/john-kerry-s-dumb-talk.

4. Karl E. Meyer, *The Dust of Empire: The Race for Mastery in the Asian Heartland* (New York: Century Foundation, 2003), 31.

5. Colin Thubron, *The Lost Heart of Asia* (New York: Harper Collins, 1994), 1–2.

6. Maira Kalman and Rick Meyerowitz, "New Yorkistan" cover for the *New Yorker*, December 10, 2001.

7. Halford J. Mackinder, "The Geographical Pivot of History," *Geographical Journal* 23, no. 4 (April 1904): 421–37.

Chapter 2: Sacred Mountain and Silly Borders

1. "All Monuments of Lenin to Be Removed from Russian Cities," *Russia Today*, November 21, 2012.

2. Leila Saralaeva, "Lenin Toppled in Kyrgyzstan," *Institute for War and Peace Reporting*, February 21, 2005.

3. Ibid.

4. John King, *Central Asia: A Lonely Planet Travel Survival Kit* (Hawthorn, Victoria, Australia: Lonely Planet, 1996), 417.

5. UNESCO World Heritage List, "Sulaiman-Too Sacred Mountain," http://whc.unesco.org/en/list/1230.

6. Karl E. Meyer and Shareen Blair Brysac, *Tournament of Shadows: The Great Game and the Race for Empire in Central Asia* (Washington, DC: Counterpoint, 1999), 121.

7. Alexander Morrison, "Writing the Russian Conquest of Central Asia," https://www.academia.edu/1710833/Writing_the_Russian_Conquest_of_Central_Asia.

8. Madeleine Reeves, "A Weekend in Osh," *London Review of Books,* July 8, 2010, 17.

9. Ahmed Rashid, "Why, and What, You Should Know About Central Asia," *New York Review of Books,* August 15, 2013.

10. "Central Asia: Day of the Bully," *Economist,* October 25, 2001.

Chapter 3: How Do You Say "Rump Roast"?

1. John King, *Central Asia: A Lonely Planet Travel Survival Kit* (Hawthorn, Victoria, Australia: Lonely Planet, 1996), 358.

Chapter 4: Kasha, Honor, Dignity, and Revolution

1. Martha C. Merrill, "Kasha and Quality in Kyrgyzstan: Donors, Diversity, and Dis-Integration in Higher Education," *European Education* 43, no. 4 (Winter 2011–12): 5.

2. "Former Soviet Bloc Corruption Threatens Education," *Vanderbilt Magazine,* July 2008, http://www.vanderbilt.edu/magazines/vanderbilt-magazine/2008/07/former_soviet_bloc_corruption_threatens_education/.

3. Jeremy Bransten, "Kyrgyzstan: Democracy and a Free Press—Endangered Species?" *Radio Free Europe/Radio Liberty,* October 14, 1997.

4. "Kyrgyzstan: Journalist Remains a Prisoner of Conscience after Inconclusive Trial Outcome," *Amnesty International Index,* May 21, 1997; Committee to Protect Journalists, "Kyrgyz journalist sentenced for libel," e-mail to President Askar Akayev, September 29, 1997.

5. "Kyrgyzstan: A Criminal Offense," *Transitions,* June 1998, 86–87.

6. Madeleine Reeves, "Getting to the Roots of Resentment in Kyrgyzstan," *Radio Free Europe/Radio Liberty,* July 4, 2010; Reeves, "The Ethnicisation of Violence in Southern Kyrgyzstan," *openDemocracy,* June 21, 2010.

7. "Stubborn Facts on the Ground," *Economist,* April 20, 2013, 46.

8. Madeleine Reeves, "A Weekend in Osh," *London Review of Books,* July 8, 2010, 18.

Chapter 5: On and Off the Silk Road

1. Karl E. Meyer and Shareen Blair Brysac, *Tournament of Shadows: The Great Game and the Race for Empire in Central Asia* (Washington, DC: Counterpoint, 1999), 230–31.

2. "Kyrgyzstan: Gold in the Hills," *The Economist,* March 16, 2013.

3. John King, *Central Asia: A Lonely Planet Travel Survival Kit* (Hawthorn, Victoria, Australia: Lonely Planet, 1996), 251.

4. "A Seven-Star Hotel and a Seven-Dollar Breakfast" was originally published as "Seven-Star Service," *Christian Science Monitor,* September 22, 2009.

Chapter 6: To Be a Kazakh Is to Be "Brave and Free"

1. "The Best and Worst Places for Women," *Daily Beast,* September 20, 2011.

2. "Kazakhstan Announces Winners of International Journalism Competition," *Astana Times,* July 4, 2014.

3. Jason Lewis, "Oil Rich Dictator of Kazakhstan Recruits Tony Blair to Help Win Nobel Peace Prize," *Telegraph*, October 29, 2011; James Kilmer, "Tony Blair Stars in Kazakhstan Promotional Video," *Telegraph*, April 23, 2012.

4. Mike Harris, "Why Is Tony Blair Lending Credibility to Kazakhstan's Dictator?" *Telegraph*, February 24, 2012.

5. Deirdre Tynan, "Kazakhstan: Top-Notch PR Firms Help Brighten Astana's Image," EurasiaNet.org, January 18, 2012.

6. Ken Silverstein, "Dictators Rely on D.C. Front Men," Salon.com, December 14, 2011.

7. "The Can't-Win Candidate" was originally published under the same title in *Transitions Online*, March 28, 2011.

8. "Election Shenanigans" is adapted from "Independent, with an Asterisk," *Transitions Online*, April 7, 2011.

9. Asqat Yerkimbay, interview with author, November 9, 2013. All following quotations of Yerkimbay are from this interview.

10. Joanna Lillis, "Kazakhstan: The ABCs of the Alphabet Debate," EurasiaNet.org, April 3, 2013.

Chapter 7: Father of Apples

1. Andrew Osborn, "As if Things Weren't Bad Enough, Russian Professor Predicts End of U.S.," *Wall Street Journal*, December 29, 2008.

2. Interviews with Gennadiy Khonin, Aleksandr Dederer, and Viktor Kist originally published in "Between Deutschland and Karaganda," *Transitions Online*, August 29, 2011.

3. Ibid.

4. Ibid.

Chapter 8: The President's Dream City

1. Rowan Moore, "Astana: Kazakhstan: The Space Station in the Steppes," *Observer*, August 7, 2010.

2. Quoted in Natalie Koch, "Urban 'Utopias': The Disney Stigma and Discourses of 'False Modernity,'" *Environment and Planning* 44, no. 10 (2012): 2446.

3. Quoted in Joanna Lillis, "Kazakhstan: Nazarbayev Eyes Legacy as Astana Reaches Adolescence," EurasiaNet.org, July 8, 2013.

4. "Laying the Golden Egg," *Economist*, July 13, 2013, 38.

5. Koch, "Urban 'Utopias,'" 2446. See also Koch, "The City and the Steppe: Territory, Technologies of Government, and Kazakhstan's New Capital" (PhD diss., University of Colorado, 2012).

6. Koch, "Urban 'Utopias,'" 2446.

7. Ibid., 2451–52.

8. Quoted in Natalie Koch, "Why Not a World City? Astana, Ankara, and Geopolitical Scripts in Urban Networks," *Urban Geography* 34, no. 1 (2013): 109.

9. "Aaarghmola," *Economist*, July 24, 1997.

10. "A Glittering New Kazakh Capital, on the Face of It," *New York Times*, November 9, 1997.

11. "Laying the Golden Egg," 38.

12. Quoted in Michael Steen, "Kazakh President's 'Backyard' Pyramid," *Sydney Morning Herald*, October 16, 2006.

13. "Urban 'Utopias,'" 2454.

14. Steen, "Kazakh President's 'Backyard' Pyramid."

15. "Urban 'Utopias,'" 2455–56.

16. Ibid.

Chapter 9: Coal and Steel

1. John King, *Central Asia: A Lonely Planet Travel Survival Kit* (Hawthorn, Victoria, Australia: Lonely Planet, 1996), 245.

2. Lonely Planet, "Introducing Karaganda," http://www.lonelyplanet.com/kazakhstan/northern-kazakhstan/karaganda.

3. Aleksandr Solzhenitsyn, *One Day in the Life of Ivan Denisovich*, trans. Ralph Parker (New York: E. P. Dutton, 1963), 53.

4. Quoted in Maria Golovnina, "Forgotten Stalin Victims Despair in Kazakh Steppe," *Reuters*, December 21, 2009.

5. Jonathan Aitken, *Nazarbayev and the Making of Kazakhstan: From Communism to Capitalism* (London: Bloomsbury Academic, 2009).

6. "Temirtau's Businessmen Want President's Monument Carved into a Mountain," *Interfax Kazakhstan*, July 8, 2011.

Chapter 10: No Polygon, No Problem

1. Interviews with Magda Stawkowski, Robert Kopack, Naila Dusembayeva, Kaisha Atakhanova, Gulsum Kakimzhanova, and Dmitry Kalmykov originally published in "In Kazakhstan, the Grass Is Greener at the Nuclear Test Site," *Transitions Online*, June 9, 2011, and "Warming to Life in the Hot Zone," *Times Higher Education*, January 12, 2012.

2. Louise Gray, "New Life in an Atomic Wasteland," *Telegraph*, August 30, 2011.

3. Quoted by Interfax Kazakhstan, July 29, 2010.

4. "A Nuclear Dustbin?" *Economist*, September 8, 2001, 46.

Chapter 11: Wheat and Oil

1. Interviews with Viktor Simanenko, Shaurab Zhempisov, and Almabek Nugmanov originally published in "Kazakhstan Needs Its Vegetables," *Transitions Online*, May 4, 2011.

2. Nate Schenkkan, "Kazakhstan: Astana at a Turning Point," EurasiaNet.org, March 26, 2012.

3. Interview with Seytkazy Matayev originally published in "Going Digital, Playing Politics," *Transitions Online,* November 1, 2012.

4. "Is Kazakhstan's Zhanaozen to Be Wiped Off the Map?" *Radio Free Europe/ Radio Liberty,* November 1, 2012.

Chapter 12: The Seven Lessons of Stanland

1. Karl E. Meyer, *The Dust of Empire: The Race for Mastery in the Asian Heartland* (New York: Century Foundation, 2003), 207.

2. "Central Asia: Stopping the Rot," *Economist,* May 4, 2002, 14.

3. Meyer, *Dust of Empire,* 198.

4. Ahmed Rashid, "Why, and What, You Should Know About Central Asia," *New York Review of Books,* August 15, 2013.

5. Nursultan Nazarbayev, "Kazakhstan's Steady Progress toward Democracy," *Washington Post,* March 31, 2011.

6. Joshua Kucera, "Kazakhstan Rising," Slate.com, August 4, 2011.

Glossary and Acronyms

Alash Orda: political party formed by Kazakh intellectuals. It set up a provisional government after the 1917 Russian Revolution but surrendered to the Red Army in 1919; its leaders were executed or sent to labor camps

Akim(a): mayor or governor

Akimat: municipal or provincial administration

ASSR: Autonomous Soviet Socialist Republic

Babushka: grandmother

Banya: traditional Russian sauna

Basmachi: guerrillas who resisted Soviet occupation of Central Asia

Batyr: hero, knight or brave warrior, a title bestowed upon individuals for military service among Turkic and Mongol peoples

Bek: a Turkic word meaning noble or chief

Besh barmak (five fingers): traditional Kazakh and Kyrgyz dish of boiled mutton and noodles, so called because it is eaten with the fingers

Bi: sage or judge among Kazakhs

Brezhnevka: standard apartment built in Brezhnev era

Chaikhana: traditional Uzbek tea house

Dacha: a small house with a garden outside the city

Dombyra: traditional Kazakh fretless stringed instrument

Dezhurnaya: hotel floor lady

Dvor: courtyard (usually of an apartment complex)

Glavni corpus: main university building

Karlag: Karagandinskiy Ispravitel'no-trudovoy Lager' (Karaganda Corrective Labor Camp).

Kasha: literally porridge, but in slang "a little bit of this and that" or a mishmash

Khan: Mongol and Central Asian name for king or military ruler

KMG: KazMunayGaz, Kazakhstan's state oil and gas company

Kolkhoz: the contracted form of kollektivnoye khozyaystvo, meaning collective farm or economy

Kolpak: traditional Kyrgyz and Kazakh felt man's hat

Komuz: traditional Kyrgyz fretless stringed instrument

Khrushchevka: standard apartment built from prefabricated concrete panels to meet the post–World War II housing shortage

Laghman: Uighur spicy noodle and vegetable soup

Lipioshki: flat bread, baked in tandoori oven

Mahalla: Uzbek neighborhood, with courtyard houses

Manas: Kyrgyz national epic poem

Manti: a Kyrgyz and Kazakh dish, dumplings stuffed with diced lamb and onion

Marshrutka: short for marshrutnoye taksi (routed taxi), which follows a route, picking up and dropping off passengers

Microraion: microregion, usually a suburban district of apartment blocks

Nooruz: traditional Turkic New Year celebration in March

Oblast: province

Oralmans: ethnic Kazakhs (from Uzbekistan, Turkmenistan, Xinjiang, Mongolia, and Russia) who moved to Kazakhstan after independence, with government subsidies for housing and relocation

OSCE: Organisation for Security and Cooperation in Europe

OVIR: Otdel Viz i Registratsii (Department of Visas and Registration)

Perestroika: Gorbachev-era policy of social and economic transition (literally restructuring or rebuilding)

Plov: Uzbek dish common throughout Central Asia, a lamb pilaf with carrots, onions, and hot peppers

Polygon (Semipalatinsk Polygon): region of northeastern Kazakhstan where for 40 years Soviet Union conducted above- and belowground nuclear tests

Ru: Kazakh tribe

Samogon: literally "self-run," a homemade distilled alcoholic concoction, usually made from sugar, beets, potatoes, bread, or fruit

Samsa: pastry filled with spicy meat or vegetables

Shashlyk: marinated mutton or beef kebabs, grilled and served with vinegary onions

Shirdak: traditional, brightly colored Kyrgyz felt rug

SSR: Soviet Socialist Republic

Stalinka: brick or cinder-block apartment blocks built from the 1930s to 1950s, some with neoclassical architectural features

Subbotnik: community work day (usually for students)

Trudarmiya: Labor Army, convicts deported to Siberia and the Kazakh SSR during Stalin era to work in industry and agriculture

Tsum: central department store

Turksib: Turkestan-Siberia Railway (Tashkent to Novosibirsk)

Virgin Lands: Soviet scheme launched in the 1960s to convert almost 100,000 square miles of grassland in the Kazakh SSR and Ukraine into arable land to raise wheat and other grains

Wiedergeburt (Rebirth): social and cultural association of ethnic Germans in Kazakhstan

Yurt: traditional Kyrgyz nomadic dwelling of sheepskins or canvas stretched over a wooden frame

Zek: convict in Soviet labor camp

Zheltoqsan (December): nationalist protests in Alma-Ata in 1986, suppressed by Soviet troops

Zhuz: horde, or confederation of tribes; Kazakhs identify as members of the Great, Middle, or Little Horde

Acknowledgments

In the mid-1990s, when I first worked in Central Asia, the literature on the region was scant. Today, there's an expanding pool of academic scholarship, think-tank analysis, journalistic reporting, and commentary, in print and online, on almost every topic. There's no room here to list all the scholarship, so I'll just mention the works I found particularly insightful. Of the many books on the struggle for power and commerce in the region, I found Peter Hopkirk's classic, *The Great Game,* Paul Georg Geiss's *Pre-Tsarist and Tsarist Central Asia,* and Karl E. Meyer and Shareen Blair Brysac's *Tournament of Shadows: The Great Game and the Race for Empire in Central Asia* thorough and enjoyable to read. Another book by Karl E. Meyer, *The Dust of Empire: The Race for Mastery in the Asian Heartland,* offers a more contemporary, but historically grounded, analysis. On the rise of Nazarbayev and the politics of oil, the works of Martha Brill Olcott (particularly *Kazakhhstan: Unfulfilled Promise?*) are essential reading. Even though it's uncritical ("mush and slush," as one reviewer put it), Jonathan Aitken's biography, *Nazarbayev and the Making of Kazakhstan,* provides a thorough, well-researched account of the leader's rise from humble roots. For current events, I relied primarily on online news sites, including *EurasiaNet,* with Joanna Lillis's insightful reporting on Kazakhstan, *Transitions Online,* the *Institute for War and Peace Reporting, Radio Free Europe/Radio Liberty*, and *Registan.* For other takes on controversial issues, I consulted Central Asian government and Russian sources.

Many people helped me along the way. Martin Hadlow, head of the UNESCO Almaty Cluster Office for Central Asia, and Bruce McGowan, the US embassy public affairs officer (PAO) in Kyrgyzstan, sponsored my first assignment in 1995. On my Fulbright in 1996–97, I worked closely with public affairs officer Kelly Keiderling, one of the smartest, most honest and direct US foreign service officers I've ever met. The United States Information Service staff in Bishkek, particularly Turat Makanbayev, Munara Munduzbayeva, and Larisa Desyatkova, provided outstanding support; I credit Turat with helping me understand how closely media in Kyrgyzstan are related to history and culture. I was privileged to work with Tarja Virtanen who, as UNESCO Central Asia head from 2006 to 2009, made media development and professional standards in journalism a priority. I've worked with Sergey Karpov, UNESCO's regional communication and information officer, on many projects, and count him as one of my dearest friends in the region. I also owe much to university colleagues: to Anisa Borubayeva, my first dean at Kyrgyz State National University; to Galiya Ibrayeva and Karliga Myssayeva at Kazakhh National University; to John Couper and Gulnar Assanbayeva at KIMEP; Yelena Kandalina and Olga Kungarova at Kostanai State University; Togzhan Mukatayeva and Galiya Damenova at Semey State University; Tatyana Golubsova at Karaganda State University; and Zhas Sabitov at Eurasian National University in Astana. And to my media colleagues and friends—Asqat Yerkimbay, Kazakh blogger, journalist, and media educator; Andrey Tsvetkov and Talgat Acirankulov, TV station directors in Bishkek; Renat Khusainov, the first manager of the Osh Media Resource Center; Dariya Tsyrenzhapova in Almaty; and Safo Saforov in Dushanbe. Parts of several chapters were previously published as freelance articles, features, and op-eds; in particular, I'd like to thank Barbara Frye, managing editor of *Transitions Online,* and Rebecca Attwood, features editor of *Times Higher Education,* for responding to my often quirky pitches and helping me focus my stories.

Over the years, my Russian has improved. Two teachers at Ohio University—Karen Evans-Romaine (now Professor of Slavic Languages and Literature at the University of Wisconsin–Madison) and Vera Belousova—helped me grasp (if not exactly master) the basics of grammar, writing, and reading. Vera kindly reviewed the manuscript and corrected my transliterations. Credit for my speaking skills goes primarily to two teachers in Central Asia—Galina Shumkina in Bishkek and Galiya Suleimenova in Astana—although both also helped me greatly with grammar, writing, and reading. I could not have survived without excellent interpreters and assistants—Gulkhan Borubayeva at Kyrgyz State National and Aigul Karimshakova with Bishkek media, Irina Velska in Almaty and Astana, Diana Akizhamova at Eurasian National University, Dina Khamitova in Almaty, and Darya Nenakhova in Karaganda.

Others who offered support and friendship don't fit easily into categories, so I'll just mention them in turn: Martha Merrill, a professor of higher education at Kent State University, my fellow Fulbrighter in Kyrgyzstan, who stayed on much longer than I did; Harvey Flad, a geography professor, also a Fulbrighter in 1997, and his wife, Mary; Elizabeth Sammons, my coauthor for a book chapter on journalism ethics in Central Asia; Manil Cooray, deputy director of the Asia-Pacific Institute for Broadcasting Development, based in Kuala Lumpur, who provided logistical support for several workshops in Almaty; Magda Stawkowski, my guide to Kazakhstan's Polygon region; and Hal Foster, a former *Los Angeles Times* journalist, my friend (and sometime apartment mate) in Astana in 2011.

My editor at the Ohio University Press, Gillian Berchowitz, encouraged me to undertake this project, and was both a reliable guide and thoughtful critic through the writing and production process. Brian Balsley used his cartographic skills and creativity to produce maps that matched the narrative tone. My talented graduate assistant at Ohio University, Heather Porter, contributed the illustrations.

My deepest gratitude is to my wife, Stephanie Hysmith, who shared the joys and challenges of living in Kyrgyzstan for a year in the mid-1990s. Although she hasn't returned to the region with me since then, she has always supported me in my travels and encouraged me to write about them.

Index

Karaganda (Qaragandhy), 177, 188, 198, 206, 218, 219, 220, 225, 234, 236, 238, 239; climate, 216, 219; coal mining, 213–14, 225, 230; ethnic Germans, 215; growth during World War II, 214; history of, 213–15; iron and steel industry, 214; perceptions of, 213, 215–16; pollution, 213; reputation for crime, 214–15; as transportation center, 214; underground economy, 214–15

Karaganda Magnitka (Temirtau steel plant), 227–29

Karaganda State Medical University, 240

Karaganda State University, 216–17

Karakol (Przhevalsk), 94, 96, 98, 99, 102; architecture, 100, 100–101figs.; location, 100; name change, 102; settlement of, 95

Karakorum, 182, 183, 200

Kara-Kyrgyz, 33

Karimov, Islam, 35, 120, 137, 280

Karlag (labor camp system), 218–22, 225, 235

Karpov, Sergey, 128–30, 145, 300

Kashagan (oil field), 268, 270

Kashgar, 20, 250

Kazakh National University (Almaty), 170–71

Kazakh SSR, 33, 152, 162, 175, 188, 221, 228, 229, 266

Kazakhstan, xiii, 1, 4, 5, 7, 8, 19, 93, 131; agriculture, 161, 167–69, 260, 262–65; autonomous region, 146; comparison with other Central Asia countries, 277; economy, 134, 148, 158–59, 173, 188, 230–31, 276; environment, 222–25, 230–31; ethnic mix, 34–35, 147–49; as Eurasia, 135, 183, 200, 206; geography, 132; higher education, 172–73, 206, 261; human rights, 134, 274; international image, 136–37, 183, 184, 186, 205; language, 151–52, 153, 154–57, 206; map, 132; media, 139, 155–57, 274–75; migration, 148–49, 220, 229–30, 268, 271, 281; mineral resources, 150, 188, 225, 230, 242, 260, 270; oil, 188, 265–72, 281; move of capital, 183, 187–88; national identity, 146, 151–52, 153, 154, 155; Nazarbayev's vision, 276, 282, 282; nuclear zone, 188, 222, 223, 233–45; perceptions of, 132, 133–34; population and demography, 133, 148–49; presidential elections, 136, 138–42, 207, 256, 276; press freedom, 134, 156–57, 275; quality of life, 134–35;

religion, restrictions on, 201; settlement of, 143–44, 146; sports, 135, 197–98; transportation and communication, 133; wealth gap, 134, 282–83

Kazakhstan Institute for Management, Entrepreneurship and Strategic Research (KIMEP), Almaty, 173–74

KazMunayGaz (KMG), 136, 266, 268, 270, 272, 273

Keiderling, Kelly, 74–75, 299

Kerry, John, 4–5

Khan Shatyr, 202, 203fig., 204, 288

Khiva: city of, 120; khanate of, 28, 30, 45, 265

Khokand: city of, 121; khanate of, 30, 31, 44, 146, 162

Khonin, Gennadiy, 175, 177, 178, 178fig.

Khrushchev, Nikita, 46, 148, 167, 188, 189, 226, 260

khrushchevka (apartment), 46–47, 108, 163

Khudaiberdiev, Khalijan, 92–93

Khusainov, Renat, 24, 103, 300

kinship and family ties, 18, 23, 60–61, 67, 154, 257

Kipling, Rudyard, 30

Kirol, Paul, 179

Kist, Viktor, 177

Klimemko, Olesja, 179

Koch, Natalie, on perceptions and depiction of Astana, 184–86, 201, 204

Kolbin, Gennadiy, 152, 163

kolkhoz, 110, 147, 168, 221, 226, 227, 263

komuz, 5, 52fig., 77

Kopack, Robert, 233–34, 239, 241–42

Koreans, deportation of, 33, 147–48,

Kostanai (Qostanay), city of, 188;history of, 260; location, 259–60; population, 260

Kostanai oblast, 259, 261, 262; climate, 263–64; mineral deposits, 260; wheat production, 262–64

Kostanai State University, 260–61

Kozlov, Vladimir, 155, 273, 274, 279

Kulibayev, Timur, 273, 275, 283

Kumtor (gold mine), 97–98

Kunayev, Dinmukhamed, 152

Kungey Ala Too (mountain range), 17, 94

Kurchatov, Igor Vasilyevich, 235; nuclear test facility, 235, 236, 238, 246

Kurmanjan Dakta: street name, 20, 24, 26; tribal chief, 26, 31

Kyrgyz Ala Too (mountain range), 15, 17, 104, 107

Kyrgyz ASSR, 15, 33

Uighurs, 8, 281
Ukraine, 133, 188, 222, 22
Ullughbek, 122–23
United Nations Development Programme (UNDP), 111, 168
United Nations Educational, Scientific and Cultural Organisation (UNESCO), 19, 23, 24, 28, 69, 70, 158, 165, 300
United States: forecast of collapse, 165; government shutdowns (1996), 41–42; policy in Central Asia, 278–80, 281
United States Agency for International Development (USAID), 58, 82, 111, 161, 278–79
United States Embassy, Bishkek, 49, 160; Astana, 190–91, 195, 210
United States Information Service (USIS), 19, 23, 40, 47, 86, 299
Ural (river), 135, 265, 266
Uralsk, 133, 188, 246, 266
Ust-Kamenogorsk, 188, 237, 246
Uzbek SSR, 21, 33, 122
Uzbekistan, xiii, 5, 7, 8, 19, 35, 42, 107, 157, 230; human rights, 280; travel in, 120–23; US aid to, 279–80
Uzen (oil field), 272
Uzgen, 21

Valikhanov, Chokan, 250–51, 253
Vecherniy (Evening) *Bishkek,* 84–85
Velska, Irina, 169, 170, 193, 206–7, 215, 225, 231, 232, 300
Virgin Lands program, 148, 167, 188–89, 260, 263
Virtanen, Tarja, 158, 300
Volga Germans, 50, 175–76; deportation of, 33, 148, 175–76, 218–19

Weidergeburt (Rebirth) Association, 175, 179, 219
wheat, in Kazakhstan, 148, 167, 188–89, 260, 262–64
Wilhelm, Hubert, xiii, 287, 288
William of Rubruck, 182–83
Witt, Daniel, 141–42
workshops and training, 165–66, 170, 192, 269
World War I, rebellion in Central Asia, 31–32, 98
Wrangel, Baron Aleksandr, 248, 249

Xinjiang, 8, 17, 268, 281

Yeleusizov, Melis, 138–39, 138fig.
Yeltsin, Boris, 34, 69, 176, 177
Yerkimbay, Asqat, xiii, 35–36, 149–52, 158, 159, 300
yurt, 16, 60–61, 109, 111, 198, 202, 288

Zailiysky Ala Too (mountain range), 44, 114, 160, 164, 167, 188, 226; glaciers, 164, 165, 166
zek, 218, 219, 220
Zhanaozen: strike and protests by oil workers, 272–73; clampdown on opposition and media, 273–74; digital TV, 274–75; rebuilding of, 274; trials, 273–74, 279
Zheltoqsan (December) protests, 145, 152, 163
Zhempisov, Shaurab, 264
Zhezdy, 150, 158
Zhezqazgan, 150, 212, 223
Zhirinovsky, Vladimir, 188
Zhumabekov, Meiran, 217